ELECTING
JUDGES

CHICAGO STUDIES IN AMERICAN POLITICS

A SERIES EDITED BY BENJAMIN I. PAGE, SUSAN HERBST,
LAWRENCE R. JACOBS, AND JAMES DRUCKMAN

Also in the series:

ELECTING

JUDGES

THE SURPRISING EFFECTS OF CAMPAIGNING

ON JUDICIAL LEGITIMACY

JAMES L. GIBSON

THE UNIVERSITY OF CHICAGO PRESS

Chicago & London

James L. Gibson is the Sidney W. Souers Professor of Government at Washington University in St. Louis and Professor Extraordinaire in Political Science at Stellenbosch University in South Africa. He is the author or coauthor of eight books, including *Citizens, Courts, and Confirmations*, and is the recipient of an APSA Lifetime Achievement Award.

The University of Chicago Press, Chicago 60637
The University of Chicago Press, Ltd., London
© 2012 by The University of Chicago
All rights reserved. Published 2012.
Printed in the United States of America

21 20 19 18 17 16 15 14 13 12   1 2 3 4 5

ISBN-13: 978-0-226-29107-9   (cloth)
ISBN-13: 978-0-226-29108-6   (paper)
ISBN-13: 978-0-226-29110-9   (e-book)
ISBN-10: 0-226-29107-3   (cloth)
ISBN-10: 0-226-29108-1   (paper)
ISBN-10: 0-226-29110-3   (e-book)

Library of Congress Cataloging-in-Publication Data

Gibson, James L., 1951–
    Electing judges : the surprising effects of campaigning on judicial legitimacy / James L. Gibson.
        pages. cm. — (Chicago studies in American politics)
    ISBN-13: 978-0-226-29107-9 (cloth: alkaline paper)
    ISBN-10: 0-226-29107-3 (cloth: alkaline paper)
    ISBN-13: 978-0-226-29108-6 (paperback: alkaline paper)
    ISBN-10: 0-226-29108-1 (paperback: alkaline paper)
    [etc.]
    1. Judges—United States—Election.   2. Judicial ethics—United States.   I. Title.
II. Series: Chicago studies in American politics.
    KF8776.G538 2012
    347.73'14—dc23
                                                                            2012001904

♾ This paper meets the requirements of ANSI/NISO z39.48-1992
(Permanence of Paper).

To the love of my life—Monica E. Kinsella

CONTENTS

PREFACE AND ACKNOWLEDGMENTS

Those who know me or who have followed my research over the years may be somewhat surprised at this foray into the world of state judicial politics: I am not generally known for working on state courts. Becoming acquainted with the literature and the players in the field has been an interesting and occasionally challenging endeavor.

My interest in the topic was piqued by the US Supreme Court's decision in *Republican Party of Minnesota v. White*, as will become apparent throughout this book. As in many judicial decisions, assertions and assumptions about empirical reality abound. The minority in *White*, for example, propounds a theory of citizen perceptions and judgments of judicial impartiality. Campaign speech can be banned because such speech teaches citizens that judges have already reached a decision on issues prior to cases coming before them on the bench, and this variety of closed-mindedness gives the impression that fair and impartial decisions cannot be rendered. Many legal controversies are (or can be) at their root empirical questions about which social scientists may well have something to say.

Consequently, I started thinking about the various issues raised by *White* from the perspective of hard-nosed empirical social science. At the time, I did not know a lot about state courts, but I did think I knew something about the legitimacy of courts and especially about how citizens go about forming their judgments of legitimacy. The court's decision seemed so at odds with my understanding of public opinion that I vowed to investigate the question as rigorously as I knew how.

My accomplice—the banker—in nearly all of my empirical endeavors is the National Science Foundation, and in particular the Law and Social Sciences Program at NSF. This project is no exception. Research such as that reported in the book is expensive—more expensive than many casual observers may imagine—and without institutional resources no individual scholar can arrange a study like this. As always, I am profoundly impressed with NSF's commitment to social science inquiry; I have always hoped that I could live up to the expectations of what I perceive as the most prestigious and intellectually demanding social science funding agency. When it comes to social science, NSF knows no rival. I am particularly indebted to Chris Zorn, then program officer of the Law and Social Sciences Program at NSF, for his willingness to take a gamble on a novice scholar (at least when it comes to state judicial politics).

One of the many things I have learned from entering the state judicial politics area is that the subfield boasts a number of excellent scholars, and nearly all of these scholars have been both generous with their time and tolerant of my mistakes. Melinda Hall and Paul Brace stand at the pinnacle of the field, and each has been helpful to this endeavor in ways too numerous to count. The same can be said of Chris Bonneau.

At the same, I have been impressed by the degree to which ideology can almost always be found at the subsurface of the issues confronting state judicial politics. I am not devoid of ideology, but on most issues about which state judicial folks argue, I have few if any normative commitments. And so as to avoid the pitfalls of ideology in social science research—while at the same time recognizing that my research has important normative implications—I have tried to be as transparent as possible in structuring my hypotheses, collecting the relevant data, and conducting the analysis. My hope is that this research will contribute to the normative debates by setting an empirical frame of reference on many issues. I am reasonably firmly convinced, for instance, that policy talk by judges does not undermine judicial legitimacy. I hope that this empirical finding becomes accepted by the protagonists and antagonists in the various normative debates. In the end, we social scientists can contribute a great deal to contemporary discussions of a host of legal/political issues.

As I have noted, the National Science Foundation provided the resources necessary to conduct this research. The Kentucky Election Panel Survey was made possible by a grant from the Law and Social Sciences Program of the National Science Foundation (SES-0451207). Any opinions, findings, and conclusions or recommendations expressed in this material are those of the author and do not necessarily reflect the views of the National Science Foundation.

In addition, the Weidenbaum Center on the Economy, Government, and Public Policy at Washington University in St. Louis and especially its director, Steven S. Smith, have provided invaluable support and assistance. Steve Smith is a consummate social scientist and a strong supporter of my various research agendas, and the center is an invaluable resource for my work. I appreciate that very much.

I deeply appreciate the comments on the analysis reported in chapter 2 of Marc Hendershot, David Primo, Christina Boyd, Chris W. Bonneau, Richard O. Lempert, Anthony Champagne, G. Alan Tarr, Jeffrey R. Lax, Michael Dimino, David A. M. Peterson, Mary E. Outwater, Howard Gillman, Scott D. McClurg, Larry Baum, Margo Schlanger, Shanto Iyengar, Lawrence Friedman, Chris Claassen, Zachary Levinson, and especially the detailed advice of my good friend and colleague Gregory A. Caldeira. Much of the inspiration for the analysis in chapter 3 came from criticism of an earlier paper of mine by Rick Lempert. I also appreciate the help of John Geer in understanding the meanings of the responses to the attack ad experiment. Charles Geyh and Jesse Atencio provided most useful comments on the material in chapter 5. Finally, I appreciate the most helpful comments on an earlier version of chapter 6 from Jon Krosnick, Paul Brace, Ian Fisher, Benjamin Bricker, Chris Bonneau, Neil Vidmar, and Lynn Vavreck.

CHAPTER ONE

THE "NEW STYLE" JUDICIAL ELECTIONS IN THE AMERICAN STATES

In 2002, the US Supreme Court ruled that candidates for judicial offices, including incumbent judges, have free-speech rights that allow them to make policy statements during their campaigns (*Republican Party of Minnesota v. White*, 536 U.S. 765 [2002]).[1] This decision has caused considerable consternation within the legal community, including among many legal scholars, based on the fear that this newly announced judicial right will undermine the perceived fairness and impartiality of courts within the public at large. The assumption seems to be that what candidates for judicial offices say during their campaigns can cause fundamental disruptions in how citizens view and evaluate judicial institutions. If so, then this is a very high price to pay for extending these speech rights to judicial candidates. As the dissenters in the Supreme Court argued,

> Prohibiting a judicial candidate from pledging or promising certain results if elected directly promotes the State's interest in preserving public faith in the bench. When a candidate makes such a promise during a campaign, the public will no doubt perceive that she is doing so in the hope of garnering votes. And the public will in turn likely conclude that when the candidate decides an issue in accord with that promise, she does so at least in part to discharge her undertaking to the voters in the previous election and to prevent voter abandonment in the next. The perception of that unseemly *quid pro quo*—judicial candidates' promises on issues in return for the electorate's votes at the polls—inevitably diminishes the public's faith in the ability of judges to administer the law without regard to personal or political self-interest. (Ginsberg dissent, joined by Stevens, Souter, and Breyer, footnotes omitted, 536 U.S. 16–17)[2]

Although judicial candidates are not now permitted *every* type of speech (promises about how one would rule in specific cases are legitimately proscribed, at least at the moment), this Supreme Court decision has opened the door to freewheeling discussions of policy issues by both incumbents and challengers for judicial offices.[3] Consequently, judicial elections now focus on judges' ideologies and judicial policy making to a far greater degree than in the past.[4]

At the same time, interest groups and legal activists have become increasingly desirous of influencing the outcomes of state judicial elections. Their interest in state courts stems partly from the relative inactivity of the US Supreme Court (which now issues fewer than 100 full opinions per year) and partly from the realization that policies made by state courts can have enormous economic, political, and social consequences (e.g., so-called tort reform). As a result, we have witnessed in the last few years an unprecedented injection of money into state judicial elections (see the activism of the US Chamber of Commerce and the Association of Trial Lawyers America, now known as the American Association for Justice; see also Echeverria 2001). The confluence of broadened freedom for judges to speak out on issues, the increasing importance of state judicial policies, and the infusion of money into judicial campaigns have produced what may be described as the "perfect storm" of judicial elections. This storm is radically reshaping the atmosphere of state judicial elections, as it gathers strength and spreads across the nation.

No better illustration of this phenomenon can be found than in the judicial elections of 2004. According to the Brennan Center at New York University Law School, candidates spent an all-time high of $24 million on advertising in state supreme court[5] elections in 2004, a dramatic increase of almost 20% compared with 2000 (Goldberg et al. 2005; see also Goldberg, Holman, and Sanchez 2002).[6] A total of 180 ads were produced, with 42,249 airings in 15 states. This sort of campaign effort seems to be becoming increasingly common in the American states.

With this new style of free-for-all judicial elections has come a blizzard of commentaries on the likelihood of dire consequences from this politicization of state courts (on the politicization of judiciaries worldwide, see Tate and Vallinder [1995]). Many commentators fear the worst, arguing that the very legitimacy of the legal system may be eroded as people come to see law and courts as little more than ordinary political institutions and therefore worthy of their contempt and disrespect.[7] Indeed, the original justification for Minnesota's prohibition on campaign speech was precisely the desire to protect the legitimacy of the state judiciaries (but see Dimino 2003). Minnesota contended that legitimacy requires the appearance of impartiality, that the appearance of partiality can undermine the confidence citizens have in their courts (legitimacy), and that legitimacy is crucial to the effective functioning of courts (see Brief and Appendix for Respondents 2002; see also Schultz 2006). One legal scholar opines,

> When judicial decisions are seen as politicized rather than independent, or as done in the service of a special interest group or to advance judges' self-interest rather than in a neutral and independent spirit, the sense of fairness and justice that is the binding force of the Rule of Law becomes exhausted and the system is weakened. Disobedience and avoidance of legal obligations can be expected to rise in direct proportion to declining respect for law. As respect for the fairness of law diminishes, greater government force must be used to ensure obedience. (Barnhizer 2001, 371, footnotes omitted)

Alarm bells are being sounded throughout the United States, announcing the imminent demise of legitimacy in the country's elected state courts.

To date, however, little rigorous evidence has been produced (one way or the other) on whether policy statements made during campaigns actually have any consequences at all for perceptions of judicial impartiality. Voters who want to vote on the basis of policy considerations, for instance, are unlikely to be put off by hearing the policy views of judicial candidates. Others may distinguish between general statements of policy preferences and specific pre-judgments in individual cases. Indeed, permitting policy debates may have useful consequences, such as allowing citizens to base their voting decisions on more rational criteria (rather than on what analysts generally assume to be dicey criteria such as the candidates' genders or inferred ethnicities; see, e.g., Baum 1988–89; Baum and Hojnacki 1992; McDermott 1997; but see also Hall 2001; Bonneau and Hall 2009). And whatever diminished impartiality courts and judges may suffer from today may be due to factors other than policy commitments, such as the use of attack ads or conflicts of interests generated by campaign contributions from litigants, or both. We simply do not know what effect the Supreme Court's ruling will have on elected judiciaries.

We do, however, know something about how citizens perceive judicial impartiality and, more generally, procedural fairness. This well-developed body of theory has demonstrated, for instance, that impartiality is a crucial component of perceived fairness. According to Tyler (2001, 422; see also Tyler 2006), when people assess the procedural fairness of institutions, they are "especially influenced by evidence of even-handedness, factuality, and the lack of bias or favoritism (neutrality)"—in short, by impartiality (see also Baird 2001). Moreover, according to Hibbing and Theiss-Morse (2001, 2002), it is precisely the perception that members of Congress make their political decisions on the basis of partial (e.g., self-interested) criteria that threatens the legitimacy of that institution. In the judicial case, it seems highly likely that campaign contributions from those who litigate cases before a judge generate at least the appearance of self-interested partiality and procedural unfairness. Declaring a policy view in a campaign statement may also impugn procedural fairness by implying ideological bias and the unwillingness to judge each case de novo, on its own merits. Even the use of so-called attack ads can threaten perceived impartiality by portraying candidates for judicial offices as nothing more than ordinary politicians—in bed with special interest groups, supremely self-interested, and motivated by politics, not law and legality. Thus, the current debate over the campaign tactics of judges maps neatly onto theories concerned with institutional legitimacy, procedural justice, and the effects of campaigns on the attitudes, beliefs, and expectations of ordinary people.

My purpose in this book is therefore to investigate the impact of campaign activity on the perceived impartiality and institutional legitimacy of courts. I focus on judicial races in the state of Kentucky and employ a panel survey of a representative sample of ordinary Kentuckians. Since the same individuals were interviewed before, during, and after the judicial elections of 2006, my analysis focuses on how campaign activities change people's attitudes, with change being measured with greater rigor than has been possible in earlier research (based overwhelmingly on cross-sectional surveys). The analysis reported here makes uncommonly strong claims to certainty about causal relationships, based in part on the availability of data over time, but based as well on several experiments that were embedded within the representative survey. The most general conclusion of this research is that campaign activity can indeed shape the attitudes and perceptions of ordinary citizens, but not necessarily in the ways commonly assumed. Owing to its central and fundamental location undergirding this research, I begin the analysis with a thorough explication of legitimacy theory.

THE LEGITIMACY OF JUDICIAL INSTITUTIONS

Politicians and scholars worldwide have long been impressed with the fragility of judicial power. When it comes to securing compliance with their decisions, courts are said to have neither the power of the "purse"—the ability to raise and expropriate money to encourage compliance—nor the power of the "sword"—the ability to coerce compliance. In the absence of these tools, courts in reality have only a single form of political capital: legitimacy. Compliance with court decisions is contingent upon judicial institutions being considered legitimate. Legitimacy is a normative concept, basically meaning that an institution is acting appropriately and correctly, within its mandate.[8] Generally speaking, a great deal of social science research has shown that people obey law more out of a felt normative compunction deriving from legitimacy than from instrumental calculations of the costs and benefits of compliance (e.g., Tyler 1990, 2006).

As a consequence, political scientists have paid considerable attention to the legitimacy of courts. The empirical analysis of legitimacy dates back to Easton's work on "systems theory" (Easton 1965), with Easton substituting the phrase "diffuse support" for judgments of legitimacy.[9] Diffuse support is a fundamental commitment to an institution and a willingness to support the institution that extends beyond mere satisfaction with the performance of the institution at the moment ("specific support"). The idea here is that institutions—especially courts—must be free to make decisions in opposition to the preferences of the majority; indeed, it is specifically a function of courts (at least in the American and many European cases, where the judiciary is vested with the power of having the last say on the meaning of the constitution) to overturn the actions of the majority when those actions infringe upon the fundamental rights of minorities. Courts must on occasion make hard decisions that are greatly displeasing to the majority—as in freeing obviously guilty criminals due to violations of due process, restraining the majority from imposing its religious beliefs on the entire society, and spying on dissenters and malcontents who threaten the political security of the majority. If democracy can be simply defined as majority rule, with institutionalized respect for the rights of the minority, especially the rights allowing the minority to compete for political power (on democracy, see Dahl 1971), then the judiciary clearly represents the "minority rights" half of the equation. If courts are dependent upon majority approval for their decisions to be accepted, then one of the most important political functions of courts is in jeopardy.

This approach to legitimacy led Easton to coin a telling phrase: institutions require a "reservoir of goodwill" in order to function effectively.[10] Gibson and Caldeira (2009a) liken this reservoir to loyalty, even to the loyalty between two friends. One may disappoint a friend without necessarily destroying the friendship. Loyalty to another requires standing by that other even when one might disapprove of the other's actions. Indeed, it is easy to be loyal to another who acts in an approving fashion; the test of loyalty involves disapproval or discontent. In a similar fashion, institutions do not require legitimacy when they are satisfying people with their policies. Legitimacy becomes crucial in the context of dissatisfaction; legitimacy requires an "objection precondition." Problems of compliance do not typically arise when court decisions align with the preferences of the institution's constituents; when they do not align, legitimacy or institutional loyalty provides the rationale for accepting or acquiescing to the ruling of a court.

This concept of legitimacy is related to unwillingness to punish institutions for their actions, which is historically important in the American case and of considerable contemporary relevance in the European case.[11] The federal judiciary, including the US Supreme Court, is not the subject of much discussion in the American Constitution. Indeed, practically none of the important aspects of the structure and function of the judiciary are determined by the Constitution, ranging from the jurisdiction of the courts, to the size of the courts and the remuneration for judges, to fundamental powers, such as judicial review. To take just the simplest structural factor, the size of the US Supreme Court can be changed by ordinary legislation, and in fact it has been changed several times throughout American history.

Political elites who are dissatisfied with court opinions often seek to punish the institution through structural or functional "reform." The most common such ploy is to alter the jurisdiction of the federal courts; every year numerous bills are introduced in Congress to prohibit the federal judiciary from ruling on various hot-button issues: ranging from the Safeguarding Our Religious Liberties Act, H.R. 4379 (introduced by Representative Ron Paul from Texas), with the purpose of eliminating federal court jurisdiction over state and local policies regarding the free exercise or establishment of religion, any privacy claim related to issues of sexual practices, orientation, or reproduction, and any equal protection claim based on the right to marry without regard to sex or sexual orientation, to the Congressional Accountability for Judicial Activism Act of 2004 (introduced in the House of Representatives by Representative Ron Lewis of Kentucky and 26 cosponsors), which would empower Congress to reverse by a two-thirds vote any judgment of the US Supreme Court that concerns the constitutionality of an Act of Congress (H.R. 3920).[12] Specific, high-stakes court decisions have drawn vicious and legitimacy-challenging criticism—as in the direct attack by various law professors on the court's legitimacy after its ruling in *Bush v. Gore* (the case that effectively decided the 2000 presidential election)—and there is no shortage of threats to the judiciary from the religious right, right-wing terrorists and murderers, and kooks. Serious proposals to change the structure of the judiciary have been floated— for example, various plans to convert the life tenure of Supreme Court judges to a fixed term. For instance, Farnsworth (2004, 2) asserts, "In recent years at least ten distinguished scholars (as well as two distinguished judges and a distinguished journalist) have proposed abolishing life tenure for Supreme

Court Justices and replacing it with fixed terms of years in office."[13] While not all dissatisfaction with judges in the United States is focused on the Supreme Court, there can be little doubt that the justices of the court are correct to worry about the implications of the current political climate in the country for the legitimacy of law and courts in general and their court in particular. Finally, some longitudinal studies of trust in the US Supreme Court argue that partisan polarization in attitudes toward the court has risen significantly in recent times (e.g., Mate and Wright 2006).[14] From Roosevelt's court-packing scheme during the New Deal[15] to contemporary refusal to increase the pay of federal judges, the legislative and executive branches have tried to impress on judges their vulnerability to political displeasure.

Elite efforts to punish often fail owing to the fundamental legitimacy of the judiciary among the ordinary people. Institutions with a "reservoir of good-will" can survive institutional attacks if elite schemes do not resonate with the mass public. From this perspective, it is not difficult to understand how institutional legitimacy is seen by many as a more powerful form of political capital than purses and swords.

Political scientists routinely measure the legitimacy of courts via public opinion polls. Implicit in this approach, of course, is the fundamental assumption that the views of ordinary people matter. Many judges, lawyers, and legal scholars believe that only elite opinion is relevant, in part because ordinary people are insufficiently well informed to have meaningful opinions of courts and judges. As it turns out, the empirical evidence from the American case is that the American people do indeed have meaningful attitudes toward the US Supreme Court (Caldeira and Gibson 1992) and that the court is among the most legitimate judicial institutions in the world (Gibson, Caldeira, and Baird 1998).

In-depth research on public attitudes toward courts other than the US Supreme Court is sparse, but far from nonexistent. In the American case, the theory of institutional legitimacy advanced by Gibson and Caldeira and others has been applied to lower federal courts (e.g., Benesh, Scherer, and Steigerwalt 2009), state high courts (Gibson et al. 2011), and to the American state court systems (Benesh 2006). Outside the United States, Gibson, Caldeira, and Baird (1998) reported an analysis of public support for the high courts of the EU member states in Europe—Baird (2001) extended this research with a more detailed study of the legitimacy of the Federal Constitutional Court in Germany. In general, this research finds that older courts are more legitimate than younger courts, in part because courts are able to claim credit for "good decisions" but shirk blame for "bad decisions," that legitimacy is acquired in part from meeting the expectations of citizens (which themselves are not uniform), and that those more informed about courts tend to support them more. Their research also indicates a considerable degree of variability across countries in the legitimacy accorded to their national high courts.

Thus, a great deal of research effort has been devoted to analyzing the attitudes of ordinary citizens toward judicial institutions under the theory that those institutions require the support of their constituents in order to function effectively.

Change in Institutional Support

But is legitimacy obdurate? Is it responsive to the influences either from within the court itself (e.g., its decisions) or from external forces (e.g., campaign activity)? Extant research has not answered this question very definitively; the need to answer this question with rigorous evidence is the primary motivating force of this project.

From the initial empirical studies of legitimacy came the view that beliefs about institutions were inculcated early in the life cycle, perhaps even in adolescence, and changed little over time (hence the great interest in research on political socialization). The view that public attitudes toward institutional legitimacy are obdurate, however, is no longer tenable. While beliefs and values acquired early in life may shape perceptions and evaluations of institutional outputs to some degree, legitimacy is nonetheless not immune to forces of change. We know, for instance, that the views of African Americans toward the US Supreme Court have changed over time from strong support to considerable suspicion (Gibson and Caldeira 1992). We also know that attitudes are to some degree responsive to policy outputs, either through salient decisions (e.g., Grosskopf and Mondak 1998; Gibson, Caldeira, and Spence 2003a) or through decisions with particular local relevance (e.g., Hoekstra 2003). Indeed, the very theory upon which so many studies of legitimacy rely (Easton's theory of diffuse support) recognizes that *sustained* disappointment with the outputs of an institution can empty the "reservoir of goodwill." Like interpersonal trust and loyalty, a single incident may not destroy a relationship, but repeated violations of expectations over time can entirely deplete loyalty. Few social scientists today believe that support for political institutions is impervious to influence from institutional performance or exogenous shocks and events.

What we do *not* know, however, is whether/why/how/under what conditions change takes place. Did, for instance, the controversies over the Bork and Thomas nominations to the US Supreme Court have a lasting effect on public perceptions of the institution? No evidence with which to answer this question exists. Moreover, it is even unclear from the research literature whether sizeable short-term reactions to individual judicial decisions have lasting effects. From available evidence, it seems that the US Supreme Court may actually have *enhanced* its institutional legitimacy via its ruling in *Bush v. Gore* (e.g., Gibson, Caldeira, and Spence 2003a), but even that conclusion is based only on a comparison of aggregate statistics over time, and some recent evidence suggests that the court's legitimacy has surrendered any gains it might have made from the disputed presidential election of 2000 (e.g., Gibson 2007). When it comes to the question of how legitimacy is created, maintained, and destroyed, social scientists have some theories and conjectures, but precious few data and little understanding of processes of opinion updating and change.

There are many good reasons why we know so little about the dynamics of change, but perhaps the most exculpatory is that longitudinal data are woefully scarce. Consider the evidence we use to understand changing attitudes toward the US Supreme Court. Apart from one-shot surveys, scholars rely on aggregate time series data from the General Social Survey (measuring confidence in the leaders of the Supreme Court—e.g., Caldeira 1986, 1987), some small collections of individual surveys conducted over time (e.g., my data from 1987, 1995, 2001, and 2006—see Gibson 2007), a handful of before and after media polls (e.g., Grosskopf and Mondak 1998), simulations and mathematical models (e.g., Mondak and Smithey 1997), and a tiny number of studies (outside the laboratory/campus, that is) that directly assess individual-level change (e.g., Murphy and Tanenhaus 1990; Hoekstra 2003; Gibson and Caldeira 2009a).

Of course, the major impediment to panel studies of individual-level stability and change lies in the unwillingness of scholars (and funders) to mount t_1 surveys *prior to* important events taking place. Change can only be assessed when baseline data are available, which means that measurements must be taken in advance of calamitous events. Unlike the periodicity of elections, the events that shape institutional legitimacy occur irregularly and are often difficult to predict. Hence, the data and knowledge deficit is enormous.

We do, however, have some theory about processes of attitude change. According to positivity theory, as developed by Gibson and Caldeira (2009a), attention-getting judicial events (e.g., nominations to the court; highly controversial decisions; salient campaign activities) "wake up" dormant attitudes toward law and courts by providing a salient window into the operation of the judiciary. To take just a simple example, the theory of mechanical jurisprudence—according to which, judges make decisions not on the basis of their ideologies but rather strictly according to the syllogisms of stare decisis—is placed under strain during confirmation hearings since nearly all actors are focusing (to at least some degree) on the ideology of the nominee. Thus, the central legitimizing symbols upon which the court relies—its impartiality and its strict adherence to the law—are potentially compromised during politicized judicial selection processes. An opportunity for attitude updating occurs.

Elections provide a similar opportunity for attitude updating, especially if campaign ads are eye-catching. Outside the campaign season, citizens may not even be aware that their judges are elected; during the campaign, advertisements for judicial candidates are commonplace, and citizens are provided an opportunity to learn about the structure and function of their judiciary.[16] However, if the campaign activity is highly politicized, as is increasingly the case in state judicial elections, then the lessons learned may be ones that subtract from rather than add to institutional legitimacy.

The positivity theory of Gibson and Caldeira (2009a) posits that when citizens pay attention to the judiciary they are inevitably exposed to symbols of judicial authority that reinforce institutional legitimacy. Thus, under most circumstances, to "know courts is to love them" (Gibson and Caldeira 2009a, 122).

However, Gibson and Caldeira have also shown that exposure to politicized processes of confirming nominees to the US Supreme Court can have legitimacy-reducing consequences. More specifically, to the extent that citizens view ads portraying the courts as "just another political institution," legitimacy is undermined. Gibson and Caldeira show that debate about judicial philosophy and ideology does not necessarily cost the institution some of its legitimacy; the American people understand that courts are policy-making institutions and, consequently, that discussions of philosophy and ideology are appropriate and perhaps even desirable (see also Gibson and Caldeira 2011). But when the judiciary is equated with ordinary political institutions, the lack of esteem of ordinary political institutions seems to rub off on the courts. Therefore, it is reasonable to hypothesize that being exposed to the rough and tumble of judicial campaigns has consequences for public support for courts and that the attitude change that takes place is not beneficial to the judiciary.[17]

Summary
While it is undoubtedly true that judicial campaigns have become vastly more costly and more focused on legal and political issues (e.g., Goldberg et al. 2005), to date, little rigorous evidence has been produced to document the alleged decline in the legitimacy of courts. Many assume that judicial legitimacy is at risk, but practically no empirical evidence on this score exists. The

purpose of this book is therefore to provide some much needed analysis of the consequences of judicial campaign activity. To do so requires an important new theoretical approach to understanding the effects of campaigns.

EXPECTANCY THEORY AND THE LEGITIMACY OF STATE HIGH COURTS

How *specifically* do campaign activities undermine institutional legitimacy? Gibson and Caldeira (2009a) have argued that judicial legitimacy is maintained and reinforced by exposure to legitimizing judicial symbols that tend to distinguish courts from other political institutions. The message of these powerful symbols is that "courts are different," and owing to these differences, courts are worthy of more respect, deference, and obedience—in short, legitimacy.

However, just as citizens can come to see courts as different due to the influence of exogenous legitimizing symbols, citizens may also come to understand courts as *quite like* other political institutions if that is the message to which attentive people are exposed during campaigns. Indeed, this is precisely the most worrisome consequence of the politicized style of judicial elections: To the extent that campaigning takes on the characteristics of "normal" political elections (see Pozen 2008), courts may be seen as *not* special and different, with the consequence that their legitimacy may be undermined. At the most general level, I hypothesize that those who become aware of and attuned to judicial campaigns in politicized judicial elections will judge courts and other political institutions similarly and will therefore extend less legitimacy to courts. Consequently, politicized judicial campaigns may seriously disrupt the normal supply of judicial legitimacy by portraying judges as nothing more than ordinary politicians.[18]

However, one mistake that those who think about state judges and their constituents sometimes make is to assume uniformity in the expectations citizens hold of the judiciary. This can be readily seen in survey questions cast in *empirical* terms rather than *normative* terms—for example, it is typically assumed that agreement with the statement "judges' decisions are influenced by political considerations" necessarily indicates disapproval of judges taking political considerations into account in making their decisions (see Pozen 2008, 45). Among at least some Americans, that may not be so. More generally, it is commonplace to assume that virtually all Americans strongly favor judicial independence. Unfortunately, assumptions about citizen expectations of judges and courts are rarely buttressed by rigorous empirical evidence.[19]

It seems quite unlikely that expectations are as uniform as typically portrayed. Indeed, Gibson and Caldeira (2009a) have shown that, at least when it comes to the expectations of the US Supreme Court, considerable disagreement exists among the American people. For instance, while 75.5% of Americans expect judges to appear to be fair and impartial (and, no doubt, an even larger percentage expects them *to actually be* fair and impartial), only 37.3% expect Supreme Court justices to "respect existing Supreme Court decisions by changing the law as little as possible." Almost one in five (17.8%) believe that justices should "base their decisions on whether they are a Republican or a Democrat," and nearly one-third (32.9%) believes that justices should "give [the respondent's own ideological position] a strong voice in how the constitution is interpreted." These figures (and others) belie the notion that Americans prefer mechanical jurisprudes who do nothing more than "interpret" the law (see Gibson and Caldeira 2011). But most important, they reveal considerable variability in the expected qualities and functions of American judges.

A national survey I conducted in 2008 strongly reinforces this point when it comes to campaign activity by state judges (see figure 1.1). In this survey, three questions about judicial campaigning were put to the respondents.[20] The questions asked about the appropriateness of accepting campaign contributions from lawyers and law firms, attacking opponents on issues that might come before the court, and expressing views on issues such as abortion, gun control, the death penalty, and gay marriage. The replies vary enormously according to the activity. Only 14% of the respondents believe that judges should accept campaign contributions, which is not surprising.[21] On the other hand, however, 60% of the respondents believe that judicial candidates *should be allowed* to attack their opponents' positions on issues of public policy, and an even larger percentage of the respondents—86%—assert that candidates for judicial office should make their policy views known, even on controversial policy issues. Thus, policy talk by judicial candidates seems to be *expected* by most Americans, not *rejected*. Indeed, from these data, one would conclude that the only aspect of campaign activity that threatens the American state judiciaries is the current system of campaign contributions. But most important, people differ in their expectations of judges and courts.

Consequently, one cannot understand the effects of campaign activity on citizen attitudes without first understanding the nature of the expectations citizens hold of the institutions and its incumbents. Expectations matter, and citizens differ in their expectations. As a result, I hypothesize that the effect of campaign activity depends upon the expectations one holds for the campaign and the office.

Previous research has not paid much attention to expectations, largely I suspect because that body of work has rarely focused on courts.[22] Even despite

FIGURE 1.1. THE CAMPAIGN EXPECTATIONS OF THE AMERICAN PEOPLE: SEE THE TEXT FOR THE WORDINGS OF THE QUESTIONS SUMMARIZED IN THIS FIGURE.

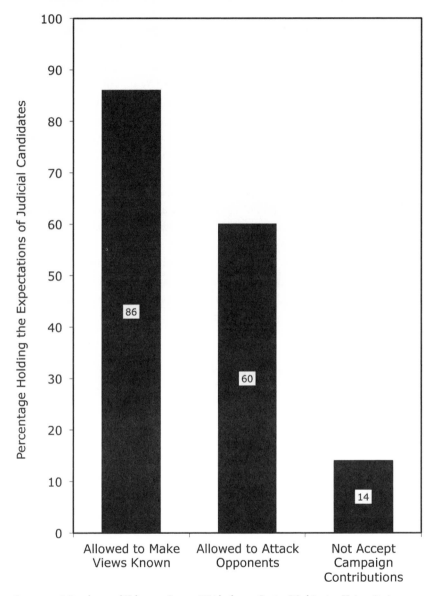

Source: 2008 Freedom and Tolerance Survey, Weidenbaum Center, Washington University in St. Louis.

considerable similarities in the expectations citizens hold of different institutions, it is probably rare in the American context to find citizens who judge courts in exactly the same terms as they evaluate legislatures and executives; courts are much more susceptible to expectations of fairness and impartiality than other political institutions. I suspect that expectations in general have much to do with how campaign activities are received and evaluated (e.g., differences in acceptance of politics as a form of limited "war"), but in the judicial case, I hypothesize that expectations are particularly potent. Thus, a central contribution of this research can be found in the development of expectancy theory in the context of judicial campaigns and court legitimacy.

Of course, campaign activity must first be perceived before it can be evaluated. Once activities are perceived, expectations become influential by attaching a valence to the perceptions. Consequently, I hypothesize an interactive effect between expectations and perceptions (just as was found by Gibson and Caldeira [2009a] in their study of expectations and perceptions of the Alito nomination).[23] Learning about state courts is a dynamic process involving the interaction of experiences and aspirations.

Thus, the purpose of this book is to determine if and how campaign activity by judicial candidates affects institutional legitimacy, using a theory of normative expectations. Although the research is far from voluminous, some earlier work does indeed address public perceptions and evaluations of state judicial institutions.

EXTANT RESEARCH ON STATE HIGH COURT LEGITIMACY

Although scholars typically recognize the importance of state courts as makers of public policy,[24] only a handful of studies of the legitimacy of these courts exists (and much of the literature is quite dated).[25] Among the best of the lot are two recent national studies, one by Benesh (2006) and the other by Cann and Yates (2008). Both of these studies, however, had to cobble together a dependent variable based on surveys fielded for nonacademic purposes. In general, scholars interested in how citizens perceive and judge their state judicial institutions have been seriously constrained by lack of public opinion data and the shortcomings of surveys conducted by nonacademic organizations (largely motivated by the desire to shape public policy).

For instance, several extant studies have been forced to rely on dependent variables that seem to measure the considerably less significant specific support (performance satisfaction), rather than diffuse support (institutional legitimacy).[26] As Cann and Yates note (2008, 300), "this is not a trivial distinction," since legitimacy is indicative of a political capital this is invaluable *particularly when* citizens are displeased with the short-term policy outputs of an institution.[27] Some have struggled valiantly to reconceptualize indicators of public attitudes into something akin to institutional legitimacy (for perhaps the most convincing such effort, see Cann and Yates [2008]),[28] but practically none of the measurement technology developed for use with the US Supreme Court (and widely accepted within the discipline) has been implemented in earlier studies of state courts.[29]

Unfortunately, methodological issues other than measurement affect another important aspect of findings from research on public opinion and state courts: Unless national samples are specifically drawn to be representative of the individual states, aggregation from the level of the individual respondent to the state-level is fraught with potential bias and error. Consider, for instance, the 2001 Justice at Stake Campaign (JaS) survey. First, few methodological details are available on how the sample was selected. Second, as with all national surveys, the numbers of respondents in specific states are small. Indeed, in 15 states, the number of respondent is less than 10. In only four states were 50 or more respondents interviewed. When respondents are aggregated by the type of selection system used by the states, as in several contemporary, scholarly analyses, states are by no means treated equally but are instead weighted by population size. Statements about citizens living in states in which judges serve life terms would therefore refer to the attitudes of the four residents of Rhode Island interviewed in the JaS survey.

I readily acknowledge that no researchers have made claims about systems in which state judges are appointed for life, but this sort of problem afflicts all cross-level (macro/state versus micro/individual respondent) conclusions. For instance, the American Judicature Society lists eight states as using partisan elections for the initial selection of judges on the state court of last resort. In the JaS database, 286 respondents are drawn from these eight states. But how the residents of West Virginia feel about their courts is practically trivial since only nine of the 286 respondents hail from that state. Louisiana and Alabama also contribute disproportionately less to the subsample of 286 respondents, with Texas and Pennsylvania represented by 119 respondents. Thus, how the residents of these two states feel about their judges contributes substantially to any overall conclusions about the consequences of partisan selection systems. Perhaps an argument could be made that our understanding of the effects of selection systems should not focus on the states individually but should instead weight the state by the size of its population, but, at a minimum, this is a controversial argument to make, and one about which those who have reported on this sort of cross-level analysis have been entirely silent.

As a consequence of these shortcomings, we at present know very little about the origins of public attitudes toward state courts in general and, more specifically, about how campaign activity and selection systems might change these attitudes. The analysis reported in this book goes some distance toward remedying this shortcoming.

CAN CAMPAIGNS CHANGE CITIZENS' VIEWS OF JUDICIAL IMPARTIALITY AND THE LEGITIMACY OF COURTS?

Precious few studies have investigated the question that defines this section of this chapter. Indeed, so far as I am aware, only a handful of studies has ever addressed campaign effects with rigorous data. Those studies have generated a mix of findings, including some disconcerting ones.

Gibson and Caldeira (2009a) examined the impact of the ad campaigns mounted in support of or opposition to the nomination of Samuel Alito to the US Supreme Court. Perhaps the most important finding of that research is that the campaigns by interest groups favoring and opposing the confirmation of Alito seemed to undermine the legitimacy of the court itself. The campaigns were politicized and taught the lesson that the court is just another political institution and, as such, is not worthy of high esteem. Interestingly though, those who paid attention to the debate in the Senate actually came away with more, not less, respect for the court. Since that study is based on a three-wave panel design, allowing the measurement of change in attitudes toward the Supreme Court, its findings are uncommonly persuasive.

On the other hand, other research has shown that public attitudes toward the US Supreme Court are remarkably resistant to alteration by the decisions of the court. We know, for instance, that the court's controversial ruling in *Bush v. Gore* did not undermine the legitimacy of the institution (Kritzer 2001; Yates and Whitford 2002; Gibson, Caldeira, and Spence 2003a; Nicholson and Howard 2003); indeed, it may have even enhanced it (Gibson 2007). Although not based on panel data, that research suggests that even controversial decisions need not necessarily detract from the legitimacy of the US Supreme Court.

Of course, the entire question of whether studies of attitudes toward the US Supreme Court can be generalized to the state judiciaries is open. State courts of last resort are obviously far less salient than the US Supreme Court, with the likely consequence that institutional attitudes at the state level may be more malleable. It is simply unclear whether findings drawn from research on the US Supreme Court apply to the state courts. Perhaps campaign activities uniquely shape state court attitudes.

The second most important lacuna in the existing literature on institutional legitimacy is the lack of understanding of change. With the exceptions I discuss below, nearly all research in the field is based on cross-sectional analysis. And even most of the limited dynamic analysis that exists examines aggregate patterns of change, not individual-level change. Here, I analyze a three-wave panel survey as a means of assessing how attitudes toward institutions are formed and how they are updated on the basis of perceptions of judicial campaigns.[30]

Some earlier research has indeed considered the dynamics of opinion toward the court. Scholars have analyzed aggregate time series (e.g., Caldeira 1986; Marshall 1989; Mondak and Smithey 1997), generational or cohort change (e.g., Gibson and Caldeira 1992), change in response to major court decisions (Franklin and Kosaki 1989; Kritzer 2001; Gibson, Caldeira, and Spence 2003a), a few true panel studies have been conducted (e.g., Murphy and Tanenhaus 1990; Hoekstra 2000, 2003), some work has tried to develop a formal model of opinion change (e.g., Mondak and Smithey 1997), and of course several scholars have attempted to induce change in the experimental laboratory (most notably, Mondak—[e.g., 1993]—and Hoekstra [1995]). Unfortunately, many of these efforts are seriously hampered by the lack of valid measures of court legitimacy extending over time (see Gibson, Caldeira, and Spence [2003b] on the deficiencies of the readily available "confidence" measure). Extant theory and data sources are simply not up to the task of providing many useful insights into how legitimacy is formed or acquired and how it is reinforced or eroded. Much more research, especially based on longitudinal data, is essential. Many fear that campaign activities are an important source of change in citizen attitudes.

Thus, the purpose of this project is to determine if and how campaign activity by judicial candidates affects institutional legitimacy. The project combines national and state-specific surveys, allowing us to overcome the significant limitations of earlier research (including our own).

THE DESIGN OF THIS STUDY

This research is based primarily upon a three-wave panel survey conducted before, during, and after the 2006 Kentucky elections.[31] The survey interviewed a representative sample of Kentucky residents. Technical details on the survey can be found in appendix B.

Perhaps one of the most important questions to be asked of this research design is, Why Kentucky? Why Kentucky, and what limits on generalizability flow from this research design?

The optimal design for a study of the impact of campaigning on judicial legitimacy would be longitudinal in nature, tracing change in public attitudes over a period of time as new types of campaign tactics are introduced within a state. Such a study is prohibitively expensive to implement and has never been conducted.

An alternative strategy would be to focus on a state in which politicized campaigns are relatively new but not unheard of and then to track the impact of campaigns on legitimacy. That is the design of this research. At this point in history, states like Ohio and Texas are not particularly revealing since citizens of those states have long witnessed highly political campaigning for judicial office. At the other end of the continuum, some states have been immune to politicization. For instance, in the high court elections of 2004, all of the candidates in 10 states reported raising *no contributions* as part of their campaigns for a seat on the state court of last resort (Goldberg et al. 2005, 14).

Kentucky lies between the extremes on this continuum. For instance, in the election of 2004, the candidates were Janet Stumbo and Will Scott, and together they raised nearly one-half million dollars in campaign contributions (Goldberg et al. 2005, 14). By all accounts, the campaign of 2004 was fairly politicized, with candidate Scott running attack ads and candidate Stumbo running ads contrasting the two candidates (Goldberg et al. 2005, 48). Among the 21 states in which judicial candidates raised at least some contributions in 2004, Kentucky defined the median, with candidates in 10 states raising less than $239,317 and candidates in 10 raising more than this figure. Moreover, also in 2004, abortion-related questionnaires were distributed by interest groups to judicial candidates in Kentucky. Some candidates refused to answer the questionnaires, which prompted a well-publicized lawsuit by the Family Trust Foundation challenging legal and ethical constraints on speech that appears to commit a candidate to a position that might come before the courts. The Family Trust Foundation was successful in its litigation.[32] Thus, in terms of the prior judicial election and the political context to which these respondents had most recently been exposed, some but perhaps not a very high degree of judicial politicization existed. So although statistical theory provides little basis for generalizing these findings to other state judiciaries, I can identify no obvious reasons why they cannot be generalized, and, on the contrary, Kentucky satisfies a number of design criteria that make it a useful state for an inquiry such as this.[33]

The Context: Judicial Legitimacy on the Eve
of the 2006 Elections in Kentucky

How much legitimacy did the Kentucky Supreme Court enjoy prior to the election campaign of 2006? With recourse to some fragmentary national data, some tentative answers to this question can be derived.

As I noted above, in 2001, JaS conducted a national survey on public attitudes toward the state and local courts (for earlier analyses of these data, see Cann and Yates [2008]). One of the questions they asked their respondents is, "How much trust and confidence do you have in courts and judges in your state?" Responses were collected on a four-point scale that varies from "nothing at all" to "a great deal." The data reveal that most Americans think quite highly of their state courts, with 25% asserting a great deal of trust and confidence and another 53% expressing some confidence, for a total 78% asserting at least some confidence in the institutions.

All 50 states are included in the JaS data set, although many states are represented by a tiny number of respondents. The average number of interviews per state is 19.3 (with a standard deviation of 18.1), with the number ranging from 1 to 84. A total of 16 states has fewer than 10 respondents in the sample. Of the states with 10 or more respondents, the average percentage of citizens expressing at least some confidence in their state judiciary is 78.4. Figure 1.2 reports the distribution across these states.

The first conclusion from this figure is that *not* a great deal of variability in court confidence exists across the states. In every state, a majority of the respondents express confidence in their state courts, and in most states, the majority is a quite sizable one.

In this data set, there are 22 respondents from Kentucky (which is slightly above average for the states). In terms of how much they trust their courts and judges, they are *not* statistically distinguishable from the rest of the respondents in the sample ($p = .770$). Overall, 78% of Americans trust their courts and judges to at least some degree. Among Kentuckians in the sample, the figure is 72%. Although I realize these data provide only a weak test of whether Kentucky is aberrant, they seem to provide some empirical support for my assertion that there is no obvious reason for thinking that empirical findings from Kentucky are atypical. Generally, the Kentucky judiciary was held in reasonably high esteem by the citizens of that state prior to the 2006 elections.

The National Replication Survey

Finally, owing specifically to this question of the generalizability of the Kentucky findings, some of the Kentucky findings reported below are replicated with a

FIGURE 1.2. CONFIDENCE IN STATE COURTS.

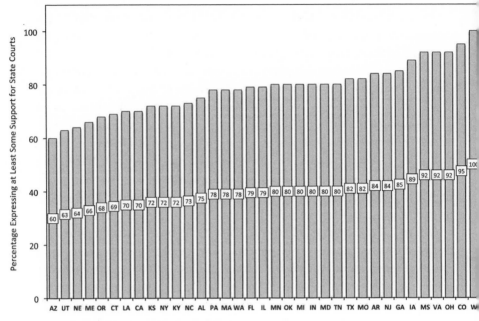

Source: Justice at Stake Campaign 2001 Survey.

national survey (the details of which can also be found in appendix B). Readers concerned about whether findings from a single state can be generalized to the nation as a whole will likely be pleased to find that there is a very close fit between the conclusions from Kentucky and those from the rest of nation.

CHAPTER-BY-CHAPTER OVERVIEW

My interest in the subject of state judicial elections originated in the decision of the US Supreme Court in *Republican Party of Minnesota v. White*. Therefore, I begin this book with a chapter specifically designed to assess whether the empirical assumptions made by the justices are in fact valid and accurate.

Chapter 2 reports the results of an experiment I designed to measure the influence of three types of campaign activity on perceived judicial impartiality and legitimacy: policy pronouncements, the use of attack ads, and the acceptance of campaign contributions. Because cross-institutional comparisons are always useful when it comes to understanding courts, the experiment also varied the institution about which the respondents were questioned—either the Kentucky Supreme Court or the Kentucky State Senate.[34]

Many of the criticisms directed against judicial elections in fact are generic to all low-salience elections (e.g., McDermott 1997). Indeed, nearly all of the complaints about state judicial elections (e.g., low turnout) probably apply with equal force to state legislative elections, even though few serious observers propose that state legislators should be freed of electoral accountability. In the analysis reported in chapter 2, it is useful, therefore, to compare the impact of these campaign activities on both judges and state legislators. The overarching hypothesis of the vignette is that the judgments and evaluations of people vary little across institutional contexts.

Finally, the experiment was replicated in a national survey fielded in 2007; the results from that survey are compared to the findings from the Kentucky sample. The strength of the analysis in this chapter is that it is based on an experimental design, allowing uncommon confidence in the causal inferences drawn. The weakness of the experiment, however, is that it presents a hypothetical context, and, as such, much of the detail of real campaign activity is simplified and stripped away. Therefore, additional analysis of the effects of campaign activity is essential.

Chapter 3 continues the investigation of campaign effects but uses a somewhat different methodological approach. Here, I use both post hoc and experimental methods to assess whether public perceptions of courts are influenced by various sorts of campaign activity. In general, my finding is that different types of campaign activity have quite different consequences. For instance, policy pronouncements by candidates do not undermine judicial legitimacy, whereas policy promises do. Throughout the analysis, I compare perceptions of courts and legislatures and often find that courts are far less unique than many ordinarily assume. Still, the most important finding of chapter 3 is that there is indeed a line of appropriateness in the minds of most citizens and campaign activity that crosses this line can in fact damage the legitimacy of state courts.

In chapter 4, I focus on measuring institutional support for the Kentucky Supreme Court. I begin with an explication of legitimacy theory because it provides useful conceptual guidance for how attitudes toward institutions ought to be measured. The analysis in this chapter also fixes the dependent variable that is used throughout the rest of the book, establishing both its validity and reliability. But because so little is known about how citizens judge state-level institutions, the chapter is perhaps valuable as a substantive contribution to the literature on public opinion and judicial institutions.

Expectancy theory is the subject of chapter 5. Here, I first develop the theory of expectations and then proceed to map the expectations Kentuckians hold of their state high court. Two important conclusions emerge from this analysis. First, considerable variability exists in the expectations of these respondents, making it difficult to think of the court's constituents as some sort of unified whole. Second, the constituency for a relatively politicized model of judging is much higher than might have been expected. These findings are important on their own terms; perhaps more important is the role that expectations play in interaction with perceptions of actual campaign activities.

Chapter 6 focuses on the elections of 2006 in Kentucky and is the most important chapter in this book. The essential question addressed by the analysis in this book has to do with the effects of campaign activity on public perceptions of judicial institutions; this is the chapter in which that question is answered. Relying upon measures of attitude changes (made possible through the use of a panel survey in which the same individuals were interviewed at three points in time), the hypotheses tested in this chapter all relate perceptions of campaign activity to changes in institutional loyalty. My findings are nuanced, but the most significant conclusion is that, while some campaign activities do indeed harm judicial legitimacy, the overall effect of judicial elections is beneficial to legitimacy. This is a very important finding, one that should fundamentally reframe how we understand the benefits and costs of electing judges.

In the final chapter (chapter 7), I move away a bit from strict reliance on the survey to discuss more generally issues surrounding the election of judges in the American states. The most important conclusion I draw about elections and campaign activity is that their effects must be understood within the American context in which preferences for judicial accountability are fairly widespread. Because elections are preferred by most Americans, elections, by themselves, with all of their warts and odorous smells, contribute to the legitimacy of elected courts in the United States. Thus—contrary to Professor Charlie Geyh's (2003) famous declaration that judicial elections stink—it appears from this analysis that judicial elections may smell in part, but overall the blend of odors from electing judges is not in fact foul!

CHAPTER TWO

REPUBLICAN PARTY OF
MINNESOTA V. WHITE
AND PERCEPTIONS OF
JUDICIAL IMPARTIALITY

The Supreme Court's decision in *Republican Party of Minnesota v. White*—which extended the First Amendment to the US Constitution to campaign statements made by candidates for judicial office—has been predicted to "make a change in judicial election campaigns that will downgrade the pool of candidates for the bench, reduce the willingness of good judges to seek reelection, add to the cynical view that judges are merely 'another group of politicians,' and thus directly hurt state courts and indirectly hurt all our courts" (Schotland 2002, 8). Professor Schotland is certainly not alone these days in fretting about the consequences of the "new style" of state judicial elections for the perceived legitimacy of law and courts. Indeed, even Justice Sandra Day O'Connor has expressed serious regrets about her deciding vote in *Republican Party of Minnesota v. White*, owing to fears that the campaigning genie has come out of the bottle with a vengeance (Hirsch 2006).[1] If these observers are correct that judicial legitimacy is imperiled, it seems a sizable cost to pay in order to extend free-speech rights to candidates for state judicial office.

It is perhaps surprising that analysts are so convinced of the effect of electioneering on judicial legitimacy given that the scientific evidence on such effects is so scant. Indeed, so far as I am aware, no rigorous empirical research has investigated the impact of campaign activity on attitudes toward the judiciary. Although we know a fair amount about the more general origins of attitudes toward courts (e.g., Caldeira and Gibson 1992; Gibson 2007), we know practically nothing about whether the activity unleashed by *Republican Party of Minnesota v. White* will harm elected courts. Obviously, this is an empirical question of considerable import.

More generally, scholars are rethinking and reinvestigating the question of whether and how campaign activity influences citizens. For instance, the long-standing conventional wisdom has been that the use of negative attack ads drives turnout in ordinary elections down (Ansolabehere and Iyengar 1995). Brooks (2006), however, claims to have undermined the finding that negative campaigning lowers voter turnout. She concludes, "Ultimately, Americans are more resilient to campaign attacks than many wedded to the normative idea of cleaner campaigning might be inclined to believe" (Brooks 2006, 693). Similarly, Geer (2006) actually touts the *value* of negative advertising and attack ads in his comprehensive analysis of advertisements in presidential campaigns. Although scholars of elections rarely consider such "dependent variables" as institutional legitimacy (just as they rarely consider judicial elections), we know at a minimum that the effects of campaigning on citizens are not simple and that they often vary considerably from what many anticipate (for a meta-analysis of this voluminous literature, see Lau, Sigelman, and Rovner [2007]).

The purpose of this chapter is to carefully consider how campaign activity by judges influences the legitimacy of state courts. Based on the Kentucky survey and a representative national survey conducted in 2007, this analysis uses experimental methods to discern how specific types of campaign activity affect the legitimacy the public accords state supreme courts. Specifically, I investigate the influence on perceived impartiality of three types of campaign activity:

- the use of attack ads
- the acceptance of campaign contributions
- the announcement of policy positions by candidates for judicial office

Each of these represents a causal factor in an experimental vignette embedded in the surveys. Because this is a true experiment (with random assignment of respondents to treatments), I am entitled in this analysis to an uncommon degree of certainty about the causal connections between campaign activity and institutional legitimacy. In addition, external validity (the ability to make inferences from this sample to the larger population of Americans) is enhanced by the use of a representative national sample.

One of the mistakes that many critics of judicial elections make is the failure to compare elections for judges with elections for other state officials. For example, scholars sometimes argue that people know so little about judges and judicial elections that different methods of selecting judges should be adopted (but see Gibson and Caldeira 2009b). But the value of cross-institutional analysis is that we also learn that people know little about state legislators and legislatures, even though few calls can be heard for the elimination of legislative elections. Consequently, the experiment reported here varies a fourth factor: the institution involved. Half of my respondents were queried about their state supreme court; the other half, about their state legislature. Thus, an important contribution of this analysis is that the effects of campaign activity can be compared across two important political institutions: courts and legislatures. As a preview of the findings, this comparison often fails to conclude that courts are unique institutions with highly fragile legitimacy. In the concluding section of this chapter, I speculate more broadly about two issues: the expectations and understandings citizens have of their judiciaries and the consequences of these empirical findings for judicial independence and accountability.

THE *WHITE* DECISION AND ITS AFTERMATH

As I have noted, the Supreme Court's decision in *Republican Party of Minnesota v. White* is regarded by many as momentous. While ongoing litigation is still attempting to identify whether any limits at all can be placed on the campaign activities of candidates for judicial office (see Hasen 2007; see also Bopp and Woudenberg 2007a, 2007b), the *White* decision is unambiguous in granting the right to candidates to announce their positions on important legal and political issues, including those likely to come before courts in subsequent litigation. The decision turned on the question of impartiality: whether speech restrictions were justified by the state's legitimate interest in protecting the impartiality and/or appearance of impartiality of the state judiciary. The majority in *White* wrestled with various definitions of "impartiality" but in the end concluded that "preventing judicial candidates from announcing their views only during the limited period of the judicial campaign would neither keep judges openminded nor create the public perception of openmindedness" (Hasen 2007, 20). In the final analysis, the majority asserted that if a state decides to hold elections for its judicial offices, then legitimate elections, with all the attendant campaign activity, must be allowed.[2]

Although not at the center of the arguments of the litigation, the *White* decision is crucially dependent upon empirical assumptions about how ordinary people form their impressions of courts. The causal process posited by the dissenters on the court goes something like this.

- Courts, lacking in the powers of the purse and of the sword, must rely heavily on legitimacy to get their decisions accepted and respected by those who disagree with such decisions.
- The legitimacy of courts is heavily dependent upon perceptions that judges are impartial.
- Perceptions of impartiality are susceptible to short-term factors, such as campaign activity by candidates for judicial office.

- Citizens who hear judges proclaim their positions on important legal and political issues during campaigns will conclude that such judges cannot be impartial in their decision making on the bench.
- The legitimacy of courts is therefore threatened by policy pronouncements by candidates for judicial office.[3]

To many, the consequence of this loss of perceived impartiality and institutional legitimacy may be dire.

What does extant research (primarily conducted by political scientists—e.g., Gibson and Caldeira 2009a) reveal about the determinants of the legitimacy of judicial institutions? In particular, do perceptions of campaign activity affect perceptions of courts? Unfortunately, the social science literature on this issue is scarce. We know, for instance, that the Supreme Court's highly controversial ruling in *Bush v. Gore* did not undermine the legitimacy of the institution (Gibson, Caldeira, and Spence 2003a); indeed, it may have even enhanced it (Gibson 2007). On the other hand, there is some recent evidence that the ad campaigns by interest groups in connection with the nomination of Samuel Alito to the US Supreme Court may have damaged the legitimacy of the court itself (Gibson and Caldeira 2009a). This evidence is persuasive since it is based upon a three-wave panel survey, which means that change in the attitudes of individual citizens could be observed rather than merely inferred.[4] Apparently, the message conveyed by the ads was that the Supreme Court is just like any other political institution, and as such, is not worthy of high esteem. These activities cost the Supreme Court some of its institutional support.

While it is certainly true that judicial campaigns have become vastly more costly and more focused on legal and political issues (e.g., Goldberg et al. 2005), to date, practically no rigorous evidence has been produced to document the alleged decline in the legitimacy of courts. It is crucial that this question be investigated via rigorous empirical methods. The legitimacy experiment does exactly that.

To reiterate, the threat of politicized judicial campaigns is that electioneering may undermine the belief that courts are essentially nonpolitical institutions. Citizens may learn that courts are quite like other political institutions if that is the message to which people are exposed. Indeed, this is precisely the most worrisome consequence of the politicized style of judicial elections: to the extent that campaigning takes on the characteristics of "normal" political elections, courts will be seen as *not* special and different, with the consequence that their legitimacy may be undermined. At the most general level, I hypothesize that those who become aware of and attuned to campaigns in politicized judicial elections will judge courts and other political institutions similarly and will therefore extend less legitimacy to courts.[5] Consequently, politicized judicial campaigns may seriously disrupt the normal supply of legitimacy by portraying judges as nothing more than ordinary politicians. Thus, the general hypothesis of this research is that politicized campaign activity undermines the perceived impartiality of judicial institutions. The campaign activity I consider here has to do with (1) the use of attack ads, (2) the receipt of campaign contributions by candidates, and (3) statements of policy positions given by candidates for office.

Attack Ads

A voluminous literature addressing the effects of negative campaigns on citizens exists, even if little consensus has been reached.[6] Ansolabehere and Iyengar 1995 (and others) document a significant drop in voter turnout associated with negative ads (presumably due to "tuning out" the electoral process). Challenges to this conclusion, however, are many (e.g., Finkel and Geer 1998; Geer 2006) and growing (e.g., Brooks 2006). Nonetheless, it seems transparently obvious that candidates for political office *believe* such campaigns to be effective (as do the critics of negative advertising). Mendelberg (2001) shows that the infamous "Willie Horton" ad was successful in framing many issues in racial terms. Yet, in a very important meta-analysis of the research literature, Lau et al. (1999) conclude that negative campaign ads have little effect, although they acknowledge that virtually no research examines the long-term implications of such ads (860), as in the consequences for institutional legitimacy (see also Lau and Pomper 2004; Mark 2006; and Lau, Sigelman, and Rovner 2007). From the perspective of this research on institutional legitimacy, not much of the extant literature on negative campaigning is relevant or informative, because no research has examined judicial campaigns and because quite different dependent variables are analyzed.[7]

On this dimension, however, courts are likely to differ from other political institutions, if for no other reason than that the use of attack ads in judicial elections is a relatively new phenomenon. Anyone accustomed to viewing advertisements touting the legal qualifications of a candidate for judicial office will surely take notice of an advertisement like the one run for Gordon Maag in the 2004 supreme court race in Illinois:

[Announcer]: Multi-national corporations, HMOs, and the insurance industry are spending millions to buy Lloyd Karmeier a seat on the Supreme Court. [At this point in the advertisement, the logos of Pfizer, Allstate, Honeywell and other corporations are shown on the

screen.] They know Lloyd Karmeier will continue to support them as they outsource American jobs and eliminate healthcare for workers and retirees. Law enforcement, teachers and working families choose Gordon Maag because they know Maag can't be bought.
Gordon Maag: Making the law work for working families.
PFB: Justice for All PAC.

Such ads portray judicial candidates as little different from any other political figure, thereby potentially undermining the distinctiveness of the judiciary. Many judicial campaigns today use extremely negative advertisements that aggressively attack their opponents (see Goldberg et al. 2005).[8]

Campaign Contributions

Scholars have become interested in the influence of campaign contributions on state judiciaries.[9] For instance, research has shown that campaign contributors in fact appear in courts before judges to whom they have given campaign contributions (e.g., Dubois 1986; Hansen 1991). Furthermore, anecdotal evidence can be found on the relationship between such contributions and individual court decisions (e.g., Schotland 1985; Champagne 1986, 1988; Banner 1988). Some rigorous evidence suggests a connection between contributions and decisions (e.g., Ware 1999), but contrary evidence also exists (e.g., on the Wisconsin Supreme Court, see Cann [2002]). No clear conclusions emerge from this literature on whether contributions *actually* affect decisions.

In some respects, however, it matters little if there is in fact a connection between contributions and votes; what people believe about the connection may be of greater significance for the legitimacy of courts. Poll data suggest that many believe a relationship exists between contributions and court decisions (e.g., Jackson and Riddlesperger 1991; Texas Office of Court Administration 1998).[10] It is not clear, however, how widespread this perception is, and the research findings are also difficult to square with evidence that the vast majority of Americans express considerable confidence in their state courts.[11] Even Texas's scandal-ridden courts are fairly positively evaluated by ordinary Texans (Cheek and Champagne 2004, 174–76).[12]

The question of whether campaign contributions corrupt officeholders—or whether such contributions contribute to the perception of corruption—is central in contemporary research on campaign finance. For example, the litigation over campaign finance focuses on whether the current system of campaign contributions adds to the appearance of corruption in American politics, thereby undermining American democracy.[13] In the litigation on the

Bi-Partisan Campaign Reform Act (BCRA), public-opinion experts directly addressed this question (e.g., Shapiro 2003). But in what is perhaps the definitive study on the issue, Persily and Lammie (2004) conclude that although Americans view campaign contributions as tending to corrupt legislators, the causal nexus between campaign contributions and perceptions of corruption has *not* been established; instead, they strongly argue that observed correlations do not necessarily imply causation and that perceptions of corruption more likely reflect generalized attitudes and propensities. They claim, for instance, that the American National Election Study's "respondents who are unhappy with their position in society, with the incumbents who run the government, or with government or people in general are more likely to deem government corrupt" (2004, 150)—rather than such attitudes being a consequence of the direct effects of campaigns (e.g., 2004,137). They also "note the irony that the share of the population perceiving corruption declined even as soft money sky-rocketed and that the share increased after passage of the soft money ban" (2004, 123). Primo (2002) expresses the same concern about the issue of causality and argues pointedly that "the claim that money drives cynicism toward politics on a macro, historical level is simply false" (2002, 217). He then goes on to draw the same conclusion from microlevel evidence.[14] Thus, although many Americans perceive governmental corruption, and an even larger proportion favor campaign-finance reform, the evidence to date that contributions *cause* perceptions of corruption is ambiguous.

Nonetheless, one might still hypothesize that, in the judicial case, campaign contributions have a particularly corrosive influence on perceptions of impartiality. When contributions come from the very law firms and corporations that litigate before the judges whom they help elect, then the generally tawdry aura of contributions takes on an even more unseemly and sinister tint.[15] Therefore, I expect that accepting campaign contributions threatens the legitimacy of both institutions and their officeholders.

Policy Commitments and Prejudgments

Of the factors considered here, the influence of policy commitments is least well understood, in large part owing to the recency of the Supreme Court decision and the quite different role of policy pronouncements in campaigns for courts and other political institutions. As I have noted, the theory of the states that prohibited judicial candidates from making policy commitments is that judges will be perceived to be biased and unable to evaluate future cases solely on the merits of the individual dispute.[16] So far as I am aware, no extant empirical research has ever investigated this hypothesis.[17]

One of the most telling critiques of using survey data to test hypotheses is that causal inferences are suspect, especially when the independent and dependent variables are measured at the same time. But, when experiments are embedded within representative surveys, not only are findings generalizable to the larger population from which the sample is drawn (external validity), but great confidence can also be placed on causal inferences (internal validity).[18] With random assignment of respondents to treatments, the proverbial "all else" can indeed be considered equal.

Consequently, I included within the survey an experimental vignette on campaigning and judicial legitimacy. The vignette allows me to investigate how people form their assessments of impartiality and institutional legitimacy. Vignettes are a particularly useful means of incorporating the context of judicial campaigns within survey research. These short stories can reveal processes of reasoning perhaps not even directly accessible to the respondents themselves (and have been used widely in the past—e.g., Hamilton and Sanders 1992; Gibson and Gouws 1999, 2001; Gibson 2002; Duch and Palmer 2004).[19] For the purposes of the questions addressed in this book, experimental vignettes—especially when embedded in a representative survey—provide an optimal methodology (on experimentation in political science, see Kinder and Palfrey [1993]; see also Gibson, Caldeira, and Spence 2002).

The experiment on which this research is based is structured around a story about candidates for public office. The story manipulates various aspects of the campaign (e.g., the use of attack ads) in an effort to estimate the effects of such activity. At the end of the vignette, the respondents are asked a series of questions about the impartiality of the officeholders (the candidate in the story is always said to be elected to office) and the institution itself. Stories such as these have the virtue of mundane realism through verisimilitude, in the sense that they depict a set of circumstances that are concrete and easily understood by the respondents.[20]

The Experimental Manipulations and Hypotheses
Technically, this experiment is a $2 \times 3 \times 3 \times 2$ fully crossed factorial design. This is a between-subjects study, with each respondent told only one version of the vignette. The respondents were randomly assigned to one of the 36 vignette versions (by the CATI program). With less-than-perfect response rates, minor imperfections inevitably creep into survey experiments, and the number of respondents per version varies from 42 to 78. Because the experimental

manipulations are orthogonal to each other, the sets of dummy variables used to represent the interventions are themselves unrelated.

The Institution. The tendency to study judicial institutions in isolation, without comparison to other comparable political institutions, has long impeded our understanding of courts. Exceptions exist (e.g., Bonneau 2005), and no one has shown us better than Hall (2001) the value of cross-institutional analysis in thinking about judicial elections and politics (see also Gibson and Caldeira 1998).

Many of the criticisms directed against judicial elections in fact are generic to low-salience elections (e.g., McDermott 1997). Indeed, nearly all of the complaints about state judicial elections (e.g., low turnout) probably apply with equal force to state legislative elections, even though few serious observers propose that state legislators should therefore be freed of electoral accountability. In the analysis that follows, it is useful to compare the impact of these campaign activities on both judges and state legislators. The experiment consequently began with a random assignment of the respondent to either a story about the Kentucky Supreme Court or the Kentucky State Legislature. (See table 2.1 for the text of each of the elements of the vignettes.) The overarching hypothesis of the vignette is that the judgments and evaluations of people vary across institutional contexts.

Campaign Contributions. The first substantive manipulation in the experiment has to do with campaign contributions. I sought to vary contributions by the degree to which a conflict of interest is implied (on conflicts of interest, see Stark [2000]). Rejecting all contributions is the condition under which no conflicts can occur; the opposite extreme involves accepting contributions from parties who do business directly before the institution, and an intermediate position involves contributors without direct business with the institution but who seek to shape public policy more generally. I hypothesize a monotonic relationship between the degree of conflict of interest and institutional legitimacy, and I suspect the relationship will deviate from linearity since the refusal to accept campaign contributions will most likely have a disproportionate effect on the protection of institutional legitimacy.

Policy Prejudgments. Policy prejudgments—to the extent they suggest to citizens that judges are deciding cases not on their individual merits, but rather on preexisting ideological preferences—may also impugn legitimacy. The judicial and legislative versions of this vignette posit equivalent variability in

TABLE 2.1. VIGNETTE MANIPULATIONS AND VERSIONS

	INSTITUTION	
	STATE SUPREME COURT	STATE LEGISLATURE
Campaign contributions		
Strong conflict— Contributions from litigants	Judge Anderson receives campaign contributions— that is, money—from corporations and public interest groups that regularly try cases before his court, the Kentucky Supreme Court.	Senator Anderson receives campaign contributions— that is, money—from corporations and public interest groups that regularly receive contracts and public spending approved by the Kentucky Senate.
Moderate conflict— Contributions from interest groups	Judge Anderson receives campaign contributions— that is, money—from corporations and public interest groups that are interested in influencing legal decisions, but which do *not* try cases before Judge Anderson's court, the Kentucky Supreme Court.	Senator Anderson receives campaign contributions— that is, money—from corporations and public interest groups that are interested in influencing legislation, but which do *not* receive any contracts or public spending approved by the Kentucky Senate.
No conflict— No contributions	Judge Anderson has been offered campaign contributions—that is, money—from corporations and public interest groups, but he declines to accept any contributions whatsoever, saying that he wants to avoid any threats to his impartiality when deciding cases before the Kentucky Supreme Court.	Senator Anderson has been offered campaign contributions—that is, money—from corporations and public interest groups, but he declines to accept any contributions whatsoever, saying he wants to avoid any threats to his impartiality when voting on legislation in the Kentucky Senate.
Policy commitments		
No commitment— No policy statement	Judge Anderson's campaign refuses to talk about issues of public policy, saying that a judge should not discuss issues that his court may have to decide some day. Instead, his television ads focus mainly on his qualifications to be a judge—things like what his background is and where he went to law school	Senator Anderson's campaign refuses to talk about issues of public policy, saying that a legislator should not discuss issues that the senate may have to vote on some day. Instead, his television ads focus mainly on his qualifications to be a senator—things like what his background is and where he went to school

	Judge Anderson	Senator Anderson
General policy— Gives policy views	Judge Anderson's campaign broadcasts some ads on television that focus mainly on his views and positions on important legal issues like abortion, lawsuit abuse, and the use of the death penalty in Kentucky.	Senator Anderson's campaign broadcasts some ads on television that focus mainly on his views and positions on important policies like abortion, lawsuit abuse, and the use of the death penalty in Kentucky.
Specific case decisions— Promises to decide certain way	Judge Anderson's campaign broadcasts some ads on television that focus mainly on his views and positions on important legal issues like abortion, lawsuit abuse, and the use of the death penalty in Kentucky. He promises that, if reelected, he will decide these kinds of cases in the way that most people in Kentucky want them decided.	Senator Anderson's campaign broadcasts some ads on television which focus mainly on his views and positions on important policies like abortion, lawsuit abuse, and the use of the death penalty in Kentucky. He promises that, if reelected, he will vote on these kinds of issues in the way that most people in Kentucky want them decided.

Attack advertising

	Judge Anderson	Senator Anderson
No attack ads	Judge Anderson's campaign ads rarely mention his opponent, instead focusing on providing voters information about himself, and claiming that, if elected, he will make fair and impartial decisions on cases before the court.	Senator Anderson's campaign ads rarely mention his opponent, instead focusing on providing voters information about himself, and claiming that, if elected, he will make fair and impartial decisions on legislation before the senate.
Attack ads	Judge Anderson's campaign ads vigorously attack his opponent, claiming that his opponent is biased in favor of insurance companies and other such businesses, and would therefore not be able to make fair and impartial decisions if elected to the supreme court.	Senator Anderson's campaign ads vigorously attack his opponent, claiming that his opponent is biased in favor of insurance companies and other such businesses, and would therefore not be able to make fair and impartial decisions if elected to the senate.

the degree to which the candidate for public office commits in advance to a particular policy position, with the range defined by the old judicial rules (no policy statements allowed) to the current rules (only general policy statements allowed) to a position beyond that which is generally deemed appropriate today (specific policy pledges are made). Consequently, the story varied the degree to which the candidate makes specific policy commitments, ranging from refusing to discuss issues at all to making general policy statements to making a specific pledge to make decisions the people of the state want (see table 2.1).[21] Obviously, I hypothesize that the stronger the policy precommitment, the less the judge and the institution will be thought to be impartial and legitimate.

Attack Ads. Finally, a third issue for judicial campaigns has to do with style of campaigning and in particular the use of so-called attack ads. This manipulation is a dichotomy, varying from innocuous campaign statements to vigorous attacks on the impartiality and fairness of the opponent.

The full text of all 36 vignettes is reported in appendix C.

The Dependent Variables

At the conceptual level, the overarching dependent variable for the vignette is the perception of whether the political actor can serve as a fair and impartial governmental policy maker. This analysis focuses on two types of measures: perceptions of the individual candidate/officeholder and perceptions of the institution itself. Regarding the individual, the respondents were asked whether the officeholder "can serve as a fair and impartial" judge/senator. The question focused on the institution posits that all judges/senators are selected in the same way as Judge/Senator Anderson and then asks directly about the perceived legitimacy of the institution. Finally, the respondents were asked whether they would accept the decisions he made as legitimate. The full text of these questions is reported in appendix D.

The vignette was highly successful in generating variability in the perceived impartiality of the officeholder (the winning candidate for judicial/legislative office). For example, within the judicial context, the percentages asserting that Judge Anderson can be fair and impartial range from 31.4% to 88.0%; in the legislative context, the percentages vary from 33.4% to 84.0%. Thus, the vignettes seem to have captured factors that are indeed meaningful to the respondents.

One limitation of many vignette-based studies is that the dependent variable is poorly measured, often with a single-item indicator (e.g., Gibson 2002). The advantage of such an approach is that substantive research findings can be clearly and simply reported; but low reliability has, of course, many highly undesirable consequences for statistical analysis. Consequently, in the hypothesis testing here, I focus for illustrative purposes on the specific items (especially the question about whether the judge/senator can be fair and impartial), but for statistical purposes, I employ a continuous indicator of reactions to the vignette. This variable is a latent construct represented by a factor score derived from a Common Factor Analysis of the three vignette judgments. For both the judicial and legislative analyses, the results reveal strongly unidimensional structures.[22] For the supreme court, the factor loadings on the first unrotated factor are

Believe the judge can be fair and impartial	.82
Accept decisions as fair and impartial	.75
Consider the Kentucky Supreme Court legitimate	.71

This set of items is extremely reliable: alpha = .80. For the state senate, the factor structure is similar:

Accept decisions as fair and impartial	.80
Believe the senator can be fair and impartial	.75
Consider the Kentucky State Senate legitimate	.67

Cronbach's alpha for the set of items is .78. Thus, the dependent variables for the statistical analysis of the vignette are quite valid and highly reliable.

The dependent variable in this analysis should be thought of as a contextualized assessment of judicial impartiality and legitimacy, and as such, contrasts with the oft-used measures of institutional support and legitimacy found in the research of Gibson and Caldeira (e.g., 2009a; see also chapter 4). For purposes of an experiment such as this, one obviously requires a specific reaction to the impartiality, fairness, and legitimacy of the people and institutions in the vignette, rather than generalized and abstract attitudes toward an institution.

Manipulation Checks

In experimental studies such as this, the manipulations are not always perceived as they are intended (for a classic example, see Gibson and Gouws [2001]). Thus, it is necessary to assess empirically how the respondents reacted to the elements of the stories they heard. Table 2.2 reports data relevant to checking the effectiveness of the manipulations. As is conventional with manipulation checks, the questions asked assess the degree to which the respondents heard and understood the attributes of the stories (see appendix D for the text of the items used to check the manipulations).

The results of checking the manipulations are both methodologically and

TABLE 2.2. MANIPULATION CHECKS

Manipulation/Condition	Manipulation check		
	Mean	s.d.	N
Campaign contributions—Whether received			
Kentucky Supreme Court[a]			
Contributions from litigants	6.37	3.21	323
Contributions from interest groups	6.31	2.84	349
No contributions	4.62	3.25	319
Kentucky Senate[b]			
Contributions from contractors	6.42	3.02	367
Contributions from interest groups	6.45	2.94	340
No contributions	4.96	3.29	324
Policy commitments—Made positions known			
Kentucky Supreme Court[c]			
No policy statement	5.47	3.23	353
Gives policy views	6.42	2.82	330
Promises to decide certain ways	6.79	2.85	309
Kentucky Senate[d]			
No policy statement	4.78	3.13	367
Gives policy views	6.27	3.04	341
Promises to decide certain ways	6.77	2.88	326
Policy commitments—Made policy promises			
Kentucky Supreme Court[e]			
No policy statement	4.95	3.23	353
Gives policy views	5.49	2.86	330
Promises to decide certain ways	6.77	2.92	309
Kentucky Senate[f]			
No policy statement	4.47	2.96	366
Gives policy views	5.39	2.86	341
Promises to decide certain ways	6.64	2.96	326
Attack advertising—Whether used attack ads			
Kentucky Supreme Court[g]			
No attack ads	3.67	3.13	485
Attack ads	6.60	3.33	506
Kentucky Senate[h]			
No attack ads	3.47	2.99	497
Attack ads	6.97	3.16	533

Note: The manipulation checks are as follows (see also appendix D for the question wordings):

Campaign contributions: Degree of certainty about receipt of campaign contributions
Policy commitments: Degree of certainty that policy positions were made known
Degree of certainty that promises were made about how cases would be decided
Attack advertising: Degree of certainty that attack ads were used.
In all instances, the response set varies from 1 to 10 (very certain).

[a] Difference of means test: $p < .000$, $\eta = .25$. [e] Difference of means test: $p < .000$, $\eta = .24$.
[b] Difference of means test: $p < .000$, $\eta = .22$. [f] Difference of means test: $p < .000$, $\eta = .29$.
[c] Difference of means test: $p < .000$, $\eta = .19$. [g] Difference of means test: $p < .000$, $\eta = .41$.
[d] Difference of means test: $p < .000$, $\eta = .27$. [h] Difference of means test: $p < .000$, $\eta = .50$.

substantively revealing. Consider campaign contributions first. In the story versions in which contributions were given, most respondents perceived the contributions accurately, and practically no differences exist in perceptions of the vignette according to whether the story depicted a judge or a senator.[23] Perhaps reflecting some degree of cynicism, roughly one-third of the respondents who were told that the judge rejected campaign contributions nonetheless were certain to some degree that he in fact had received some. The results for the senate version of the vignette are similar. Nonetheless, this manipulation was generally correctly perceived by a significant majority of the respondents.[24]

As with the policy commitment manipulations, when the candidate was depicted as making policy promises, the respondents were substantially more certain that such promises were made (see "Made policy promises" in table 2.2). It is perhaps noteworthy that only marginal differences are found on the "Made positions known" manipulation check between the expression of policy views and the making of policy promises. The former seems, to many respondents, to imply the latter. Nonetheless, this manipulation was also accurately perceived by the respondents. Finally, the attack ad manipulation was extremely successful in both the judicial and legislative contexts, with the vast majority of respondents able to recall correctly whether such ads were used.

In general, the vignettes succeeded in the sense that the respondents perceived correctly the various manipulations. It remains then to consider whether these manipulations in fact influenced perceptions of impartiality and legitimacy.

MULTIVARIATE RESULTS

The most efficient means of assessing these hypotheses is to create dummy variables from the manipulations and then regress the legitimacy factor scores on these indicators.[25] In that analysis, the excluded category for the campaign contribution manipulation is the scenario of no contributions; for policy commitments, it is the condition of expressing no policy views. Table 2.3 reports the results. So that the institutional hypothesis can be readily assessed, I report the judicial and legislative results in the same table.[26]

The first observation about table 2.3 is that institutional legitimacy is reasonably well predicted (see the R^2 statistics), especially because each of the independent variables is nothing more than a dichotomy. Second, in general, the equations produce remarkably similar coefficients, indicating that cross-institutional differences, with one important exception, are largely trivial. How people evaluate the court does not differ much from how they assess the legislature.

TABLE 2.3. MULTIVARIATE ANALYSIS OF THE CONSEQUENCES OF CAMPAIGNING FOR INSTITUTIONAL LEGITIMACY

Manipulation/Value	Supreme court			State legislature		
	b	s.e.	β	b	s.e.	β
Campaign contributions						
From litigants/contributors	−.24	.02	−.40***	−.24	.02	−.42***
From interest groups	−.18	.02	−.31***	−.17	.02	−.29***
Policy commitments						
Policy views	−.03	.02	−.05	.05	.02	.09**
Promises	.01	.02	.01	.10	.02	.17***
Attack ads						
Uses ads	−.09	.02	−.17***	−.09	.02	−.17***
Equation statistics						
Intercept	.79	.02		.71	.02	
Standard deviation—				.28		
Dependent variable	.28					
Standard error of estimate	.26			.25		
R^2			.16***			.18***
N	983			1,024		

Note: All the independent variables are dichotomies, scored at 0 or 1. The dependent variables also vary from 0 to 1.
Standardized regression coefficients (β): *** $p < .001$ ** $p < .01$ * $p < .05$

Third, the strongest effects on institutional legitimacy come from campaign contributions. When groups with direct connections to the decision maker give contributions, legitimacy suffers substantially. Furthermore, there appears to be nothing at all idiosyncratic about courts: campaign contributions have nearly identical consequences for judicial and legislative legitimacy. One can see in both contexts the particularly damaging consequences of contributions from parties having direct business with the institution (litigants/contributors), an effect that significantly exceeds that of ordinary policy-oriented interest groups. In the absence of campaign contributions, the legitimacy of both institutions is high (see the intercepts, which of course also reflect the conditions of no policy commitments and no attack ads). Figure 2.1 depicts the bivariate relationship within each institution, using the individual item about whether the policy maker can be fair (because the manipulation variables are by definition orthogonal to each other, bivariate and multivariate conclusions are identical). The effect of campaign contributions on institutional legitimacy is highly significant, statistically and substantively, and, with each type of contributor, differs little across institution. When contributions are given by parties having a direct stake in the decisions of the officeholder, fewer than one-half of the people believe that the policy maker can be fair.

In contrast to the findings on campaign contributions, policy commitments have no impact whatsoever on the legitimacy of the supreme court, even while having a *positive* influence on the legitimacy of the state legislature. These relationships are depicted in table 2.3 in the OLS analysis and in figure 2.2 for the specific question about institutional legitimacy. For the legislature, promises to make specific decisions influence legitimacy more than do general policy statements, a finding presumably grounded in the popular expectation that legislators should make and honor campaign promises. *But for the judicial candidates, even promises to decide cases in specific ways have no consequences at all for the legitimacy of the institution.* This is an important finding that may

FIGURE 2.1. THE IMPACT OF CAMPAIGN CONTRIBUTIONS ON PERCEPTIONS OF FAIR AND IMPARTIAL POLICY MAKING.

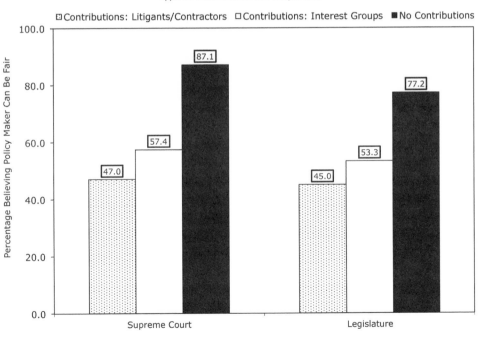

Type of Contribution to Policymaker

☐ Contributions: Litigants/Contractors ☐ Contributions: Interest Groups ■ No Contributions

Which Institution is the Vignette About?

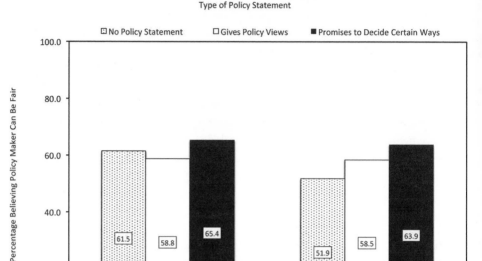

Type of Policy Statement

indicate that people recognize that judges make policy and that, in a democracy, some degree of political accountability ought to be imposed on policy makers. It also seems as if people are thinking in terms of policy, not necessarily individual cases. When they think about issues like the right to abortion, they are probably not focusing on the specific individual seeking an abortion (or those who would prohibit it) but rather on *legal policy* about whether (and when) abortions can be had. Given the widespread debates in American society about judicial philosophies and ideologies, it would be perhaps surprising were this otherwise. The data are striking and compelling in revealing that making policy statements during campaigns does not seem to render a judge unable to make fair and impartial decisions on the bench, at least in the eyes of ordinary people.

The contrast between the judicial and legislative findings is especially striking. Conventional wisdom holds that if judges express policy views in campaigns, institutional legitimacy will suffer, because the function of courts (based on minoritarianism and independence; e.g., McGuire 2004) is different from the function of legislatures (majoritarianism and accountability). These findings indicate that courts are indeed different—judicial legitimacy does not *profit from* explicit position assertions: courts are not mirror images of legislatures in the sense that policy commitments do not have the opposite effect of undermining institutional legitimacy. Elites may expect judicial independence and see policy commitments as a threat to independence and impartiality, but these data suggest that ordinary people are not similarly worried about judicial candidates making policy statements during campaigns. The judicial coefficients in table 2.3 strongly challenge the assertions of the dissenters in *Republican Party of Minnesota v. White* (2002).

Between the strong impact of campaign contributions and the nonexistent influence of policy commitments lies the moderate influence of the use of attack ads. When candidates for office, judicial or legislative, use attack ads, legitimacy suffers. This effect is moderate and is not nearly as large as the effect of campaign contributions; and it is virtually identical within both the judicial and legislative contexts. Of course, this experiment cannot demonstrate one way or the other whether the negative consequences of attack ads persist over time; but, in this context, attacking one's opponent, judicial or legislative, detracts from the appearance of impartiality and fairness.

Finally, these findings demonstrate the value of cross-institutional analysis. At least with regard to campaign contributions and attack ads, the data reveal little about courts that is unique. To the extent that campaigning affects the legitimacy of institutions, it does so similarly for courts and legislatures.

Conditional Analysis

Experiments have the invaluable asset of being self-contained sets of hypotheses. Nonetheless, conditional effects may still be present—the experimental stimuli may be received differently by different people. Consequently, one further analytical step can shed important additional insight into the consequences of politicized judicial campaigns.

Two obvious conditional hypotheses occur. First, general support for a court may cause people to perceive the experimental stimuli differently, with those more loyal toward the judiciary being more offended by politicized campaign practices. This hypothesis is grounded in the theory of positivity bias, advanced by Gibson and his colleagues (e.g., Gibson, Caldeira, and Spence 2003a; Gibson and Caldeira 2009a): Those with high loyalty toward courts tend to see them as unique, relatively nonpolitical institutions (even if these citizens do not necessarily accept naive theories of mechanical jurisprudence). Consequently, politicized campaigning is likely to be considered a threat to judicial legitimacy.

Second, knowledge may moderate these relationships: Just as with institutional support, those who are more knowledgeable about courts are more likely to view them as distinctive institutions, with nonpolitical characteristics. They therefore are more likely to be negatively influenced by politicized campaigning, judging such activity as inappropriate for courts and judges.

Thus, the hypotheses predict that the negative effects of campaign contributions, attack ads, and policy promises are greater among those more knowledgeable and who express greater support for the court, and therefore the interactive coefficients are expected to be negative (exacerbating the undermining influence on judicial legitimacy of the campaign stimuli). Given the limits of the survey, these hypotheses can only be tested for those respondents who heard the vignette about the supreme court. The measures of both institutional loyalty and knowledge of the Kentucky judiciary are discussed in appendix D and chapter 4.

Consider first the impact of institutional support (which varies from 0 to 8). When the interaction terms are added to the equation reported in table 2.3, including of course the direct effect of institutional support, the only significant interactive effect is between support and policy promises—no effect is observed for campaign contributions or for the use of attack ads.[27] When support is at its lowest (0), the effect of policy promises on legitimacy is significantly positive ($b = .14$): promises *enhance* perceived judicial legitimacy. As support for the court increases, the effect of promises declines ($b = -.04$), so that at the highest level of institutional support (8), the coefficient for policy promises is $-.21$. This coefficient is substantial, achieving roughly the magnitude of the effect of campaign contributions from policy-minded groups (although smaller than the effect of contributions from those litigating before the court; see table 2.3). As citizens become more supportive of the Kentucky Supreme Court, the effect of policy promises becomes corrosive.

However, two important caveats must be attached to this finding. First, the number of citizens at the highest level of support for the court is small (about 3% of the sample), so that for most citizens of Kentucky, policy promises have few meaningful consequences for institutional legitimacy. Second, I observe no interactive effect whatsoever between institutional support and the simple expression of policy views (in contrast to policy promises). Even among the most supportive citizens, this sort of campaign activity has no negative consequences at all. Thus, the hypothesis of an interaction between institutional legitimacy and campaign activity is supported, but only for the most extreme form of policy promises and only among a fairly thin slice of the total population.

The hypothesized interaction between knowledge and campaign activity receives even weaker support. The only significant interaction is between knowledge and the expression of policy views (not policy promises). But contrary to the hypothesis, as knowledge of the courts increases, the negative effect of policy statements weakens ($b = .06$), so that at the highest level of knowledge, the coefficient for policy statements is +.08. Although this effect is statistically significant, it is relatively small, and, to reiterate, no such effect is observed on the impact of policy *promises*. Thus, the prudent conclusion is that the effect of campaign activity varies little according to levels of knowledge of the Kentucky judiciary.[28]

Perhaps the most important conclusion emerging from this analysis has to do with variability across the three types of campaign practices. The detrimental effects on institutional legitimacy of campaign contributions are substantial and uniform across various subgroups in the total population. The same can be said of the influence of attack ads (except that the influence is considerably weaker than that of contributions). Some evidence suggests that explicit policy promises undermine legitimacy among those already most supportive of the court, but this is a small portion of the population, and the effect is not observed under the condition of general policy statements by candidates. Thus, it appears that there is a consensus of expectations regarding the undesirability of campaign contributions and attack ads, but with more disagreement about whether explicit policy promises are appropriate. In general, the results of this conditional analysis are illuminating but change little the overall conclusions from the experiment.[29]

REPLICATING THE RESULTS AT THE NATIONAL LEVEL

To what degree are the results from Kentucky generalizable to the nation as a whole? I have argued that Kentucky has some attributes that render it useful for analysis, but without national data, we cannot be sure that the results extend beyond the borders of the commonwealth.

Fortunately, national data are available; the campaign experiment was embedded within a representative national survey conducted in the summer of 2007. The experiment, with random assignment of respondents to treatments conditions, was in nearly every respect a replicate of the Kentucky experiment.

Appendix E provides further methodological details. The hypotheses, manipulations, and indicators are the same in both the original Kentucky experiment and the national replication.

The Dependent Variable

All of the hypotheses of this research predict an effect of campaign activity on the perceived legitimacy of political institutions. Consequently, the dependent variable, measured by a series of questions following the presentation of the vignette to the respondent, concerns whether the officeholder is thought to be able to make fair and impartial decisions as a governmental policy maker. The questions asked address both perceptions of the individual candidate/officeholder and perceptions of the institution itself. Regarding the former, the respondents were asked whether the officeholder "can serve as a fair and impartial" judge/senator. Regarding the latter, a question asked whether an institution in which all judges/senators are selected in the same way as Judge/Senator Anderson is legitimate. Finally, the respondents were asked whether they would accept the decisions the officeholder makes as legitimate. The full text of these questions is reported in appendix C.

The first empirical question to be asked of the vignette data is whether the various versions of the story are associated with different judgments about the impartiality of the officeholder (the winning candidate for judicial/legislative office). For example, within the judicial context, the percentages asserting that Judge Anderson can be fair and impartial range from 25.0 to 95.5 across the 18 versions of the judicial vignette; in the legislative context, the percentages vary from 30.0 to 92.9. Thus, the stories seem to have captured contextual factors that are indeed meaningful to the respondents' perceptions of the institutions.

As I have noted, the experiment employs multiple indicators of the dependent variable, perceptions of the impartiality and legitimacy of the institution. Multiple indicators, of course, provide numerous advantages over single-item measures, as in the ability to estimate both the validity and reliability of the latent variable represented by operational indicators. In terms of validity, for both the judicial and legislative analyses, the results reveal strongly unidimensional structures.[30] For the supreme court, the factor loadings on the first unrotated factor are

Accept decisions as fair and impartial	.89
Believe the judge can be fair and impartial	.73
Consider the [state] supreme court legitimate	.62

This set of items is extremely reliable: alpha = .79. For the state senate, the factor structure is similar:

Accept decisions as fair and impartial	.82
Believe the senator can be fair and impartial	.75
Consider the [state] senate legitimate	.65

Cronbach's alpha for the set of items is .79. Thus, the dependent variables for the statistical analysis of the vignette are quite valid and highly reliable.

For the statistical analysis that follows, I employ a continuous indicator of reactions to the vignette. This variable is a factor score derived from a Common Factor Analysis of the three vignette judgments. For illustrative purposes, however, I report the responses to the specific item about whether the judge/senator can be fair and impartial. In every instance, the illustrative findings strictly parallel the analytical results.

Manipulation Checks

In experimental studies such as this, checks must be implemented to determine the degree to which the respondents accurately comprehended the manipulations. On occasion, manipulations "fail" in the sense that they are not understood as they were intended. For the national legitimacy experiment, table 2.4 reports data relevant to checking the effectiveness of the manipulations, based on conventional questions determining whether the respondents heard and understood the attributes of the stories.[31]

Important methodological and substantive conclusions emerge from the manipulation check analysis. For example, regarding campaign contributions, in the story versions in which contributions were given, most respondents perceived the contributions accurately, and only minor differences exist in perceptions of the vignette according to whether the story depicted a judge or a senator. No doubt reflecting some degree of cynicism, roughly one-fourth (28.4%)[32] of the respondents told that the judge rejected campaign contributions nonetheless were certain to at least some degree that he in fact received some. The results for the senate version of the vignette are similar (26.5%). In general, a substantial majority of the respondents seemed to understand the contributions manipulation as it was intended to be understood.

The same conclusion applies to the policy commitment manipulations: when the candidate was depicted as making policy statements or promises, the respondents were substantially more certain that policy positions were made known (see the means in the "Made positions known" section of table 2.4). Similarly, based on the "Made policy promises" check, those told that the

TABLE 2.4. MANIPULATION CHECKS, 2007 NATIONAL DATA

Manipulation/Condition	Manipulation check			Difference of means test	
	Mean	s.d.	N	eta	p
Campaign contributions—Whether received					
[State] Supreme court				.30	<.000
Contributions from litigants	6.25	3.28	110		
Contributions from interest groups	6.57	3.39	109		
No contributions	4.17	3.50	109		
[State] Senate				.30	<.000
Contributions from contractors	6.02	3.38	111		
Contributions from interest groups	6.17	3.31	117		
No contributions	3.91	3.36	117		
Policy commitments—Made positions known					
[State] Supreme court				.18	<.005
No policy statement	5.03	3.32	114		
Gives policy views	6.31	3.23	108		
Promises to decide certain ways	6.29	3.41	108		
[State] Senate				.34	<.000
No policy statement	4.16	3.40	102		
Gives policy views	6.58	3.12	131		
Promises to decide certain ways	6.85	3.25	112		
Policy commitments—Made policy promises					
[State] Supreme court				.28	<.000
No policy statement	4.89	3.45	114		
Gives policy views	4.89	2.88	108		
Promises to decide certain ways	6.79	2.87	108		
[State] Senate				.27	<.000
No policy statement	4.21	3.34	103		
Gives policy views	5.31	3.10	131		
Promises to decide certain ways	6.54	3.33	112		
Attack advertising—Whether used attack ads					
[State] Supreme court				.46	<.000
No attack ads	3.68	3.39	164		
Attack ads	7.04	3.15	166		
[State] Senate				.50	<.000
No attack ads	3.28	3.15	180		
Attack ads	7.08	3.46	166		

Note: The manipulation check indicators are as follows (see also appendix D for the question wordings):

Campaign contributions: Degree of certainty about receipt of campaign contributions

Policy commitments: Degree of certainty that policy positions were made known

Degree of certainty that promises were made about how cases would be decided

Attack advertising: Degree of certainty that attack ads were used.

In all instances, the response set varies from 1 to 10 (very certain).

candidate made promises are markedly more likely to perceive such promises. In general, most respondents also accurately perceived this manipulation.

Finally, most respondents were able to recall correctly whether attack ads were used in both the judicial and legislative contexts. In general, then, the vignette was a success in the sense that the respondents correctly perceived the various manipulations. The question that remains is whether these factors in fact influenced perceptions of the impartiality and legitimacy of these two political institutions.

ANALYSIS

Table 2.5 reports the results from the experiment (*among those living in states in which judicial elections take place*).[33] So as to be able to clearly compare across institutions, I have reported the results separately for judgments of the state court and state legislature. Two of the manipulations are represented by three conditions; therefore, two dummy variables are necessary to model the effects

TABLE 2.5. MULTIVARIATE ANALYSIS OF THE CONSEQUENCES OF CAMPAIGNING FOR INSTITUTIONAL LEGITIMACY

Manipulation/Value	Supreme court			State legislature		
	b	s.e.	β	b	s.e.	β
Campaign contributions						
From litigants/contributors	−.18	.04	−.29***	−.19	.04	−.30***
From interest groups	−.15	.04	−.25***	−.18	.04	−.29***
Policy commitments						
Policy views	−.01	.04	−.02	.06	.04	.10
Promises	.04	.04	.06	.08	.04	.13*
Attack ads						
Uses ads	.01	.03	.02	−.14	.03	−.25***
Equation statistics						
Intercept	.66	.04		.69	.04	
Standard deviation—				.29		
Dependent variable	.29					
Standard error of estimate	.28			.27		
R^2			.08***			.17***
N	327			342		

Note: All the independent variables are dichotomies, scored at 0 or 1. The dependent variables also vary from 0 to 1.
Standardized regression coefficients (β): *** $p < .001$ ** $p < .01$ * $p < .05$

of those manipulations. The excluded categories are "no contributions" and "no policy promise." The use of attack ads is a dichotomous condition, which of course can be represented by a single dummy variable.[34]

First consider the impact of campaign contributions on legitimacy.[35] For both the state high court and the legislature, the acceptance of campaign contributions significantly detracts from the legitimacy of the institution. Interestingly, however, for courts, it makes a relatively small difference whether the contributions are from a group interested in general policy ($\beta = -.25$) or one directly involved in advocating its interests before the institution ($\beta = -.29$). My original speculation was that contributions from those with immediate self-interests involved would be judged much more harshly than the contributions from those with only general policy interests, but the judicial vignette provides only marginal support for that hypothesis. In the legislative context, that hypothesis fails to receive any support whatsoever. In general, both institutions suffer when candidates accept campaign contributions, irrespective of the specific motives of the contributors.

When it comes to policy commitments from candidates, the differences across institutions are entirely trivial. For candidates for judicial office, neither expressions of policy views nor even policy promises have any consequences for institutional legitimacy (the significance of the judicial coefficient just barely exceeds the .05 critical value: $p = .065$). The coefficient for policy promises in the legislative context is statistically significant, even if only marginally influential. But to the extent that there is a consequence, policy talk generally *increases* legitimacy. Perhaps the most certain conclusion here, however, is that *policy talk by candidates for judicial office has no negative consequences for the perceived impartiality and legitimacy of state courts of last resort.*

So as to better illustrate this lack of relationship, figure 2.3 reports the answers to the simple question of whether the judge can be fair and impartial according to the three experimental conditions on policy talk. The figure strikingly depicts the small differences across the three types of speech. To the extent that any relationship at all can be found in these data, it is that the widely feared "promises to decide" speech is the *least harmful* type of speech, even if the most conservative statistical conclusion from this figure is that policy talk of any sort does not undermine institutional legitimacy.

So as to drive this point home, figure 2.4 reports the same sort of relationship between campaign contributions and perceived fairness. Here, there can be no ambiguity about the cost for perceived impartiality of campaign contributions. The differences between figures 2.3 and 2.4 are stark indeed.

Finally, returning to table 2.5, the data indicate that attack ads are harmful

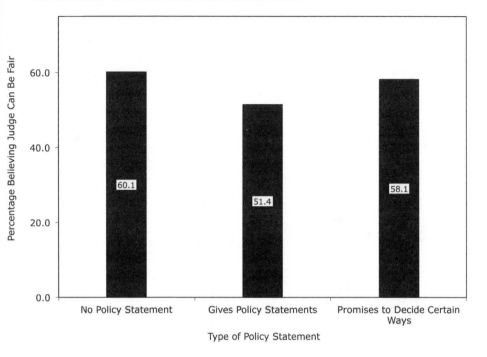

to the legitimacy of legislative institutions but have no effect whatsoever on judicial institutions. This is also a surprising finding in that one might have predicted that attack ads are the stock and trade of "normal" politics but a violation of the norms of gentility among candidates for judicial office. Figure 2.5 depicts this total absence of any relationship in the judicial context.

In general, the findings of this analysis of national data are not greatly different from the findings I reported based on the Kentucky sample. To summarize: (1) the effect of campaign contributions was found to be more corrosive in Kentucky than in the national sample, even though its effect is substantial and negative in both studies; (2) few differences exist in the consequences of policy pronouncements; and (3) attack ads had a weak negative effect on candidates for judicial office in Kentucky, but none in this national sample.

Subnational Differences
A national survey of course represents people residing in states using vastly different methods of selecting judges for their high bench, including those

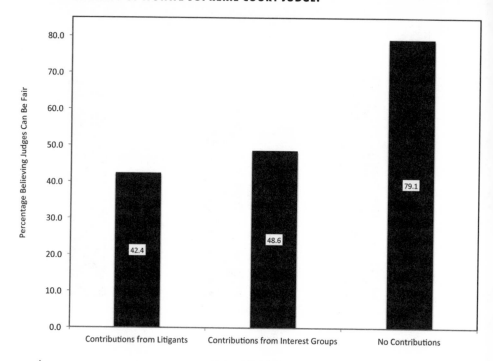

living in states that do not ever force judges and candidates for judicial office to face the electorate. To this point, I have only considered those who live in states using elections to select or retain their judges. The data set allows me to assess the degree to which the views of citizens are dependent upon the type of selection/retention system used by the states.[36]

I therefore created a dichotomy indicating whether supreme court judges in the respondent's state were subject to a vote of the people (partisan elections, nonpartisan elections, retention elections) or not (legislative and gubernatorial appointments, and "Missouri Plan" appointments without retention elections). To reiterate, nearly three-fourths of the respondents (73.3%) live in states using elections to select and/or retain their judges.

The most revealing way to model this relationship is to add to the equation shown in table 2.3 (1) a dummy variable indicating whether elections are used and (2) interaction terms between each of the manipulations and the dummy variable (and to analyze all respondents in the sample). The central hypotheses concern whether the effects of campaign activity differ according to whether judges in the respondent's state must face the electorate. The proper statistical test asks whether the addition of the interaction terms leads to a statistically significant increase in explained variance in perceived institutional legitimacy and whether any of the sets of interaction terms achieve significance (see Cohen et al. 2003; Kam and Franzese 2007).

The analysis reveals that only two of the interaction terms are statistically significant. Both have to do with the policy talk variables. When these two interaction terms are added to the basic equation, R^2 changes by 1.8%, which is statistically significant at $p < .05$.[37] The interaction terms are quite interesting: In states with elected judges, the coefficient for the condition under which the candidate expresses his policy views is a trivial .04. However, in states without elections, the coefficient is $-.24$, indicating that policy talk *detracts* from legitimacy. Similarly, while the coefficient for the policy

FIGURE 2.5. ATTACK ADS AND THE PERCEIVED IMPARTIALITY OF A STATE SUPREME COURT JUDGE.

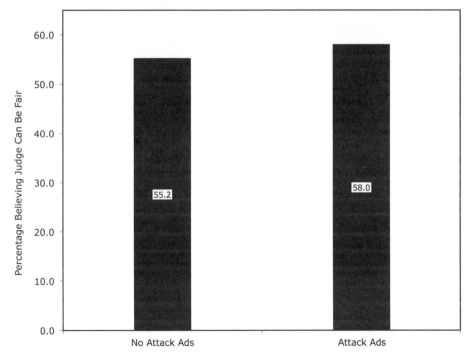

promises condition is +.11 in states with elections, it is −.16 in states without elections.[38]

From this analysis, an important amendment to the findings reported in table 2.3 emerges: the general conclusion that policy statements by judicial candidates have no deleterious effects on institutional legitimacy is confined to states employing elections to select and/or retain their judges. In states without such processes, citizens (presumably) have little direct experience with judicial campaigning, and they therefore find it objectionable when they are exposed to such activity in the experiment.[39]

Care must be taken, however, with this finding, for two reasons. First, the sample was, of course, not designed to be representative of individual states, and, second, this interactive effect is *not* confirmed on the issues of campaign contributions and attack ads. Perhaps this indicates that campaign contributions are ubiquitous and widely disliked, attack ads are also ubiquitous but are seen as part of everyday politics and are therefore widely thought to be acceptable, but policy talk by judges, a relatively new phenomenon even in states with elected judges, is still seen by some as inappropriate (or at least unusual) behavior by judges. Thus, it appears that people without experience with voting for judges are considerably more put off by policy talk than people living in states selecting their judges by popular elections.[40]

DISCUSSION AND CONCLUDING COMMENTS

This analysis does not purport to be a comprehensive account of all factors affecting the legitimacy of judicial institutions. No doubt legitimacy is influenced by momentous court decisions and many other factors. The contribution of experiments is *never* to test complete theories. (Of course, it is the random assignment of individuals to orthogonal vignette versions that renders these incomplete models *not* misspecified.) Instead, experiments allow us to take processes apart and to focus on testing hypotheses concerning individual components of complex causal models.

I have limited my attention in this analysis to the influence of campaigns on perceptions of judicial impartiality and institutional legitimacy. One of the most perplexing questions arising from earlier research has to do with the causal nexus between campaigns and institutions. The strength of experiments lies in the degree of confidence one can have in causal inferences. Given the research design employed in this analysis, I am entitled to conclude with considerable certitude that when candidates for public office receive campaign contributions from those with direct business interests before the institution, many (if not most) citizens perceive policy making as biased and partial and the policy-making institution as illegitimate. Similarly, the use of attack ads causes many to question institutional legitimacy. Just as certain are my conclusions that policy pronouncements by judicial candidates cause little harm to courts, and that the same sort of policy pronouncements enhance the legitimacy of legislatures. Owing to the structure of the experiment and the two independent surveys, both the internal and external validity of these conclusions is unusually robust.

Of course, it is possible to imagine that more extreme policy talk could in fact threaten court legitimacy. Were a candidate to declare that he or she would decide a certain way in a specific *case*—in contrast to taking a position on a specific *issue*—perhaps citizens would view that declaration as illegitimate. At present, the evidence indicates that at least some policy commitments and promises do not harm courts; we do not know the point at which such talk "crosses the line" of acceptability, if it does, and thereby generates the appearance of partiality. The research reported in the next chapter considers this question more thoroughly.

At the same time, the current system of campaign contributions does appear to be injurious to courts. Two aspects of this finding are important. First, it pertains with equal force to courts and legislatures. Nothing seems to be peculiar about the judiciary. Second, only a small difference is observed between the effects of campaign contributions from those with direct business before the institution and those with more general interests in influencing policy. This finding is worrisome from the point of view of democratic theory and is, of course, contrary to the hypothesis undergirding this portion of the experiment. One can easily imagine a system of mandatory recusal for instances in which campaign contributors are litigating before a judge who is the beneficiary of their contributions. But the American people seem to make minor distinctions between specific conflicts of interests in individual cases and more general efforts to shape public policy by getting the "right" people on the bench and in the legislature. The current system of campaign contributions seems to have such a thoroughly disreputable reputation that the American people are unable to distinguish between relatively benign and relatively corrosive types of contributions and influence. I do not want to oversell this finding since it is based on only a moderate statistical relationship. Nonetheless, future research should explore whether there are any means of contributing to the campaigns of candidates for public office that would not impugn the integrity of American political institutions.

If these findings indicate that we must worry about campaign contributions, they do not seem to mandate a similar need for concern about so-called attack ads, at least in the judicial context. When attack ads are used in judicial campaigns, few consequences for institutional legitimacy emerge. This is not so for legislative institutions. While the explanation of this finding is not obvious, it seems possible that legislatures have a lesser supply of legitimacy in the first place, and therefore attack ads enhance a preexisting propensity to view legislative institutions negatively. Courts, on the other hand, have a deeper reservoir of goodwill, which may provide a prophylactic against unseemly behaviors like attacking one's opponents (see Gibson and Caldeira 2009a)—even if the reservoir is not sufficiently deep to shield against the perceived conflicts of interest associated with campaign contributions.

Many judicial analysts seem to believe that campaigns present unique problems for courts. That position is decidedly not supported by this analysis. Those who worry about the corrosive effects of campaign contributions and attack ads on courts would do well to expand their concern to legislatures (and, most likely, other political institutions as well). Indeed, it is remarkable how similar these findings are for both the court and the legislature.

When it comes to policy pronouncements, the judiciary does seem to differ from the legislature, but not in the way ordinarily assumed. Perhaps the single most important finding of this chapter is that *candidates for judicial office can engage in policy debates with their opponents without undermining the legitimacy of courts and judges.* I have speculated that this finding reflects the sophistication of the American mass public in recognizing that judges do (and perhaps must) make public policy, that on broad policy issues some degree of accountability is desirable, and that the expression of policy views does not prejudice the rights of individual litigants to fair and impartial hearings before a court. To the extent that the state judiciaries are threatened today by campaign activity it is not because the US Supreme Court awarded judicial candidates free-speech rights in its 2002 decision.

What I cannot conclude from this analysis, however, is whether the legitimacy-threatening effects of campaign contributions and attack ads will persist over time. Grosskopf and Mondak (1998) have suggested, for instance, that the half-life of the effects of exogenous events can be quite short (see also Hoekstra 2003). Citizens may be put off by campaign activity, but we do not know whether their displeasure endures. One possibility is that there are so many other legitimizing symbols associated with courts that the effects of campaigning quickly dissolve (i.e., the so-called positivity bias asserted by Gibson and Caldeira [2009a]). Obviously, the connection between cause and effect (the manipulation and the response) is highly compressed in this experiment (as in all experiments); no single survey can ever document that changes that occur during the interview are in fact obdurate. Further research on this issue is reported in chapter 6.

Nonetheless, it seems clear that perceptions of institutional legitimacy are shaped to some degree by exogenous events: campaign activity matters to institutions. Loyalty toward institutions is not unalterable, even if it is relatively insensitive to policy debates among judges. Those concerned about threats to the legitimacy of elected state courts would do well to turn their attention away from substantive policy pronouncements and focus instead on the corrosive effects of politicized campaigning and especially campaign contributions from those having business before the bench.

As I have noted, the analysis suggests some important differences between states that use elections to select and retain their judges and those that do not. Given the limitations of the survey design, these findings must be regarded as tentative, especially as concerns the nonelected states. Future research must pay considerably more attention to interstate differences and in particular to differences across states in the perceptions and expectations citizens hold of their judges. As costly as it will be, this objective can only be accomplished through samples that are representative of individual state populations. When it comes to judicial politics, states are the important units of analysis, and future research must recognize and capitalize on this basic fact of American politics.

Nonetheless, these findings may indicate that experience with campaigning leads to acceptance of it. Politicized judicial campaigns may provide a "shock" to an electorate, but that shock may not have enduring consequences as citizens alter their expectations of proper behavior for candidates. The perceived legitimacy of institutions may be more resilient than is sometimes assumed. The process of learning from the electoral environment is undoubtedly interactive and nonrecursive, and only through dynamic research designs can we come to understand better the processes by which citizens update their attitudes and expectations toward political institutions.

There are, of course, some important limitations to these findings. Most significant, this experiment is based on reading respondents' statements about ads, which is a relatively tepid presentation of the genre. Were the experiment to expose the respondents to actual attack ads—many of which are extraordinarily gruff, at least from the conventional viewpoint of judicial advertisements—perhaps the effect would be stronger. Like policy talk, a threshold may well exist at a more extreme point than is portrayed in this experiment. Additional research should do more to try to identify and delineate that threshold, if indeed one exists. That is the purpose of chapter 3 of this book.

I should also note that numerous types of dicey campaign activities are not represented in this experiment. As Hasen has expertly demonstrated (2007), issues such as the appropriateness of direct solicitation of campaign contributions from parties with business pending before courts remain to be decided by litigation. We also know little about the effects of involvement in partisan political activity (e.g., making campaign contributions to the campaigns of other elected officials). "Partisan" is not a word that is endearing to most Americans; whether judges can (and should) act as partisans in their off-the-bench behavior without harming the legitimacy of the judiciary is at present unclear. Indeed, much more research is needed for us to understand the processes by which ordinary citizens draw conclusions about the partiality or impartiality of their judges.

Ultimately, the majority in *Republican Party of Minnesota v. White* was probably correct about at least one thing: if elections are employed as a means of selecting judges, then the elections must be legitimate, and all campaign activity that is allowed in elections for other offices must be tolerated in judicial elections. Critics complain that it is nearly impossible to do away with elected selection/retention systems because most Americans favor such processes for selecting their judges. Perhaps this is so. But to restrict policy talk among candidates for public office seems to strike at the very essence of elections as a means of selecting policy makers in a democratic polity. And instead of merely stipulating various undesirable consequences of judicial elections, researchers ought to be more focused on conducting rigorous research on the crucial empirical issues that undergird current policies governing systems of electing judges. Answering these empirical questions will not only contribute significantly to public policy debates over methods of selecting judges but will also greatly enrich and expand extant theories of judicial legitimacy and of the consequences of the politicization of campaigns for judicial office.

CHAPTER THREE

CAN CAMPAIGN

ACTIVITY CROSS

THE LINE?

The evidence from chapter 2 is that campaign speech by candidates for judicial office, including policy pronouncements and the use of attack ads, does little to undermine the legitimacy of elected state courts (even if campaign contributions are an entirely different matter). These findings pertain to both the Kentucky and national samples and therefore seem to warrant some confidence in their generalizability.

In another sense, however, the findings from chapter 2 are suspect in their generality. The material presented in the interviews is actually fairly tepid compared to the intense ads that are often broadcast in judicial races these days. One would not, for instance, claim that every single type of policy speech and every version of attack ads are innocuous based on the findings from chapter 2. Instead, it is important to try to determine the degree to which campaign activity can "cross the lines" in the minds of citizens and therefore damage the legitimacy of courts. Investigating this problem is the purpose of this chapter.

Specifically, the purpose of this chapter is to consider in greater detail the consequences of various types of campaign statements for public views of courts. In particular, I assess the impact of campaign activity by judges—including actual ads broadcast in judicial races in Kentucky—on the public's attitudes toward the Kentucky judiciary. The issues I consider are whether the activities are deemed appropriate for candidates for judicial office and whether such ads influence perceptions of the impartiality of judges and the legitimacy of the Kentucky Supreme Court. In order to provide some important perspective, a portion of the investigation that follows continues to rely upon cross-institutional analysis, comparing reactions to the Kentucky Supreme Court and the Kentucky State Senate.

The analyses in this chapter are drawn from three separate sections of the interview. In the first, the respondents are asked in a straightforward manner to judge three types of campaign activity by candidates for judicial office. In particular, I investigate the consequences of campaign activity for perceived fairness and impartiality. Here I discover an important difference between general policy talk and specific policy promises.

The second portion of the analysis is based upon a formal experiment in which people are exposed (via random assignment) to actual ads broadcast by judicial candidates in Kentucky elections. All of the ads are attack ads, but, according to the results, considerably different types of attacks are portrayed in the advertisements.

Finally, a second experiment directly addresses cross-institutional similarities and differences in the effects of promises to decide issues in a certain way. This analysis is particularly revealing in its documentation of the relatively minor differences in the judgments citizens make of legislators and judges. Here, too, the evidence is that promises to decide are often judged as inappropriate.

The analysis I report here is based on both post hoc and experimental designs, allowing uncommon confidence in the causal inferences that are drawn. My most general conclusions are that not all campaign activities undermine judicial impartiality—some do, others do not—and consequently that much more research is needed to ascertain how different aspects of campaigning fit with the expectations citizens hold of their judges and courts.

ANALYSIS

The analysis reported in the preceding chapter is limited in at least one very important sense: the data are drawn from a hypothetical vignette. Hypotheticals have their virtues, but they also have important limitations. For instance, in the Kentucky experiment, attack ads are represented by the following language:

> Judge Anderson's campaign ads vigorously attack his opponent, claiming that his opponent is biased in favor of insurance companies and other such businesses, and would therefore not be able to make fair and impartial decisions if elected to the Supreme Court.

This is certainly one representation of attack ads; but it also seems a tame version compared to the vigorous attacks one sees these days in television ads, and the ad is presented without much context or emotion. Hypothetical vignettes such as these represent one way to study the effects of campaign activity on legitimacy, but only one way.

Threats to Impartiality from Campaign Activity

All respondents in the third-wave survey were asked to evaluate three types of activities said to be engaged in by a judge during a campaign. The actions are

Issuing a campaign statement saying: "I believe the constitution gives women the right to have abortions."

Issuing a campaign statement saying: "If elected, I will change Kentucky's law on abortion."

Accepting campaign contributions from groups seeking to change Kentucky's law on abortion.

The respondents were asked about what consequences such activity would have for whether the individual can serve as a fair and impartial judge.[1]

I selected the issue of abortion because it is salient in Kentucky (e.g., the various political and legal activities conducted by the Family Trust Foundation) and because the issue is quite relevant to state courts and state judicial elections. Many scholars (e.g., Caldarone, Canes-Wrone, and Clark 2009) agree about the importance of abortion decisions for state judiciaries. Abortion is typically a state issue (Brace, Hall, and Langer 1999), and abortion cases are routinely heard in state courts. In addition, abortion is often a significant issue in campaigns for state high courts (Baum 2003; Brennan Center for Justice 2006). Consequently, questions about judges and abortion policy most likely seemed quite realistic to the respondents.

Table 3.1 reports the percentages of respondents asserting that the judge can be fair and impartial in spite of the specific activity in which the judge engaged during the campaign.[2] So, for instance, for all respondents, over one-half (55.6%) judged the statement about constitutional protection for abortion rights *not* to have impugned the impartiality of the judge.[3] I also report in this table the results according to how the respondent feels about "pro-abortion activists." The data indicate that even among those feeling negatively toward such groups (45 degrees or colder on the 100-degree feeling thermometer), a majority believes the judge can be fair and impartial. Not surprisingly, a larger percentage of those feeling favorable toward pro-abortion activists (55 degrees or higher) perceive the judge as impartial. From these data, it seems that policy statements offering broad approaches to constitutional interpretation do not threaten the perceived impartiality of judges and courts, at least among the majority of the people, and even when people disagree with the policy position.

Campaign contributions and direct promises to take policy action are quite a different matter. In both instances, only a minority of the respondents believe the judge can serve in a fair and impartial manner, and these judgments are entirely uninfluenced by the respondent's attitudes toward pro-abortion activists.[4] Even a majority of those sympathetic toward pro-abortion activists

TABLE 3.1. CAMPAIGN ACTIVITY AND JUDICIAL IMPARTIALITY

Percentage believing the judge can be fair and impartial

Activity	All respondents	Respondent's feelings toward pro-abortion activists		
		Cold	Neutral	Warm
Says Constitution gives abortion rights	55.6	51.4	53.5	71.1
Says I will change abortion law	36.5	35.0	38.9	36.9
Accepts campaign contributions from abortion groups	31.6	31.4	30.6	34.1

Note: The percentages indicate the proportion of the respondents in the category who asserted that a judge who engaged in such activity can be fair and impartial in her or his decision making on the bench. For instance, among those with "cold" (negative) feelings toward pro-abortion activists, 51.4% nonetheless believe that a judge who says the Constitution provides for the right to have an abortion can be fair and impartial in deciding cases on abortion. $N \approx 1{,}034$.

believe that the judges engaging in this sort of campaign activity cannot be fair and impartial. Although the difference is small, it is noteworthy that the effect on perceived impartiality of a direct policy promise is less severe than is the receipt of campaign contributions from a relevant interest group.

It appears from these data that, for most citizens, the line is crossed when the candidate makes a specific policy promise, but that a general assertion of one's constitutional ideology does *not* necessarily undermine perceptions of judicial impartiality. Most generally, it seems that relatively small differences in campaign statements can have significant consequences for public assessments of judges and the judiciary. Statements about constitutional interpretation seem not to violate the expectations of most citizens, while promises to decide issues in a certain way do. And, it should be noted, general policy speech and campaign contributions are quite different matters, having different effects on institutional legitimacy.

Nonetheless, I should note the size of the group that is *not* unnerved by direct policy promises and campaign contributions. It is not a majority, but it is roughly one-third of the population, for both promises and contributions. Indeed, nearly one in five respondents (19.4%) does not find *both* direct policy promises and the acceptance of campaign contributions objectionable. It is unclear at present whether any political activity by judicial candidates would cause doubt among this group about the impartiality of judges. These figures remind us that the American people are heterogeneous when it comes to their expectations of judges, with, so it seems, many being satisfied with judges who sometimes act as "politicians in robes."

The analysis reported in table 3.1 has an obvious limitation. As with all post hoc research, the nature of the causality in the relationship is ambiguous. To establish causality more confidently, I now turn to a different section of the interview in which experimental methods were employed.[5]

Judgments of Actual Attack Advertisements, Kentucky 2006

The respondents were also presented with some campaign statements actually made by judges. The respondents were randomly assigned to hear one of the following advertisements. To reiterate, each respondent heard only a single ad, with random assignment to ad version. These are ads that were actually aired in Kentucky during judicial campaigns.

A. [Announcer]: In 2003, Circuit Judge Bill Cunningham tried to make six rapists eligible for parole. One had been out on parole for only 12 hours when he raped a 14 year old and made her mother watch. Bill Cunningham already had tried to reduce their sentences, but our Supreme Court said no. Bill Cunningham said it was folly and a blatant injustice to keep these rapists in prison. Judge Rick Johnson believes that a life sentence means a life sentence. Please, vote for Rick Johnson for Justice on the Supreme Court.

B. [Announcer]: John Roach says he's tough on crime but Judge Mary Noble has put thousands of criminals behind bars. John Roach, none. Judge Mary Noble has helped dozens of lives through her Drug Court Program. John Roach, none. Judge Mary Noble has been elected by the people twice. John Roach, none. Elect a real judge to the Supreme Court. Vote for Judge Mary Noble.

C. [Announcer]: David Barber is confused. He's now airing an ad that says Janet Stumbo wrote the Supreme Court opinion in the Morse Fetal Homicide Case. Barber can't tell the boys from the girls. The Morse opinion was written by Justice Bill Cooper. More confusing is that Cooper's opinion upheld the decision with which Barber concurred. He's attacking the Supreme Court for agreeing with him. David Barber: confused about his own opinions. Is he a judge, or just another politician? On November 7th elect a judge: Janet Stumbo.

Following the presentation of the ad, the respondents were asked a series of questions, including a query about whether such an ad is appropriate for a Kentucky Supreme Court election. Figure 3.1 reports the results.

As it turns out, a majority of respondents approved of the first two statements, whereas only a very small percentage of the subjects (17.2%) thought

FIGURE 3.1. ASSESSMENTS OF THREE ATTACK ADVERTISEMENTS BROADCAST BY KENTUCKY JUDGES, 2006. SEE THE TEXT FOR THE WORDINGS OF THE STATEMENTS SUMMARIZED IN THIS FIGURE. TOTAL N = 1,032. INDIVIDUAL TREATMENT CONDITION N'S VARY FROM 332 TO 351. CROSS-CONDITION DIFFERENCE OF MEANS TESTS (ON THE UNCOLLAPSED RESPONSE SET): η = .38, P < .001.

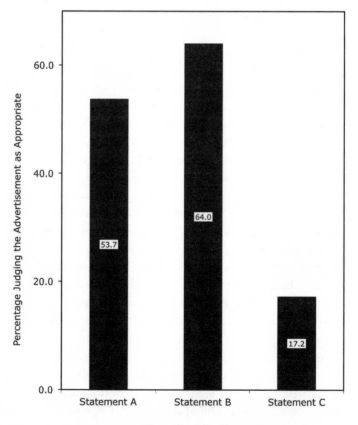

the third campaign statement was appropriate for a candidate for judicial office in Kentucky. These differences are stark and are, of course, highly statistically significant.

It seems clear that the last statement crosses some sort of line that citizens have in their minds. The ad does seem to be caustic and shrill, and includes an important reference to ordinary politics in the question: "Is he a judge, or just another politician?" My suspicion is that this statement cues the respondents to think: "This ad sounds like politics as usual, politics as I have seen in other political races, and exactly the sort of politics of which I disapprove." Consequently, a far greater proportion of the respondents are willing to deem the ad inappropriate.[6] The other ads may be caustic, but this ad seems to portray judges as run-of-the-mill politicians and therefore detracts from their impartiality. This finding is similar to that of Gibson and Caldeira (2009a), in that politicized ads by interest groups favoring or opposing Alito's confirmation to a seat on the Supreme Court seemed to subtract from the legitimacy of that institution.

Still, perhaps the most important conclusion from this analysis is that it is indeed possible to attack one's opponent, even when one is a judge, so long as the attack is strictly confined to policy disagreement. And because this analysis is based on an experimental design, we can have considerable confidence that the ad content itself actually caused the respondents' assessments of appropriateness.[7]

To this point, I have established that some types of campaign activity can indeed impugn the perceived impartiality of state courts. I have not, however, concluded that these findings are peculiar to the judiciary. It seems quite reasonable to hypothesize that all political institutions suffer from perceptions of conflicts of interest generated by campaign contributions and scurrilous attack ads. In order to pinpoint more clearly the significance, if any, of the judiciary, cross-institutional analysis comparing courts with other political institutions is necessary.

The Campaign Content Experiment

In this experiment, the respondents were asked several questions about whether particular types of campaign statements were appropriate. Several variables were manipulated in the question, including

The institution: whether the statements were made by a candidate for the Kentucky Supreme Court or the Kentucky State Senate.

The policy: Two-thirds of the respondents were presented with campaign assertions on the issue the respondent deemed most important in the second-wave interview; the remaining one-third heard statements about an issue other than the issue deemed most important by the subject.[8]

The policy position: Respondents in the "most important issue" condition were then randomly assigned to hear campaign statements that are (a) contrary to the respondent's own views on the issue, or (b) not contrary to the respondent's own view. For those few respondents who had no position on the most important issue, random assignment to campaign statements representing the differing views on the issue was used. For those hearing statements about an issue other than the one designated as most important, each respondent was randomly assigned to either a "pro" or "con" statement on the issue to which they had been randomly assigned. Because this is not the most important issue for the respondent, her or his substantive view on the policy is not known.

Thus, ignoring the specific issue about which the respondent was asked, there are eight major versions of the campaign statement experiment. The basic structure of the stimuli in this experiment is

Suppose a candidate for the [Kentucky Supreme Court/Kentucky State Senate] made a promise during the campaign that, if elected, he would [PRO/ ANTI R'S ISSUE POSITION: e.g., expand the right to abortion] in Kentucky. Would you say that this sort of campaign activity is entirely appropriate for a [INSTITUTION] election, somewhat appropriate for a [INSTITUTION] election, not very appropriate for a [INSTITUTION] election, or not at all appropriate for a [INSTITUTION] election?

As I have noted, the manipulations are (1) the institution, (2) the importance of the issue to the respondent, and (3) whether the campaign statement is agreeable or disagreeable to the respondent.

Do people think it appropriate for candidates for public office to make statements of the sort "if elected, I promise to . . . ," and do opinions vary according to whether a judge or a legislator is running for office? Perhaps surprisingly, they do not: a substantial majority (about two-thirds) of the respondents found such behavior inappropriate, with a strong tendency toward rating such statements as "not at all appropriate" (twice as many responses as "not very appropriate"). But more surprising still is the finding that, while an institutional difference exists, it is not massive, and this sort of campaign promise is deemed inappropriate for a *legislative* candidate by well over one-half of

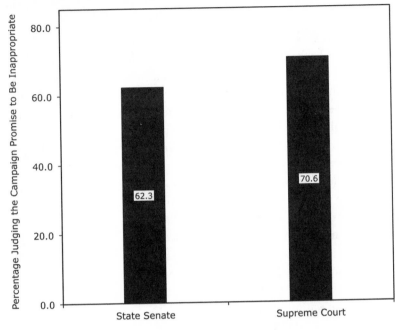

FIGURE 3.2. THE INAPPROPRIATENESS OF CAMPAIGN PROMISES, ACROSS INSTITUTIONS. $N = 1,028$. CROSS-CONDITION DIFFERENCE OF MEANS TESTS (ON THE UNCOLLAPSED RESPONSE SET): $\eta = .09$, $P = .005$.

the respondents (see figure 3.2). The difference in replies across institutions is indeed statistically significant (but not highly so), but, while 70.6% of the respondents asked about a candidate for the supreme court found the promise not appropriate, 62.3% gave the same reply to a question about a candidate for the Kentucky Senate. Thus, while it may not be surprising to find that people do not approve of judges issuing campaign promises, they also do not approve of legislators engaging in such behavior, and the difference between the two institutions is far less than might have been imagined given that the traditional role of legislators often requires them to make promises about how they will decide issues if elected. This is an important finding: many respondents who condemn campaign activity by judges also evaluate campaign activity by other political leaders as inappropriate. Without a control for the type of office under consideration (court versus not) much of the anti-campaign sentiment commonly observed might be considered to be idiosyncratic to the judiciary, when in fact the sentiments most likely generalize to campaign activity within most if not all political races.

Why do citizens object to policy promises by candidates for public office? After all, are not policy promises one of the most important reasons for holding elections in the first place? This finding is indeed unexpected and surprising.

One possible explanation of these results is that I have fundamentally misunderstood the basic objection to "promises to decide" behavior by candidates. Perhaps one implication of such promises that renders them objectionable to people is that they imply some sort of precommitment to an undisclosed *group*, perhaps even to an interest group, and not necessarily to the *issue* itself. Perhaps the objectionable part of policy promises has nothing to do with closed-mindedness and impartiality, but everything to do with "selling out" with "promises" to interest groups. Perhaps the key word in this question is "promises," which to some may imply some sort of tawdry quid pro quo. If this is so, then it explains why promises are detrimental in both the legislative and judicial contexts.[9]

This experiment also varied the importance of the issue (to the respondent) that the campaign promise was said to address. For two-thirds of the respondents (randomly selected), the issue was the one they deemed most important to them in the second interview; for the remaining one-third of the respondents, the issue was one of the six from which the respondent chose the most important, but was not the most important issue. Table 3.2 reports the difference of means on the appropriateness measure, within institution, according to whether the most important or not most important issue was described in the question about making campaign promises.

The differences in judged appropriateness according to the importance of the issue are not great. In the case of the state senate, the *t*-test approaches statistical significance; those hearing that the promise was made on the most important issue are less likely to judge it inappropriate. For those told about a campaign promise by a candidate for the Kentucky Supreme Court, a similar difference emerges, although it is far from statistically significant. The importance of the issue alone does not have much influence over judgments about the appropriateness of making campaign statements.

Among those told about campaign promises on the issue of greatest importance to them, the sample was further divided (via random assignment) according to whether the campaign promise was in accordance with the respondent's own position or whether the promise was contrary to the respondent's preference.[10] As table 3.2 also reports, policy agreement makes a tremendous difference in the judged appropriateness of the statement, for both legislators

TABLE 3.2. THE CAMPAIGN SPEECH EXPERIMENT, WITHIN INSTITUTIONS

	Inappropriateness of campaign activity			
Manipulation/Condition	Mean	s.d.	N	p—difference of means
Institution: State senate				
Importance of issue				
Not most important	3.72	1.41	188	.072
Most important	3.47	1.58	353	
Position: Most important issue				
Disagree with respondent	4.08	1.33	180	.000
Agree with respondent	2.84	1.57	173	
Position: Not most important issue				
Anti-issue	3.85	1.36	104	.167
Pro-issue	3.56	1.46	84	
Institution: Kentucky Supreme Court				
Importance of issue				
Not most important	3.89	1.18	151	.383
Most important	3.77	1.42	336	
Position: Most important issue				
Disagree with respondent	4.33	1.09	161	.000
Agree with respondent	3.27	1.50	176	
Position: Not most important issue				
Anti-issue	4.02	1.16	70	.191
Pro-issue	3.77	1.19	82	

and judges. When the promise is contrary to the respondent's own position, it is thought to be quite inappropriate. But, again, this finding pertains to both judges and legislators: campaign promises are frowned upon when the candidate promises to make an unwelcome policy decision. Moreover, these data hint at the possibility that simple policy disagreement, not more general standards of appropriateness, might be the driving force in the judgments reflected in this dependent variable.

Despite the overall conclusion that campaign promises by judges and legislators are evaluated similarly, we do see in these data a slight but interesting effect of institution on judgments of appropriateness. For those told about a legislative candidate making agreeable promises, the mean response is 2.84, indicating a low level of inappropriateness. For those told about a judicial candidate, the comparable mean is 3.27. This difference indicates that some people seem to judge legislative and judicial candidates differently and that the essential basis of that judgment is not simply policy agreement or disagreement.

Still, this difference should not be exaggerated. In the legislative context, 42.2% of the respondents find agreeable policy promises inappropriate, while in the judicial context the comparable figure is 54.5%. This is a difference, to be sure, but not one of the expected magnitude, in light of the traditional nature of judicial and legislative campaigns. And this finding must be understood within the overall context of disapproval of campaign statements promising to decide issues in a particular way.[11]

Finally, as expected, I find no significant difference in whether the promise is "pro" or "anti" the issue among those respondents in the "not most important issue" condition, which is not surprising in that random assignment produces a context in which some respondents agreed with the policy position expressed, whereas others did not.

Several important findings emerge from this experiment. First, a significant majority of the respondents found making policy promises to decide inappropriate. Second, the interinstitutional differences (i.e., between the court and the senate) are largely (but not entirely) trivial. Finally, the data hint at the possibility that the objectionable element of policy promises is not so much the inability to decide policy issues with an open mind but may instead be related to the making of promises, which may imply some sort of conflict of interest, perhaps one cemented by much-hated campaign contributions.

DISCUSSION AND CONCLUDING COMMENTS

Does campaign activity by candidates for judicial office threaten the institutional legitimacy of courts? The answer to this question offered by the data analyzed here is somewhat complicated. Evidence presented in this chapter confirms the earlier finding that campaign contributions represent a significant threat to the perceived impartiality of judges, even if a similar threat to the legitimacy of legislators also exists. When it comes to policy talk, most Kentuckians are not put off by general statements of policy positions, and most do not object to even fairly vigorous attack ads. At least some elements of traditional political campaign activity are acceptable to most people, even within the context of judicial elections.

But a line clearly exists for both types of activity. In terms of attack ads, charges that portray judges as ordinary politicians seem to be damaging to courts. Just as with the findings of Gibson and Caldeira (2009a) on the Alito nomination to the US Supreme Court, ads suggesting that judges are "politicians in robes" influence how people view judges and courts. The attack ad experiment reported here shows that candidates can indeed vigorously attack one another without overstepping the expectations of citizens; nonetheless, the invocation of "low politics" appears to cross the line in judicial races.

Similarly, specific policy promises threaten the legitimacy of both courts and legislatures. These findings diverge somewhat from those presented in chapter 2 most likely because the promises depicted in the analysis reported here are considerably more explicit and may be tied in the minds of some respondents to a quid pro quo relationship between candidates and groups. Again, it is important to stress that there seems to be little that is peculiar to the judiciary on this score. To the extent that states wish to ban "promises to decide" by judges under the theory of threats to institutional legitimacy, they should also consider banning such promises when made by legislative candidates. Most people seem to accept that candidates for judicial and legislative office hold policy views on various, relevant issues, and the expression of those views seems reasonable to most. Policy promises, however, are another matter.

The whole issue of the limits of permissible campaign activity remains to be investigated more thoroughly. It seems obvious to me that both the positions that "all policy talk is benign" and that "all policy talk is cancerous" are inaccurate as an empirical matter. Moreover, it seems possible that some serious interactions complicate the picture further. For instance, when promises to decide are offered in rebuttal to the assertions of a competing candidate, are they viewed in the same negative vein? Campaign activity is typically multidimensional and complicated. Research such as that reported here most likely does not fully capture that complexity, even if it moves some distance in that direction.

CHAPTER FOUR

DIFFUSE SUPPORT FOR

A STATE SUPREME COURT:

JUDICIAL LEGITIMACY IN

KENTUCKY

It is by now clear that the support courts enjoy from the mass public constitutes one of the most significant political resources the judiciary can marshal. When courts have legitimacy, they are efficacious; where a legitimacy shortfall exists, courts are often impotent. Understanding how judicial institutions acquire legitimacy is perhaps one of the most important tasks facing scholars of law and politics.

Legitimacy theory has been applied with full force to high courts around the world, including especially the US Supreme Court (e.g., Caldeira and Gibson 1992; Gibson, Caldeira, and Baird 1998), the German Federal Constitutional Court (e.g., Baird 2001), and the South African Constitutional Court (e.g., Gibson and Caldeira 2003; Gibson 2004, 2008b). Research on the support citizens extend to state courts of last resort has been vastly more limited.[1] Few doubt that state courts make controversial decisions displeasing to a majority of the citizenry, and that therefore institutional loyalty is valuable to these institutions. But the conventional wisdom seems to be that state courts of last resort have insufficient visibility to have developed loyal constituents, and that therefore asking citizens their views of these institutions is largely pointless.

Not all agree with this view, however. State court administrators have become increasingly interested in the views of their "constituents" and consequently have fielded a number of public opinion surveys.[2] Scholars are also rethinking the entire issue of what sort of political knowledge and information is necessary for citizens to perform their role in a democratic polity (Prior and Lupia 2008; Gibson and Caldeira 2009b). Perhaps the lack of attention to state courts constitutes little more than one further bit of evidence of the obsession of American political scientists and law professors with the institution standing at the pinnacle of the American judiciary, the US Supreme Court. Given the dearth of rigorous data, we simply do not know much about how visible and legitimate state judicial institutions are.[3]

The first purpose of this chapter is therefore to investigate the degree to which the citizens of Kentucky are aware of and knowledgeable about their highest court, the Supreme Court of Kentucky. The analysis is strengthened by its cross-institutional character: instead of considering the court in isolation, I compare public attitudes toward the judiciary and the Kentucky State Legislature. Cross-institutional analysis always provides fresh perspective on the degree to which ignorance of courts is peculiar to the judiciary or extends more broadly across state and local governments. Based on my analysis of the survey data, I find that levels of information and knowledge are in fact relatively low, even if somewhat higher than many might have expected.

The most important purpose of this chapter is to describe and explain public attitudes toward the Kentucky Supreme Court. To what degree does the institution enjoy institutional loyalty ("diffuse support")? Furthermore, what are the sources of that support? Is it contingent upon satisfaction with the outputs of the institution, or, like support for the US Supreme Court, are attitudes grounded in more fundamental commitments to democratic institutions and processes (e.g., Caldeira and Gibson 1992, 1995; Gibson 2007)? What role do political awareness and knowledge play in shaping attitudes toward these institutions? We know a considerable amount about the origins of attitudes toward the US Supreme Court; to what degree are those theories generalizable to attitudes toward state courts of last resort? Finally, like earlier research, I also consider the degree to which opinion leaders are distinctive in their attitudes toward Kentucky political institutions.

The attitudes analyzed in this chapter are quite different from those considered in the earlier chapters. In chapters 2 and 3, the respondents were asked to make judgments about judges (the hypothetical Judge Anderson) and courts (the Kentucky Supreme Court) typically after being exposed to specific ads and campaign activities. Generally speaking, the hypotheses tested were contextualized and dependent on events external to the respondent. Some might term the attitudes I considered "opinions," to indicate that they are specific judgments within stylized contexts. Experimental methods are particularly useful in ascertaining the effects of contexts on opinions.

In this chapter, more general attitudes are examined. Most generally, I refer to the attitude analyzed as institutional loyalty or support, and the attitude is thought to be a generalized orientation toward the supreme court. I hypothesize that these orientations reflect other attributes of the respondent, as in the hypothesis that those more committed to democratic institutions and processes will extend more support to the Kentucky Supreme Court. These are the attitudes that were treated as control variables in the analysis above, and they are the attitudes hypothesized to change in response to exposure to campaign activities (in the analysis in chapter 6). As I have noted, what distinguishes these attitudes is that they are generalized orientations to the Kentucky Supreme Court, not specific judgments of any actions by the justices of the court.

Since a deeply ingrained conventional wisdom asserts that citizens have no meaningful attitudes toward courts like the Kentucky Supreme Court, I begin this analysis by directly assessing the degree to which ordinary Kentuckians are aware of and knowledgeable about their supreme court and other state political institutions.

AWARENESS OF AND SATISFACTION WITH
KENTUCKY POLITICAL INSTITUTIONS

In the initial survey in the summer of 2006, we asked the respondents to describe their level of attentiveness to both the Kentucky Supreme Court and the Kentucky Legislature. As it turns out, levels of asserted awareness of the two institutions are surprisingly high, with about one-third of the respondents claiming to be "very aware" of the court and with a similar figure characterizing the legislature. Only 4.9% of the Kentuckians admitted to knowing essentially nothing about the Kentucky Supreme Court, a figure only slightly higher than the 3.0% admitting to knowing nothing about the state legislature. For both institutions, the percentages of respondents claiming to be either somewhat or very aware exceeds 80%. The correlation between awareness of the court and the legislature is .61, indicating that people do not specialize much in terms of which of the two institutions they pay attention to.

Kentuckians are also to some degree able to evaluate the performance of these institutions. When asked how well the court does its job, 9.0% volunteered that they did not know; for the legislature, the figure is slightly lower, at 6.7%. As in most studies of public opinion toward state institutions, people are generally satisfied with the job state government is doing. In these data, about three-fourths of the respondents believe the supreme court is doing a "pretty good" or "great" job. People are not so pleased with the legislature, with only 62.8% judging it to be doing a "pretty good" or "great" job. Only 5.0% of the respondents say the supreme court is doing a "poor" job; 9.2% are that critical of the legislature. How one rates these two institutions is strongly intercorrelated, even if most people rate the legislature lower than judicial institutions.

We also asked standard "feeling thermometer" questions about several Kentucky institutions and groups, including the supreme court and the legislature. Table 4.1 reports the results.

**TABLE 4.1. AFFECT TOWARD KENTUCKY INSTITUTIONS
AND POLITICAL GROUPS**

Institution/Group	% Don't know	Among those with an opinion		
		Mean	s.d.	N
Christian fundamentalists	12.2	56.9	26.5	1,767
State supreme court	11.2	56.5	21.4	1,795
Kentucky press	3.3	52.3	22.7	1,971
Kentucky court system	4.0	51.8	24.1	1,953
State legislature	7.3	50.6	20.7	1,889
Anti-abortion activists	3.6	49.4	31.1	1,950
Insurance companies and large businesses	2.3	45.7	24.6	1,992
Pro-abortion activists	5.3	36.1	28.2	1,912

Note: Question stem read:
"Next, I would like to get your feelings toward some of our political institutions
and groups. I'll read the name of a group and I'd like you to rate that group using
something we call the feeling thermometer.
You can use any number between 0 and 100 to express your feelings. Ratings above
50 degrees mean that you feel favorable and warm toward the group, while those
below 50 degrees mean that you don't feel favorable toward the group. You would rate
the group at the 50 degree mark if you don't feel particularly warm or cold toward it.
If we come to a group whose name you don't recognize, you don't need to rate that
group, just tell me and we'll move on to the next one."

The first data column in the table reports the percentages of respondents
unable to formulate an opinion toward the institution.[4] This was most common on the question about Christian Fundamentalists, followed by the Kentucky Supreme Court. For all other institutions, less than 10% of the respondents were without feelings they could express during the interview.

Among those holding opinions, the institutions receiving the warmest feelings are Christian Fundamentalists and the Kentucky Supreme Court. Mean
scores greater than 50 degrees were also registered for the Kentucky press, the
Kentucky court system in general, and the Kentucky Legislature. Pro-abortion
activists were the most disliked group on the list.[5] Among those with opinions, attitudes toward the court and the legislature are strongly correlated
($r = .53$).[6] In general, the court generates more positive feelings than the legislature among Kentuckians, although not by a great margin.[7] Comparing
the feeling thermometers for the two institutions reveals that about 11.4% of
Kentuckians feel substantially more positive toward their legislature, 9.2% feel

somewhat more positively, 39.3% feel the same, 13.7% express somewhat more positive views toward the court, and 26.4% hold substantially more positive views toward the court as compared to the legislature.[8] Thus, these data reinforce the common finding that the judiciary receives greater respect from the citizenry than does the legislature.[9]

Conclusions

Claimed awareness of the Kentucky Legislature and Supreme Court is relatively high among these respondents, as is general satisfaction with the performance of the institutions. I do not necessarily contend that these are well-informed opinions—the next step in my analysis is to determine whether they are—but most citizens claim not to be oblivious to their important state-level legislative and judicial institutions. And, as with virtually all previous research on public opinion and political institutions, Kentuckians are somewhat more favorably predisposed toward their judicial as compared to legislative institutions.

KNOWLEDGE OF THE KENTUCKY SUPREME COURT

The above analysis is of course based on little more than the respondent's self-proclaimed awareness of the institution. A more stringent test involves asking the respondents factual questions about their supreme court. The questions we asked and the percentages of respondents answering correctly are

- Whether the justices are elected or not—24.0% correct (elected).
- Whether the justices serve a life or fixed term—32.9% correct (fixed).
- Whether the justices have the "last say" on the meaning of the constitution—45.6% correct (they do).[10]

Across all three items, the average number of correct answers is 1.0, with fully one-third of the respondents getting none of the test items correct and only 7.3% answering accurately to all three. Although these questions were asked during a period of relatively low salience of the state judiciary,[11] by no means can knowledge of the state supreme court be judged to be anything but dismally low.[12] However, in comparison to the frequent alarmism about the near total ignorance of the mass public on things legal, these figures are perhaps more comforting than expected.[13]

To what degree are the objective measure of institutional knowledge and the self-assessments of awareness connected? The variables are certainly correlated, but not strongly so ($r = .19$, $p < .001$). A clear monotonic relationship exists between actual knowledge and self-proclaimed awareness. Nonetheless, the average number of correct answers among those claiming to be "very aware" of the Kentucky Supreme Court is only 1.2 (compared to .7 for those at the lowest level of awareness).

A recurring finding in the literature on attitudes toward courts is that those who hold more information about the judiciary tend to support it more (e.g., Gibson, Caldeira, and Baird 1998). I will consider this hypothesis more fully below, but, in fact, a significant but somewhat modest correlation of .16 ($p < .001$) exists between awareness of the institution and holding positive feelings toward it. The average degrees of affect for the Kentucky Supreme Court vary from 48 among those least aware of the institution to 60 degrees for those most aware. The relationship with actual levels of knowledge is not as strong ($r = .10, p < .001$), although greater information is still associated with higher levels of positive affect.

Thus, this survey documents a relatively low level of information held by Kentuckians about their supreme court, especially when compared to the information most Americans hold about the US Supreme Court (Gibson and Caldeira 2009b). At the same time, however, the survey was conducted outside the election season for Kentucky state judges, so the state judiciary was most likely not in the forefront of the consciousness of most Kentuckians.

DIFFUSE SUPPORT FOR THE KENTUCKY SUPREME COURT

We measured institutional loyalty[14] toward the Kentucky Supreme Court with reactions (collected on five-point Likert response sets) to the following statements:

If the Kentucky Supreme Court started making a lot of decisions that most people disagree with, it might be better to do away with the Supreme Court altogether.

The right of the Kentucky Supreme Court to decide certain types of controversial issues should be reduced.

The Kentucky Supreme Court can usually be trusted to make decisions that are right for the state as a whole.

Judges of the Kentucky Supreme Court who consistently make decisions at odds with what a majority of the people in the state want should be removed from their position as judge.

It is inevitable that the Kentucky Supreme Court gets mixed up in politics; therefore, we ought to have stronger means of controlling the actions of the Kentucky Supreme Court.

The Kentucky Supreme Court may have its ideas about what the
constitution means, but more important is what the majority of people
think the constitution means.

The Kentucky Supreme Court gets too mixed up in politics.

The Kentucky Supreme Court ought to be made less independent so that it
listens a lot more to what the people want.

Following earlier research on attitudes toward courts, I analyze the responses
to these questions only among what is termed the "attentive public"—those
who claim at least some level of awareness of the institution.[15] In this case, 4.9%
of the respondents are excluded as being too ill informed for their attitudes to
have much substantive meaning. Table 4.2 reports the univariate frequencies
on these court support variables.

The data in table 4.2 support a variety of conclusions. First, "don't know"
responses on these propositions were issued by about one-fifth of the respondents. The percentages of respondents without an opinion on the statements
vary from a low of 11.2 to a high of 27.6, but in general the proportion is about
one in five Kentuckians. This finding is itself somewhat surprising in that one
might have expected considerably higher rates of non-opinionation.

Across the various statements, support for the Kentucky Supreme Court
varies widely from 22.8% to 69.1% of the respondents giving supportive replies.
Only a small proportion of Kentuckians (19.7%) would do away with the court
if it made a string of objectionable decisions, although a substantial majority
(63.5%) would prefer a court that is *less* independent of the will of the people.
If a general conclusion can be drawn from the responses to these various statements, it is that the idea of an independent institution blocking efforts of the
majority of the people to have its way politically is not very attractive to a considerable number of Kentucky citizens. Judicial independence, in the minds of
many respondents, does seem to threaten majoritarianism and accountability.

A few of these items have been asked of national samples with regard to
the US Supreme Court (e.g., most recently, Gibson [2007]). As to "doing away
with the courts," 69.1% of Kentuckians would not abolish their supreme court,
compared to the 68.9% of Americans who would not abolish the US Supreme
Court. Slightly over one-half of the Americans would limit the Supreme Court's
jurisdiction (51.4%); 41.9% would limit the jurisdiction of the Kentucky court
(although some of this difference has to do with respondents who have no
opinion about the Kentucky court). As table 4.2 shows, 65.9% of the Kentucky
sample say their supreme court can be trusted; 65.5% of Americans assert that
the US Supreme Court can be trusted. Although differences in the size of the

TABLE 4.2. LOYALTY TOWARD THE KENTUCKY STATE SUPREME COURT, ATTENTIVE PUBLIC, 2006

Item	Percentage[a]			Mean[b]	s.d.	N[c]
	Not supportive	Undecided	Supportive			
Do away with the court	19.7	11.2	69.1	3.61	1.09	1,938
Trust the court	16.1	18.0	65.9	3.54	.89	1,937
Reduce right to decide issues	36.0	22.2	41.9	3.07	1.05	1,933
Remove judges who decide against majority	40.3	20.5	39.3	2.96	1.11	1,937
Majority view of constitution is most important	51.9	17.3	30.8	2.74	1.13	1,937
Court gets too mixed up in politics	45.7	27.6	26.7	2.75	.98	1,936
Make court less independent	63.5	12.9	23.5	2.53	1.04	1,939
Politics inevitable, must control court	57.8	19.4	22.8	2.56	1.06	1,938

Note: The statements read (with supportive responses in parentheses):

If the Kentucky Supreme Court started making a lot of decisions that most people disagree with, it might be better to do away with the Supreme Court altogether. (Disagree)

The Kentucky Supreme Court can usually be trusted to make decisions that are right for the state as a whole. (Agree)

The right of the Kentucky Supreme Court to decide certain types of controversial issues should be reduced. (Disagree)

Judges of the Kentucky Supreme Court who consistently make decisions at odds with what a majority of the people in the state want should be removed from their position as judge. (Disagree)

The Kentucky Supreme Court may have its ideas about what the constitution means, but more important is what the majority of people think the constitution means. (Disagree)

The Kentucky Supreme Court gets too mixed up in politics. (Disagree)

The Kentucky Supreme Court ought to be made less independent so that it listens a lot more to what the people want. (Disagree)

It is inevitable that the Kentucky Supreme Court gets mixed up in politics; therefore, we ought to have stronger means of controlling the actions of the Kentucky Supreme Court. (Disagree)

[a] The percentages total to 100 percent across the three columns (except for rounding errors).

[b] The means and standard deviations are calculated on the uncollapsed, five-point Likert response sets.

[c] N represents the institution's attentive public—those with some awareness of the institution.

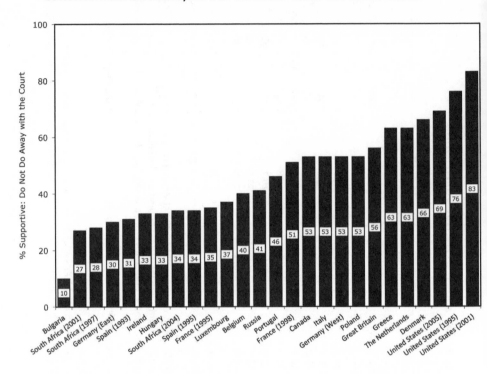

Sources: Most of these data are taken from Gibson, Caldeira, and Baird (1998, table 4, p. 350). When not otherwise indicated, the data are taken from surveys conducted in the period 1993–95. For a few countries, more than a single survey is available; for these, the year of the survey is indicated in the country label. The Canadian data are taken from Fletcher and Howe (2000); the South African data are from Gibson (2008b).

"don't know" group cloud the comparison slightly, there are more Americans who think the US Supreme Court gets too mixed up in politics (37.2%) than Kentuckians who think the Kentucky Supreme Court gets too mixed up in politics (26.7%). Finally, if one were to compare the Kentucky findings on the "do away with" question to data from nearly two dozen surveys around the world of attitudes toward national high courts, the conclusion would be that few national high courts enjoy the level of public esteem enjoyed by the Kentucky Supreme Court (Gibson 2007). Indeed, the Kentucky Supreme Court is even considerably more visible to its constituents than are many high courts around the world (Gibson, Caldeira, and Baird 1998; see figure 4.1). In general, these data seem to indicate that the Kentucky Supreme Court enjoys a considerable degree of legitimacy in the eyes of the citizens of the state (at least before the judicial elections of 2006).

When these eight items are subjected to Common Factor Analysis, a two-dimensional solution emerges.[16] However, the second factor is defined overwhelmingly by the statement about expressing trust in the supreme court.[17] When the seven items defining the first dimension are separately factor analyzed, a strongly unidimensional solution emerges. Consequently, I have extracted from the unrotated eight-item factor solution a single factor score as the indicator of institutional loyalty. The trust item has a low loading on this factor. However, the correlation between the factor score and a simple summated index of the replies to the eight items is .99.[18] Moreover, Cronbach's alpha for the eight-item set is .74, and alpha varies trivially with the deletion of the trust item (i.e., $\alpha = .75$). For simplicity, I use the summated index as the measure of institutional loyalty. I also use for some descriptive purposes a variable that is a count of the number of supportive responses (mean supportive = 3.2, among the attentive public).

As I have noted, additional measures of attitudes toward the Kentucky Supreme Court were included in the interview, including

a "feeling thermometer" for the institution
a general assessment of how well the institution does its job
an assessment of whether the institution's decisions are ideologically agreeable to the respondent

The intercorrelations of the measure of institutional loyalty with indicators of performance evaluation will provide evidence of whether diffuse support is really nothing more than satisfaction with institutional outputs.

Among the attentive public, the strongest correlation with loyalty toward the court is .30, with the indicator of the overall assessment of how well the court does its job. With the feeling thermometer the correlation is .22, and with ideological satisfaction with the court, the correlation is .14. Indeed, when the loyalty index is regressed on the three measures of performance satisfaction, an R^2 of only .11 results. Clearly, this measure of diffuse support is not the same thing as simple satisfaction with the decisions made by the Kentucky Supreme Court, a finding contributing to our confidence in the validity of the measure.

Since the focus of this research is much more on the supreme court than on the state legislature, loyalty to the state legislature was measured with only three items. As table 4.3 reports, most Kentuckians would not do away with

TABLE 4.3. LOYALTY TOWARD THE KENTUCKY STATE LEGISLATURE, ATTENTIVE PUBLIC, 2006

	Level of diffuse support					
	Percentage[a]					
Item	Not supportive	Undecided	Supportive	Mean[b]	s.d.	N[c]
Do away with the legislature	22.9	11.5	65.7	3.51	1.05	1,976
Trust the legislature	24.4	20.3	55.4	3.30	.95	1,977
Legislature favors some groups more than others	65.2	19.3	15.5	2.38	.93	1,977

Note: The statements read:

If the Kentucky legislature started making a lot of decisions that most people disagree with, it might be better to do away with the legislature altogether.

The Kentucky legislature can usually be trusted to make decisions that are right for the state as a whole.

The decisions of the Kentucky legislature favor some groups more than others.

[a] The percentages total to 100 percent across the three columns (except for rounding errors).
[b] The means and standard deviations are calculated on the uncollapsed, five-point Likert response sets.
[c] N represents the institution's attentive public—those with some awareness of the institution.

their state legislature, and most are reasonably trustful of it. The threat to the legitimacy of the state legislature lies in perceptions of partiality: a significant majority of Kentuckians believe that their legislature favors some groups more than others.

The most important comparison is between attitudes toward the Kentucky Supreme Court and Kentucky Legislature. Here we find a tiny difference in willingness to stand by the institution even when dissatisfied with its policy outputs (69.1% for the court, 65.7% for the legislature), even while generalized trust in the institution is somewhat less for the state legislature as compared to the supreme court (55.4% versus 65.9%). In general, these findings indicate that the Kentucky Legislature enjoys somewhat less legitimacy than does the Kentucky Supreme Court.

With only three items, it is not surprising that a single factor emerged from the factor analysis. The correlation between the factor score and a simple summated index is .93. I therefore use the summated index as the measure of institutional support for the legislature. Obviously, the reliability of the measure of loyalty toward the legislature is considerably lower than that of the supreme court support indicator.

The correlation between support for the court and support for the legislature is .39: those who tend to support one of the institutions tend to support the other. However, that this is only a moderate to strong relationship indicates that at least some respondents differentiate in their attitudes toward the legislature and the high court.

Knowledge of the Court and Institutional Support

A recurring finding in the literature on attitudes toward courts is that those who hold more information about the judiciary tend to support it more. As I have noted, I refer to this as "positivity bias." Those who acquire more information about courts tend simultaneously to be exposed to the potent symbols of legal legitimacy and hence wind up supporting courts more. In fact, in these data, a modest correlation of .13 ($p < .001$) exists between awareness of the institution and support for it. The relationship with actual levels of knowledge is exactly as strong ($r = .13$, $p < .001$); more information is associated with higher levels of support. For example, the average number of supportive replies given to the eight legitimacy items ranges from 2.7 among those with the lowest level of knowledge to 4.2 ($r = .19$) for those most informed about the Kentucky Supreme Court. These relationships are not very strong, but they are entirely consistent with the commonplace finding that to know more about courts is to be more positively predisposed toward them.

Benesh (2006) has shown that support for local courts is connected to the methods used to select judges in the state: citizens living in states using partisan selection of judges express less confidence in their local courts. She explains this finding as follows: "Valuing independence, respondents are less likely to highly regard elected courts" (Benesh 2006, 704). This is an important conclusion that requires some additional consideration, which these data allow.

In Kentucky, at least, only 24.0% of the respondents knew that their supreme court is elected. One might reasonably surmise that the proportion knowing whether Kentucky judges are elected on a partisan or nonpartisan ballot is even smaller. If Kentucky is not atypical, then the conclusion Benesh draws may be suspect: if citizens do not know that their judges are elected on a partisan ballot, then it is hard to imagine how the lack of independence implied by partisan selections shapes their attitudes. The microlevel foundations of Benesh's conclusion are suspect.

In Kentucky, a majority of citizens do *not* strongly favor an independent judiciary. In table 4.2, I report the reactions to the statement, "The Kentucky

Supreme Court ought to be made less independent so that it listens a lot more to what the people want." As noted in the table, 63.5% of the court's attentive public agrees with this statement; only 23.5% disagrees. Judicial independence hardly seems to be a highly revered value among a majority of the residents of Kentucky, a state using nonpartisan elections to select and retain its judges.

Knowing that the Kentucky Supreme Court is elected is only slightly related to support for the institution (among the court's attentive public): $r = .05, p = .03$. Knowledge of the length of the term of supreme court justices is completely unrelated to support, although those who know that the court has the "last say" on the law are significantly more supportive ($r = .20, p < .001$) than those ignorant of the court's power. These various data do not suggest to me that some sort of violation of expectations of judicial independence undermines the legitimacy of courts. Many citizens do not want independent courts (at least not courts independent of the majority), many do not see courts as violating their expectation regarding independence, and therefore the conclusion that elected judiciaries undermine court support owing to the lack of judicial independence associated with such systems does not seem warranted.

Summary

Institutional support for the Kentucky Supreme Court seems to be fairly widespread among the court's constituents. Indeed, in many respects, support for this state court mirrors support for the US Supreme Court. Whether the correlates of such support are the same, however, is unknown and therefore requires further consideration.

DETERMINANTS OF INSTITUTIONAL SUPPORT

Extant research on support for the US Supreme Court and other national high courts has generated a number of findings that I will test in the context of the Kentucky Supreme Court. First, and perhaps foremost, research has shown that support for courts is grounded in citizen support for democratic institutions and processes. The connection most likely has something to do with understanding the distinctive role of the judiciary within a democratic system like that of the United States. Three measures of democratic values are considered in this analysis (see appendix G for measurement details).

Second, as already noted, political knowledge seems to increase support, although some recent research on attitudes toward the US Supreme Court indicates that although knowledge is associated with enhanced support for democracy, its independent impact on court support is minimal (Gibson 2007).

Gibson (2007) has also shown that support for the US Supreme Court is *not*

TABLE 4.4. MULTIPLE PREDICTORS OF LOYALTY TO THE SUPREME COURT

Predictor	r	b	s.e.	β
Support for the rule of law	.33	.19	.02	.20***
Support for liberty over order	.33	.10	.02	.13***
Support for democratic values	.32	.16	.02	.21***
Court knowledge	.14	.03	.01	.06**
Level of education	.37	.12	.01	.22***
Political engagement	−.12	−.02	.01	−.03
African American	−.04	−.00	.01	−.00
Gender	.05	.02	.01	.06**
Age	.05	.07	.02	.09***
Home ownership	.10	−.00	.01	−.01
Party identification	.02	.01	.01	.03
Ideological identification	−.04	−.01	.01	−.01
Opinion leadership	.05	−.01	.01	−.01
Equation statistics				
Intercept		.16	.02	
Standard deviation—Dependent variable		.16		
Standard error of estimate		.14		
R^2				.27***
N		1,859		

Significance of standardized regression coefficients (β): *** $p < .001$ ** $p < .01$ * $p < .05$

related to partisan or ideological identifications. Nonetheless, it is still reasonable to consider these variables in the Kentucky context. To the extent that liberals favor minority rights and perceive courts as relatively minoritarian institutions, I hypothesize a connection between ideology and court support.

Finally, analyses of court support often include demographic variables as controls, a practice I follow here. The results of the comprehensive equation are reported in table 4.4.

I first note that a substantial amount of the variance in court attitudes can be explained: $R^2 = .27$. In Gibson's (2007) most recent study of attitudes toward the US Supreme Court, 20% of the variance can be accounted for, so, at least at this point in the analysis, it seems that attitudes toward the Kentucky Supreme Court are comprised of a significant amount of systematic variance.

A number of variables make no contribution to the explanation of support for the Kentucky Supreme Court. Partisan and ideological identification are completely unrelated to court attitudes, as are opinion leadership, race, and perhaps gender as well.[19] A couple of variables exhibit bivariate relationships with court attitudes, but in the multivariate equation the independent effects of these variables are reduced to insignificance (e.g., home ownership, political engagement). Indeed, only a handful of the variables in this table are significant predictors of support for the Kentucky Supreme Court.

The Kentucky Supreme Court's institutional legitimacy is primarily dependent upon democratic values and the respondent's level of education. Those who extend more support to democratic institutions and processes are much more likely to also support the supreme court. Indeed, these three components of democratic values alone can account for 21% of the variance in institutional legitimacy. This finding strongly reinforces the principal conclusion from years of research on the US Supreme Court. Those who appreciate democracy more (and presumably who understand it more) are more likely to view the institutions of democracy as legitimate.

An illustration of this relationship can be seen in figure 4.2, which depicts the connection between court support and responses to the democratic values indicator: "Any person who hides behind the law when he is questioned doesn't deserve much consideration." Those who strongly disagree with the statement expressed support for the Kentucky Supreme Court on 4.4 of the statements (on average), whereas those agreeing with the statement issued only 2.5 supportive responses. Belief in the rule of law and democratic due process are fairly strong predictors of the willingness to extend legitimacy to the state's highest court.

A little surprising is the relatively strong independent effect of level of education on court support.[20] Kentuckians with more education are more likely to support democratic institutions and processes, but even beyond that, they are more likely to hold their highest court in high esteem. Indeed, the three measures of democratic values and level of education by themselves account for nearly all of the variance explained by the full equation (26% versus 27%). So in the end, this account of support for the Kentucky Supreme Court is fairly simple: those with the ability to understand the role of the judiciary in a democratic system and who are committed to the rule of law, democracy, and due process are more likely to extend legitimacy to this court.

As with Gibson's (2007) analysis of attitudes toward the US Supreme Court, judicial knowledge has little direct effect on court support in the multivariate model. This is no doubt owing to the connection between knowledge and support for democratic institutions and processes and the far stronger predictive ability of the respondent's level of education.

The variables not connected to court support are also noteworthy. More important, attitudes toward the Kentucky Supreme Court are not dependent upon the respondent's ideological or partisan self-identification. Liberals sup-

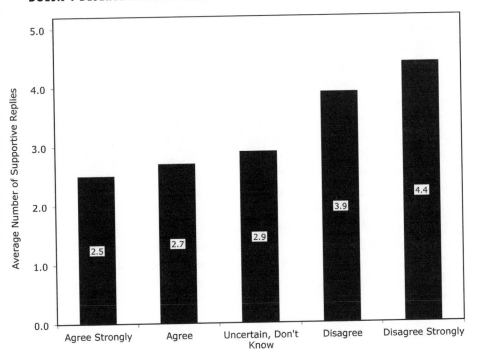

FIGURE 4.2. DEMOCRATIC VALUES AND SUPPORT FOR THE KENTUCKY SUPREME COURT. THE STATEMENT USED WAS, "ANY PERSON WHO HIDES BEHIND THE LAWS WHEN HE IS QUESTIONED ABOUT HIS ACTIVITIES DOESN'T DESERVE MUCH CONSIDERATION."

port the court at the same rate as conservatives; Democrats and Republicans support the court alike. Like Gibson's findings on the US Supreme Court (2007), institutional legitimacy crosses partisan and ideological lines.

With the possible exception of age, none of the demographic variables influences court support. This is most likely because any such influence of these relatively coarse variables is felt through more direct measures like support for democratic institutions and processes.

DISCUSSION AND CONCLUDING COMMENTS

Several general conclusions emerge from this analysis of the attitudes of Kentuckians. First, Kentucky political institutions may not be as obscure to ordinary people as is typically assumed by scholars. I definitely do not contend that ordinary people have a great deal of information about state political institutions, but my analysis suggests that attitudes are meaningful enough to be measured and systematically analyzed. I acknowledge that specific attitudes contain a strong measure of more general values, just as they do in almost all contexts. Nor do I argue that these findings from Kentucky are necessarily generalizable to the larger population of American states. But in the Kentucky context, responses to these queries about the Kentucky Supreme Court contain considerable quantities of systematic variance, and much of that variance can be explained with a fairly simple equation using only a handful of predictors.

The most important substantive finding of this analysis is that attitudes toward the Kentucky Supreme Court seem to be shaped by factors similar to those shaping attitudes toward the US Supreme Court. In both instances, court evaluations are largely determined by broader commitments to democratic institutions and processes. I speculate that willingness to extend legitimacy to judicial institutions is contingent upon understanding something about the role of the third branch in democratic politics. Presumably, citizens are unwilling to extend trust and support to an institution without some appreciation of how that institution is supposed to exercise power. To this extent, institutional legitimacy is dependent upon fairly cognitive processes.

These processes may be cognitive in nature—dependent upon information and the ability to process it—but the processes may well be stimulated by symbolic factors such as judicial robes, honored forms of address, and so on. It may be tempting to treat symbolic processes as largely emotional in nature;[21] the symbols produce awe, and hence deference. This is not the process I envisage.

Instead, these symbols promote citizens to ask, What do the symbols indicate about the functioning of the institution? Legislators wear business clothes; what is the meaning of judges wearing robes? Perhaps some are intimidated by robes and therefore submit and defer to the authority the robes symbolize. But others answer the question by concluding that what judges do is different from what ordinary politicians do. Ordinary politicians, largely strategic, self-interest maximizers, cannot be trusted and must therefore be carefully scrutinized and reined in. Judges, on the other hand, seem to make decisions on the basis of more principled processes and therefore act sincerely, not strategically, and without regard to their self-interest. The symbols impart an understanding of courts—that they are different—and that understanding provides a presumption of legitimacy. Experience can overcome that presumption—as the citizens of the old Communist regimes of Central and Eastern Europe so readily illustrate (Markovits 1995)—but because courts are different they are not laden with presumptions of illegitimacy. To reiterate, the symbols themselves are not terribly important; instead, it is the message of judicial uniqueness, once understood within even a primitive theory of democratic governance and institutions, that contributes to institutional legitimacy.

CHAPTER FIVE

EXPECTANCY THEORY AND

JUDICIAL LEGITIMACY

Many legal scholars assume that politicized processes of selecting state and federal judges in the United States contribute—and some would
say contribute mightily—to the erosion of confidence in the judiciary. The assumption of this position is that anything associated with politics delegitimizes
courts: politics poisons the judiciary. Campaigning for the bench in particular
is commonly said to pose every manner of threat to the "nonpolitical" nature
of the judiciary, the most crucial wellspring of institutional legitimacy. Courts
in the United States are at risk owing to the processes used to select judges.

As I have repeatedly noted in the chapters above, however, this assumption
has not been subjected to much rigorous, empirical investigation. In order to
assess this hypothesis with any degree of rigor, several tasks must be under-
taken. First, some definitions are in order. While it is not too difficult to define
"confidence"—a substantial literature (cited above) on attitudes toward courts
exists—more demanding is the task of deriving an agreeable definition of "politicized." And even more difficult still is the unpacking of the processes by
which politicization undermines confidence (if in fact it does). If the politici-
zation/legitimacy connection is to be considered as an empirical characterization of the American judiciary today, much more effort must be put into testing each of the linkages in what is undoubtedly a fairly complex causal model
of citizen attitude formation and change.

The overriding hypothesis of this chapter is that the consequences of politicization cannot be apprehended without direct investigation of *what it is
citizens want from their courts*. What I will refer to as the "expectancy model"
includes two crucial elements: what citizens expect of courts and what they
perceive courts to be doing. The conventional (if often implicit) assumption
seems to be that (1) nearly all citizens hold the same expectations of courts,
(2) that expectations of judicial independence trump all other possible functions courts might perform, and (3) that all citizens hold similar views of how
judges go about making decisions. Because citizens are assumed to value judicial independence above all else, deviation from independence—as in making
courts more accountable through the political process—is therefore thought
to undermine judicial legitimacy. Contrariwise, to the extent that citizens view

courts as inherently and inevitably political in nature, then politicization is unlikely to detract from judicial legitimacy. Thus, the central empirical objective of this chapter is to map citizens' expectations of the judiciary and to determine whether a connection exists between these attitudes and the willingness to extend legitimacy to courts.

Even though legitimacy theory has been thoroughly explicated above, it is perhaps useful to begin this analysis with an overview of the theory and especially how it is connected to the expectations citizens hold of institutions.

EXPECTANCY THEORY AND ITS CONNECTIONS TO LEGITIMACY THEORY

All institutions need political capital in order to be effective, to get their decisions accepted by others and be successfully implemented. Since courts are typically thought to be weak institutions—having neither the power of the "purse" (control of the treasury) nor the "sword" (control over agents of state coercion)—their political capital must be found in resources other than finances and force. For courts, their principal political capital is institutional legitimacy.

But where do courts get their legitimacy? In a democratic society, the principal sources of legitimacy for political institutions are elections and accountability. As part of the social contract, citizens grant authority to political institutions to make public policy and therefore accept the decisions they produce. The contract is enforced by accountability. Institutional decision makers who repeatedly make decisions with which citizens disagree are subject to replacement; institutions that fail repeatedly also can be radically restructured (e.g., court packing) or even abolished. Electoral accountability is perhaps the most powerful source of legitimacy for political institutions in a democratic polity.

According to Brandenburg and Schotland (2008, 102), "More than 89 percent of America's state judges must stand for election to sit on the bench or retain office," even if courts throughout the world are not typically subject to electoral accountability (Kritzer 2007). Without elections, courts begin with a legitimacy shortfall, and this is of course particularly true of the US Supreme Court, where the legitimacy shortfall is punctuated by lifetime tenure, making any sort of policy-making accountability virtually impossible. In the absence of an electoral connection, courts seek legitimacy through the rule of law, by which I mean courts are deemed to be legitimate to the extent that their decision making is principled and grounded in the universalism of law; that is, to the extent that their decision-making processes are procedurally correct and acceptable. The image of the blind Lady Justice is most apposite for this source of legitimacy.

Connected to this view of legitimacy is expertise: that is, to the extent that judges are deemed to be experts in law who ably apply their legal training to decisions within the context of the rule of law, legitimacy attaches. Even in a democratic society, a wide variety of public-policy decisions are turned over to experts—for instance, much of the control of the economy is placed within the purview of relatively unaccountable institutions. Such experts are subject to limited accountability; they are given the freedom to "do the right thing" within the context of their expertise.

Judges seek to enshroud their decision making with technical imagery, suggesting or indicating to their constituents that their decisions ought to be accepted because they are correct, in the same sense that decisions on the economy must be accepted because they represent the judgments of experts on technical issues. Judges tell us they follow the law, and because they follow the law, their decisions should be accepted. In following the law, they are giving effect to the will of the majority through its support of legislation and constitutions. To package decisions as discretionless and guided only by technical expertise is to inoculate those institutions from challenges and to confer legitimacy upon them. There can be no doubt therefore that legitimacy is one of the most highly valued forms of political capital.

As I have presented the theory here, legitimacy turns on institutional decision makers satisfying expectations regarding the procedural components of their decision making. Citizens expect judges to make decisions in a fair and impartial way and when they do so, that process of decision making virtually automatically generates an obligation to comply. Thus, the satisfaction of expectations is crucial to legitimacy.

We typically think of courts as subject to some defining sets of expectations, as I have mentioned several times already, particularly the requirement that they be fair and impartial. It seems quite reasonable to assume that the vast majority of citizens in a democratic polity expect their judges to make decisions in a fair and impartial way on the basis of the rule of law.

But these are of course not the only expectations citizens might hold of judges. They might, for instance, expect judges to make decisions that are fair and just, and it may very well be that in some instances fairness and the rule of law battle with one another. In the instance of conflict between justice and legality, some may prefer that fairness trump legality; others prefer that legality be deemed superior to fairness.

Furthermore, in many instances, the technical aspects of decisions are nearly irrelevant to rendering decisions. Under such conditions—the condition under which law is not dispositive, the condition under which discretion exists on how decisions should be made—citizens may expect that judges take into account the broader values of the society in making their decisions.[1] But not all citizens will agree with that. Some may believe that decisions ought to be made only on the basis of the intent of those creating the legislation and constitutions; others may disagree. If citizens understand decision making to be discretionary in the sense that judges must choose their course of action rather than deduce it, then it follows that law cannot be the only legitimate basis of decision making. But again, citizens likely differ on these issues. The essential point here is that expectations matter and that expectations vary across citizens.

I have presented here a simple theory of expectations. It is doubtful, however, that expectations are themselves quite so simple. Citizens may expect many things from their judicial institutions, and the things they expect may not be internally coherent or consistent. Some citizens may understand the judiciary as just another political institution, whereas others may view the judiciary as a unique institution that should act in a fashion quite distinct from other political institutions. Citizens vary on this score. In a society in which courts are very well defined, quite salient public institutions, often rendering important public-policy decisions—such as in the United States—citizens may have reasonably well developed but diverse understandings of and expectations of courts.

Thus, legitimacy is ultimately grounded in the satisfaction of the expectations of the citizenry. In the case of courts (but perhaps more broadly as well), the expectations primarily concern processes of decision making. It is crucial, therefore, to understand the nature of these expectations.

Extant Research on the Expectations Citizens Hold of Judges

Only a handful of studies has seriously considered the expectations citizens hold of judges and courts, although scholars of the legislative process have paid more attention to citizens' expectations of Congress (e.g., Kimball and Patterson 1997). For example, focusing on public attitudes toward the German Federal Constitutional Court, Baird (2001) shows that the nature of the expectations citizens hold of the FCC, and especially expectations of legalistic styles of decision making, is related to the willingness to attribute legitimacy to the institution (see also Baird and Gangl 2006).

Do the American people expect their courts to be independent? Unfortunately, the evidence is somewhat less than crystal clear. For example, in her analysis of public attitudes toward state courts and court systems, Benesh (2006, 700) argues that Americans prefer independence over accountability, citing evidence from Heagarty (2003, 1305). However, that conclusion does not seem widely supported by empirical evidence (and Heagarty's data are far from definitive on the issue). Some research supports the opposite view (see Wenzel, Bowler, and Lanoue 2003). More generally, judicial independence is most likely a multidimensional concept, with citizens supporting some types of independence (independence from the executive branch) but not others (independence from the preferences of the majority of the citizenry). So when Bybee (2011) puts a general question about judicial independence to a sample of ordinary people and finds that 73% believe that judges should be shielded from outside pressure and allowed to make decisions based on their own reading of the law, this should not be understood to mean that people expect judges to be independent *of every source* of accountability for their decisions. As he acknowledges, people hold ambivalent expectations about the judicial system.

Some data on citizen expectations exist that have not been previously analyzed. In a 2001 survey, the interest group JaS asked a question about the responsibilities of judges that can be understood as reflecting the respondent's expectations.[2] Table 5.1 reports descriptive data on the replies, providing several characteristics of the distributions of opinions. The mean is the average response, and the standard deviation indicates the degree of agreement among the respondents in their judgments. Because the distributions are skewed, I also report the percentages of respondents who assigned the attribute a "10," the highest point on the scale. The column labeled "Loading" reports the factor loading of the item that resulted from a Common Factor Analysis of the set of items.[3] In general, these responses are strongly intercorrelated (mean interitem correlation = .50), indicating a pervasive tendency for the respondents to rate the various responsibilities similarly (i.e., they did not discriminate very much across the various characteristics).

Most Americans want judges to defend constitutional rights and freedoms, to ensure fairness, to protect civil liberties and individual rights, and to make impartial decisions, which is perhaps neither surprising nor particularly interesting. Much more intriguing are the areas where people disagree. On the substantive responsibility to advance social and economic justice, the respondents are quite divided, with (as noted) 18.1% of the respondents assigning a score of "10" to this responsibility, but 5.3% assigning a "0," and 41.6% scoring this type of justice at less than or equal to 5.0 on the 11-point scale. People also adopt different views on whether judges should resist political pressure (whatever that might mean to the respondents), with 35.2% asserting this is very important and 5.4% rating it as unimportant.

TABLE 5.1. EXPECTATIONS OF JUDGES, JUSTICE
AT STAKE NATIONAL SURVEY

Responsibility	Mean	s.d.	% at 10	Loading
Defending constitutional rights and freedoms	8.19	2.50	51.8	.79
Ensuring fairness under law	7.85	2.61	47.3	.83
Protecting civil liberties	7.85	2.59	43.4	.76
Protecting individual rights	7.69	2.67	42.0	.80
Making impartial decisions	7.58	2.74	41.6	.76
Dispensing punishment for crimes	7.45	2.67	36.1	.67
Providing equal justice for rich and poor	7.22	3.30	47.6	.84
Resisting political pressure	6.85	3.10	35.2	.69
Being an independent check on other branches of government	6.55	2.75	23.0	.52
Advancing social and economic justice	6.23	2.79	18.1	.44

Source: Justice at Stake national survey.
Note: The question read: "Now, I am going to read you a list of phrases which some people say are responsibilities of courts and judges. Please rate each one on a scale of 0 to 10, with '10' meaning it is the single most important responsibility of courts and judges, and '5' being in the middle. If you have no opinion, please say so." A handful of "don't know" and "no opinion" replies were recoded to the center point of the 11-point scale. The items are ranked according to their mean score. $N = 1,000$.

These data are inadequate for a comprehensive analysis of citizens' expectations, in part because so few of the items refer to procedural aspects of decision making. The one conclusion the data seem to support, however, is important and apposite: the American people do not uniformly subscribe to any given view of judging, and particularly not to the view that judges ought to be entirely and perfectly insulated from accountability to the people.[4]

Summary: The Research Question

Do politicized judicial selection processes undermine judicial legitimacy, and, if so, how widely? To the extent that people expect and prefer a judiciary that is well insulated from the political process, politicization of selection processes may undermine the legitimacy of courts. But to the extent that citizens instead expect political accountability for their judges, politicized campaigning is unlikely to affect legitimacy. The effect of judges' activities in their pursuit of a judgeship depends mightily on what people want from their judges, not what legal judicial elites think people should want from their judges. Thus, it is crucial to map the expectations people hold and to determine whether those expectations are connected to the willingness to extend legitimacy to judicial institutions.

ANALYSIS
Expectations of Kentucky Judges

We asked the respondents to give us their views of the characteristics of a good Kentucky Supreme Court judge, and their replies are reported in table 5.2. Note that some obvious attributes—for example, *being* fair and impartial in decision making—were purposefully excluded from the questionnaire because I thought it safe to assume (based in part on pretest results) that virtually all Kentuckians wanted their judges to decide cases in a fair and impartial manner. So rather than being an exhaustive list of judicial traits, this question focused on areas where I expected some disagreement among Kentuckians.

Two characteristics stand out from the rest in this table: Kentuckians are strongly united in the view that their supreme court judges ought to "strictly follow the law no matter what people in the state may want" and ought to "be especially concerned about protecting people without power from people and groups with power." On their faces, these items seem contradictory. "Strictly following the law" seems to indicate a procedural characteristic, especially when it is juxtaposed with an outcome—what the people of the state may want. On the other hand, protecting people without power smacks of substance, not of procedure. Moreover, the former seems highly legalistic (following the law); the latter item seems much more political in the sense that it addresses power differentials in the larger society, not necessarily the strength of legal arguments. Of those rating following the law as very important, 75.1% also rate protecting people without power as very important (even though the responses to these two items are practically uncorrelated).[5]

I also note from table 5.2 that the constituency for a very explicitly political view of judging is perhaps small but far from trivial. While only 18.5% of the respondents favor partisanship as a basis for judicial decision making, 43.7% expect to have their own ideological views given weight by the judges, and nearly one-third (30.1%) believe in majoritarianism as a basis of judicial decision making. Indeed, nearly one-half (46.5%) of the respondents agree that judges ought to be "involved in politics, since ultimately they should represent the majority." This majoritarian politics view of judging is attractive to a substantive proportion of the people of Kentucky.

These data certainly suggest complex, if not confused, views of judges (see Bybee 2011). Indeed, for some of these characteristics, it may be that the responses are not particularly high in substantive content. Considering the en-

TABLE 5.2. EXPECTATIONS OF THE CHARACTERISTICS OF A GOOD SUPREME COURT JUSTICE, KENTUCKY 2006

Characteristic	% rating it very important	Mean[a]	s.d.	N
Protect people without power	72.9	3.64	.69	1,438
Strictly follow the law	71.8	3.62	.68	1,437
State policy positions during campaigns	64.2	3.49	.80	1,438
Refuse to accept campaign contributions	48.2	3.17	.96	1,435
Respect existing decisions	47.2	3.32	.76	1,437
Represent the majority	46.5	3.07	1.05	1,436
Give my ideology a voice	43.7	3.18	.88	1,435
Use contributions to get issue stands out	40.9	3.06	.97	1,436
Decide the way the majority wants	30.1	2.72	1.09	1,435
Base decisions on party affiliations	18.5	2.11	1.13	1,433

Note: The items read:
"Now I would like you to focus on thinking about the characteristics of a good supreme court judge, that is, what a good judge ought to be like. First, how important would you say it is for a good Kentucky Supreme Court judge to . . .

Be especially concerned about protecting people without power from people and groups with power.

Strictly follow the law no matter what people in the country may want.

State how they stand on important legal and political issues as part of their campaigning for a position on the Kentucky Supreme Court.

Refuse to accept any campaign contributions from anyone—individuals, groups, and political parties.

Respect existing Kentucky Supreme Court decisions by changing the law as little as possible.

Be involved in politics, since ultimately they should represent the majority.

Give [conservatives/liberals] a strong voice in how the constitution is interpreted.

Use campaign contributions to get their messages out about where they stand on important issues likely to come before the court.

Decide cases the way the majority of the people in Kentucky prefer, even if it goes against existing laws.

Base their decisions on whether they are a Republican or a Democrat."

[a] The response varies from (1) not at all important/don't know to (4) very important. Thus, higher mean scores indicate greater ascribed importance to the characteristic.

tire set of 10 items, the squared multiple correlation coefficients between the item and the set are below .08 for the following statements: strictly follow the law (.06), protect people without power (.05), respect existing decisions (.07), and refuse to accept campaign contributions (.03). These small coefficients may indicate that the responses contain a great deal of idiosyncratic variance,

variance that may be random because little substance underlies the answers of the respondents. These findings suggest that characteristics such as following the law and protecting those without power are largely platitudes, to which nearly all subscribe, but which, at the same time, have little practical meaning in the minds of many if not most citizens. The remainder of the items are all reasonably intercorrelated.

In fact, when these remaining six items are factor analyzed (Common Factor Analysis), a unidimensional structure is revealed.[6] All items load on the first unrotated factor at .40 or higher, with the strongest loading associated with the represent the majority (be involved in politics) item. Cronbach's alpha for the six-item set is .65, indicating modest reliability (mean interitem correlation = .23). The latent dimension suggested by these factor analysis results is one that seems to indicate the degree to which the respondents favor a politicized view of judging.

Because the correlation between the factor score and a simple summation of the responses to the six items is .99, I will use the former as the indicator of the expectation of a politicized judiciary. I also use for some purposes a simple count of the number of items of the six that the respondent rated as "very important." The distribution of this count variable is reported in figure 5.1, where it can be seen that a very small percentage of respondents (2.8%) has entirely politicized expectations of judges. The mean of the distribution is 2.4, which is decidedly skewed toward holding less political expectations of judges. The most important finding from this analysis is that Kentuckians vary in what they expect from their judges, even if a highly politicized view of judging is rejected by a majority, but not a great majority, of the people.[7]

Summary

As I have noted, the most important conclusion of this portion of the analysis is that the expectations people hold of their judges vary. Not everyone accepts that mechanical jurisprudence constitutes the best form of judging; not everyone accepts that judicial independence is a value trumping all other considerations. Instead, people have different conceptions of judging, leading them to hold different normative models about what constitutes a good judge. The importance of this finding is that, because people have different conceptions of judging, campaign activity (and other off-the-bench judicial behavior) is unlikely to be uniformly evaluated. Most specifically, if some citizens expect the judiciary to make ideologically based decisions, then those citizens are unlikely to be put off when judges express their ideological views during the selection process. The conclusion that policy talk and other forms of politicized

FIGURE 5.1. THE DISTRIBUTION OF POLITICIZED JUDICIAL EXPECTATIONS.

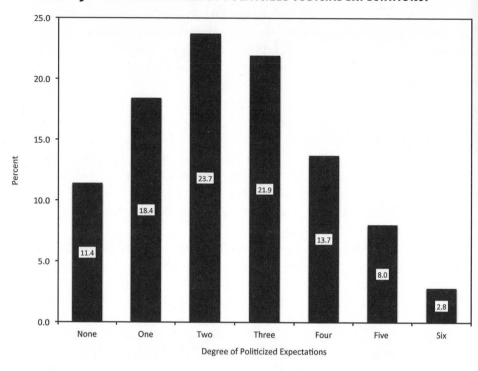

campaigning would cause these citizens to evaluate the judiciary as illegitimate is most likely wrong, at least for a substantial portion of the population.

Expectations and the Institutional Legitimacy of the Kentucky Supreme Court

To what degree are the expectations people hold of the judiciary connected to the willingness to extend legitimacy to judicial institutions? One might hypothesize that those with more politicized expectations of courts hold the judiciary in lesser esteem because they are less likely to subscribe to a mythical view of judging. As Gibson and Caldeira (e.g., 2009a) have argued in the context of the US Supreme Court, support for the Supreme Court results from exposure to the institution and its legitimizing symbols. Consequently, it is revealing to explore the interconnections of expectations and institutional legitimacy.[8]

I measured loyalty toward the Kentucky Supreme Court with the items explicated above in chapter 4. As I noted in that chapter, the measure is reasonably valid and reliable and produces an index of institutional support.

As expected, those holding more politicized expectations of courts are decidedly less supportive of the Kentucky Supreme Court ($r = -.38, p < .000$).[9] Figure 5.2 depicts this relationship. Those with politicized expectations are much less willing to extend the legitimacy to the court that it needs to be effective.

The Relationship between Institutional Support and Knowledge of the Courts
Because it is typically assumed that more knowledgeable citizens are more important to the judiciary—and that the more knowledgeable hold attitudes that differ from the less knowledgeable—the next interconnection that must be considered is that between loyalty toward the Kentucky Supreme Court and knowledge of the Kentucky judicial systems. To do so, a measure of judicial knowledge is necessary.

As I have noted, the expectations questions were asked at the opening of the t_2 interview. So as to avoid clouding the issues of causality, I have used a measure of knowledge derived from the t_1 interview, during which we asked

FIGURE 5.2. THE RELATIONSHIP BETWEEN INSTITUTIONAL SUPPORT AND POLITICIZED EXPECTATIONS. $R = -.38, P < .001$.

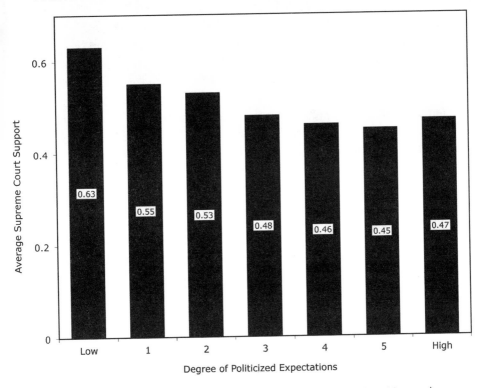

Expectancy Theory and Judicial Legitimacy | 97

the Kentuckians factual questions about their supreme court. To reiterate, the questions we asked and the percentages of respondents answering correctly are (1) whether the justices are elected or not—24.0% correct (elected); (2) whether the justices serve a life or fixed term—32.9% correct (fixed); and (3) whether the justices have the "last say" on the meaning of the constitution—45.6% correct (they do). Interestingly, the correlation between the general court knowledge index and awareness of the candidates in the election (measured at t_2) is only .11, which most likely reflects the fact that two different types of knowledge are being measured: general information about the institution and specific information about who is running at the moment in the respondent's judicial district.

Extant research has uniformly revealed that greater knowledge of courts is connected to greater support for them (e.g., Gibson, Caldeira, and Baird 1998; Gibson and Caldeira 2009a). Kentucky is no exception to this general rule: the correlation between the support index and knowledge is .13 ($p < .001$), which comes as no surprise.

Connecting Expectations with Knowledge of the Courts

A few commentators acknowledge that some citizens distinguish little between courts and other political institutions, and, for those folks, finding that the politicized view of judging has a nontrivial constituency will be of little surprise. Most of these observers dismiss this model of judging as inappropriate, and they do so on normative grounds (e.g., judicial independence and the rule of law trump everything). Some believe that the politicized view of judging is only embraced by the politically ignorant and that, were they better informed, they would abandon this position. For instance, Jamieson and Hardy (2008, 12) assert, "With ignorance about the judiciary comes an increased disposition to believe that judges are biased and a reduced tendency to hold that the courts act in the public interest" (see also Jamieson and Hennessy 2007).

The degree to which views of judging are connected to knowledge and ignorance is an important empirical question. Consequently, the simple hypothesis guiding this portion of the analysis is that those more knowledgeable about the Kentucky judiciary will tend to reject the view that the courts should respond to political inputs and pressures. Knowledge and the politicized view of judging should be inversely related.

The specific hypothesis I test in this section is that those most knowledgeable about courts hold distinctive expectations of judging. Table 5.3 reports the relationships between court knowledge and the importance assigned to different judicial characteristics.

TABLE 5.3. THE IMPACT OF JUDICIAL KNOWLEDGE ON EXPECTATIONS

Characteristic	Amount of judicial knowledge				tau-beta
	0	1	2	3	
Protect people without power	72.2	72.6	73.5	76.3	.02
Strictly follow the law	70.2	71.3	71.3	**82.5**	.03
State policy positions during campaigns	65.9	64.9	64.3	**53.5**	−.04
Refuse to accept campaign contributions	44.2	49.8	54.9	**39.5**	.03
Respect existing decisions	48.4	47.4	43.7	50.9	−.01
Represent the majority	54.4	40.7	53.7	**25.4**	−.11***
Give my ideology a voice	45.5	41.3	46.6	40.7	−.03
Use contributions to get issue stands out	40.2	41.2	43.2	36.0	−.02
Decide the way the majority wants	30.7	30.7	31.2	22.8	−.07**
Base decisions on party affiliations	19.2	18.4	19.6	14.0	−.07***

Note: The entries shown are the percentages of respondents rating the characteristic as "very important," the most extreme point on the response set. The correlation shown is calculated from the full distribution of importance ratings. $N \approx 1{,}436$. Boldface entries for the highest level of knowledge indicate that the difference between those high in knowledge and all others is significant at $p < .05$. For the full text of the items, see the note to table 5.2.
Differences across all levels of judicial knowledge: *** $p < .001$ ** $p < .01$ * $p < .05$

The most common finding of this table is that those with high levels of knowledge *differ little* from those with relatively low levels of knowledge (see the tau-beta column). For instance, the vast majority of Kentuckians, irrespective of the information they hold about the Kentucky judiciary, expect that judges should protect people without power from those with power. Those high and low in knowledge do not differ on whether a judge should strictly follow the law, respect existing decisions, or even give the respondent's ideology a voice. In terms of campaign activity, no knowledge differences exist on whether judges should refuse to accept campaign contributions, use contributions to get their issue stands out, or state their policy positions during their campaigns (although the difference on the last item approaches statistical significance: $p = .062$). It is noteworthy that the strongest difference between the more and less knowledgeable is on the statement about representing the majority. Empirically, those high in knowledge are a minority in Kentucky (7.9%). If they think of themselves as in the minority, then that might explain their reluctance to agree that courts should represent the majority.

Those with high levels of knowledge are distinctive in their expectations on three of the characteristics reported in table 5.3. The knowledgeable are less

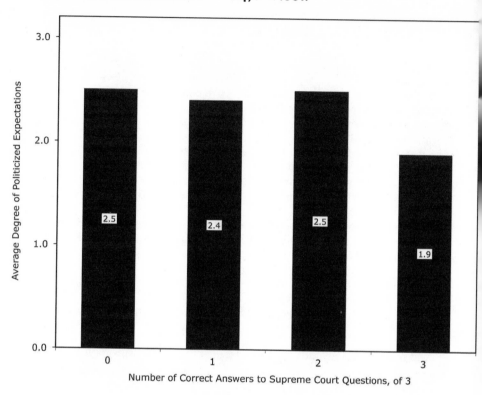

FIGURE 5.3. THE RELATIONSHIP BETWEEN KNOWLEDGE AND POLITICIZED EXPECTATIONS. $r = -.14$, $P < .001$.

Number of Correct Answers to Supreme Court Questions, of 3

likely to assert that judges should represent the majority, that they should base their decisions on their party affiliations, and that they should decide the way the majority wants. Using the full index of politicized expectations, a highly significant but not particularly strong relationship exists between levels of knowledge and the politicization of judicial expectations (see figure 5.3). The correlation between knowledge and holding politicized expectations is $-.14$, indicating that more knowledge is associated with less emphasis on political orientations for judges.[10]

Table 5.3 also reports the items upon which those highest in political knowledge (i.e., who score a "3" on the knowledge index) are distinctive from the remainder of the sample. On four items, the difference is statistically significant at $p < .05$. The most knowledgeable are distinctive in their views of strictly following the law, stating policy positions during campaigns, refusing to accept campaign contributions, and representing the majority. Not all of these relationships are substantively meaningful: for example, on refusing to accept campaign contributions, those highest in knowledge hold about the same views as those lowest in knowledge. Overall, the correlation between a knowledge dichotomy (high versus all else) and the index of politicized expectations is −.15, which is the same as the relationship with the more finely tuned measure of knowledge.

Are Judges Just Politicians in Robes?

These findings are decidedly mixed. One conclusion is that the more knowledgeable place less emphasis on political aspects of judging, as in their rejection of the view that courts should represent the majority. At the same time, however, those high in knowledge are little more committed to a mechanical view of judging than those low in knowledge. Furthermore, *a majority of those with high knowledge assert that judges should state their policy positions during their campaigns for a seat on the bench*, and a large majority believes that judges should protect the powerless. These findings seem to indicate a complex, if not confused, view of what it is judges should be doing.

Perhaps what these data indicate is something like the following. Perhaps only a small portion of the population views mechanical jurisprudence as feasible or desirable. Everyone most likely favors judges who prefer justice over legality, to the extent that the two conflict. And most people also recognize that judges make public policy and that great discretion is available within many if not most cases. Consequently, a sizeable proportion of the population wants to know something about the ideologies of those who put themselves forward for a seat on the high court.

Where the more and less knowledgeable differ, however, is on the degree to which judges are little more than politicians in robes. The less knowledgeable seem to hold the view that judges should represent majority opinion, implementing the ideological views of the majority, even if not their partisanship. In this sense, low levels of knowledge seem to be associated with the view that judges are representatives, perhaps even in the mold of other elected public officials. We might even refer to this as an "instructed delegate" style of representation, in the sense that the job of the representative is to take policy instructions from her or his constituents.

The more knowledgeable do not completely eschew representation but are perhaps more attracted to the "trustee" style of representation. Trustees are elected because they hold values similar to the majority but, at the same time, once elected, are expected to exercise their own independent judgment and, to the extent possible (i.e., where law does not conflict with justice), follow extant law. In this view, judges are not mechanical jurisprudes—they are instead policy makers with a great deal of available discretion—and their ideologies are entirely relevant to judging. At the same time, they are different from other representatives in the sense of being expected to exercise independent and principled judgment. All agree, however, that in one form or another, judges should reflect the views of their constituents; in this sense, the constituency for strict judicial independence is small.

This then leads to the question of whether those holding politicized expectations of judges also hold distinctive views of courts. Are courts then just the same as legislatures and executives? Is there anything distinctive about the judiciary when it comes to its relationships with its constituents?

We asked the respondents to agree or disagree with the statement that "supreme court judges are little more than politicians in robes." Fully 40% of the respondents (40.2%) agreed with this statement, and another 13.0% was uncertain about it. The remaining 46.7% of the respondents, a plurality but not a majority, rejects this view of judges. Obviously, Kentuckians are quite divided in their views of their judges and politics.

Most important, the expectations one holds of the judiciary are strongly connected to the belief that judges are politicians in robes. Figure 5.4 reports this relationship ($r = .27, p < .001$). A large majority of those holding politicized views of judges believe that judges are politicians in robes; only a very small percentage of those not holding politicized expectations agree with the statement. To state the relationship in the opposite direction (since the nature of the causal connection between the two variables is ambiguous), those who believe that judges are politicians in robes are quite likely to hold politicized expectations ($r = .27, p < .000$), a finding that may indicate that believing that judges are politicians in robes is not necessarily a disparaging view. It seems clear that a substantial proportion of the constituents of the Kentucky Supreme Court view that institution in explicitly political terms.[11]

DISCUSSION AND CONCLUDING COMMENTS

Perhaps the most important conclusion of this chapter is that Kentuckians vary in many of the expectations they hold of their judiciary. Many of the constituents of the Kentucky Supreme Court expect that institution to represent their views on the policy issues it decides. If directly asked to choose between the independence and accountability of judges, a substantial proportion of Kentuckians would select accountability, even if it is the accountability of the trustee, not the instructed delegate.

As a consequence of the variability in expectations, I predict that citizens

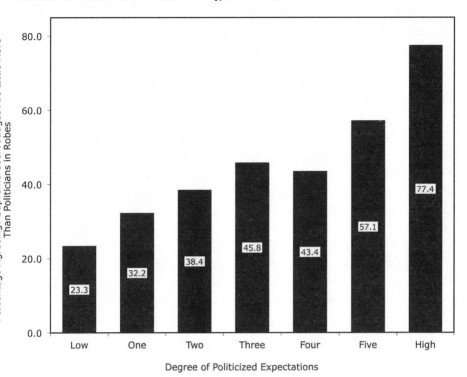

also vary in how they are affected by the behaviors of judges. If citizens expect judges to make public policy, then it stands to reason that they are unlikely to be put off when judges announce their policy views in their campaigns for a judgeship. If citizens expect judges to represent the views of the majority of their constituents, then it hardly would be surprising to find that judges representing the views of the majority are viewed favorably. The simple point of this analysis has been only to suggest that citizens' views of the appropriateness of certain types of judicial activities have a great deal to do with whether those activities undermine judicial legitimacy—a hypothesis tested in the next chapter of this book.

This view runs deeply contrary to almost all judicial understandings of public confidence and faith in the judiciary. Legal elites typically begin with either assumptions about what citizens expect from the courts, or, more likely, presumptions about what citizens *ought to expect* from their courts. Legal elites, I conjecture, overwhelmingly support strong judicial independence with little direct accountability to the people (just as professors overwhelmingly support strong professorial independence with little direct accountability to students or administrators). They most likely also support both impartial judicial decision making and the appearance of impartiality, and I do not doubt that most Americans support these values as well, at least at the abstract level.

But here is the rub: legal elites presume that activities such as discussion of legal ideologies during judicial campaigns are offensive to citizens, not because they are, but because they ought to be. The explorations of this chapter suggest that legal elites are wrong in assuming that public expectations of judges are uniform,[12] in assuming that the constituency for a politicized model of judging is minute, and therefore in assuming that a wide variety of off-the-bench judicial behavior threatens the legitimacy of elected state courts. To the extent that popular confidence in the judiciary is a standard for evaluating the behaviors of judges, we must be aware that the sources of confidence are disparate and perhaps even contested and that popular and elite expectations of judges may not be consonant. We must also investigate the processes through which these expectations intersect with perceptions of the judiciary—and especially with perceptions of campaign activity—and in turn affect levels of institutional support. Beginning that investigation is the purpose of chapter 6.

CHAPTER SIX

JUDGES, ELECTIONS, AND THE AMERICAN MASS PUBLIC: THE EFFECTS OF JUDICIAL CAMPAIGNS ON THE LEGITIMACY OF COURTS

The premise of this book is that a new era has emerged in the ways in which candidates for state judicial office campaign. In the past, judicial elections were largely devoid of policy content, with candidates typically touting their judicial experience and other preparation for serving as a judge. Today, in many if not most states, such campaigns are relics of the past. Modern judicial campaigns have adopted many of the practices of candidates for other types of political office, including soliciting campaign contributions, using attack ads, and even making promises about how they will decide issues if elected to the bench. As Gibson et al. (2011, 1) put it: "campaigning for state judgeships in America has entered a new era. In the past, campaigns might be described as decent, docile, and dirt-cheap, even if drab and dull. Today, they are said to be 'nosier, nastier, and costlier' (Schotland 2001)."

Not surprisingly, this new style of judicial campaigning has caused considerable consternation among observers of the courts, with many fearing that such activity will undermine the life-giving legitimacy of these fragile legal institutions. For instance, Caufield (2007, 10) exclaims, "When we look at the landscape of judicial elections today, we see a clear and troubling trend—sitting judges and judicial candidates are being forced to behave like candidates for the legislative and executive branches. The same factors that emerge in legislative and executive elections—the partisanship, the special interest influence, the negative campaigning, the money, and the bitter rhetoric—are all now shaping judicial elections as well. . . . But judicial independence, the only thing that can ensure fair and impartial justice across the country, is facing an uncertain future in today's electoral landscape. In the end, it is the most basic of American values—the rule of law—that is at stake." Such fears, however, are grounded in extremely limited empirical evidence on the effects of campaign activity on public perceptions and evaluations of judicial institutions. Pronouncements of impending doom are commonplace; rigorous and dispositive evidence, however, is much more scarce.

Providing evidence of the effects of campaigns on citizens is methodologically demanding. The most probative research design is one that measures actual change after exposure to advertising—preferably after some period of time elapses between the exposure and the measurement, so as to ensure that change is not epiphenomenal—and that deals to at least some degree with the likelihood that exposure to ads is itself endogenous. Such designs are difficult and costly to implement. At least some of the rationale for poorly understanding the effects of campaigns on citizens is grounded in formidable research design requirements.

At the same time, however, theories of campaign effects are also much underdeveloped, with little research attempting to develop understandings of individual differences in reactions to campaign ads. Citizens most likely do not respond uniformly to campaign advertisements; citizens most likely differ in what they regard as offensive and inoffensive campaign content. Especially when it comes to the judiciary, expectations about what is and what is not appropriate for candidates for judgeships are likely to play a major role in moderating the effects of campaign activities on attitudes toward and support for judicial institutions.

Consequently, the purpose of this chapter is to investigate the effects of judicial campaigning on the support citizens extend to elected state courts of last resort. Utilizing all the components of my three-wave panel survey of a representative sample of Kentucky residents, with interviews before, during, and after the election period, this analysis seeks to assess the degree to which campaign activity affected the legitimacy of the Kentucky Supreme Court. At least from the research design aspect, this project has the potential to rigorously document campaign effects on the constituents of courts with an unusual degree of causal certainty.

The theoretical contribution of this chapter lies in the extended development of expectancy theory, a theory accounting for individual differences in reactions to judicial campaigns. This theory is normative in the sense that it focuses on what citizens think is appropriate campaign activity. Legitimacy-stripping dissatisfaction with courts is hypothesized to flow from the intersection of citizens' expectations and perceptions, with those believing that certain activity is inappropriate for judicial campaigns withdrawing support from the institution. In general, that hypothesis is supported by the data analyzed in this chapter, although perhaps the most surprising aspect of the analysis is that the size of the constituency for politicized judicial campaigns is remarkably large. This then leads to the conclusion that politicized campaign activity violates the expectations of only a slice of the electorate, and therefore such activity is *not* catastrophic for courts.

My most important finding is that judicial elections by themselves enhance judicial legitimacy. So even if campaign activity drains some of the judiciary's reservoir of goodwill, the *net effect* of judicial elections is positive. Most earlier research (and speculation) on the damaging consequences of judicial campaigns for institutional legitimacy fails to recognize the inherent boost provided to courts by elections. Thus, the research reported in this chapter is unusually rich in its data and theory, and unexpected and significant in its conclusions.

I begin this analysis with a review of the limited literature on the effects of campaign activity on perceptions and evaluations of judicial institutions.

RESEARCH ON THE EFFECTS OF CAMPAIGNS ON COURT LEGITIMACY

Especially in our post–*Citizens United* world, scores of commentators complain about the impact of campaign activity on the perceived impartiality, and hence legitimacy,[1] of elected state courts.[2] For instance, a variety of interest groups have mobilized in response to what they see as threats to fairness and impartiality posed by elections, including NYU's Brennan Center (e.g., Sample, Jones, and Weiss 2007) and Sandra Day O'Connor's effort to eliminate judicial elections (see Wyatt 2009; see also her post–*Citizens United* assessment that "if both sides unleash their campaign spending monies without restrictions, then I think mutually-assured destruction is the most likely outcome" [Liptak 2010]). Few of these complaints, however, cite empirical evidence because practically none exists. Even the research on campaign effects on citizen attitudes in other institutional contexts has little to say about this issue because legitimacy is rarely one of the consequences receiving scholarly attention.[3]

Indeed, most research testing legitimacy theory hypotheses is static, making it difficult to determine how campaign activities affect popular attitudes (for an exception, see Gibson et al. [2011]). Conversely, the limited research adopting a dynamic framework largely ignores election campaign activity, either because it focuses on federal courts or because it was conducted in an era before judicial campaigns became politically significant (e.g., Franklin and Kosaki 1989; Marshall 1989; Murphy and Tanenhaus 1990; Gibson and Caldeira 1992; Mondak and Smithey 1997; Kritzer 2001; Gibson, Caldeira, and Spence 2003a; Hoekstra 2003; Gibson and Caldeira 2009a). Unfortunately, many of these efforts are also seriously hampered by the lack of valid measures of court legitimacy (see Gibson, Caldeira, and Spence 2003b) and, most crucially, by research designs that do not allow the assessment of individual-level attitudinal change. Extant theory and data sources are simply not up to the task of providing many useful insights into how legitimacy is formed or acquired and how it is reinforced or eroded.

Only a handful of studies have addressed campaign effects with rigorous data, and the findings from those studies are mixed. For example, Gibson and Caldeira (2009a) examined the impact of the advertising campaigns mounted in support of or opposition to the nomination of Samuel Alito to the US Supreme Court. They discovered that the ad campaigns by interest groups seemed to have undermined the legitimacy of the court itself. The ads run both for and against Alito's confirmation were highly politicized and portrayed the court as "just another political institution." From these messages, citizens seemed to conclude that, as an ordinary political institution, the court is not worthy of high esteem.

At the same time, some research has shown that public attitudes toward the US Supreme Court are remarkably resistant to alteration by the court's decisions. The justices' controversial ruling in *Bush v. Gore* did not undermine the court's legitimacy (Kritzer 2001; Yates and Whitford 2002; Gibson, Caldeira, and Spence 2003a; Nicholson and Howard 2003; Price and Romantan 2004); and, indeed, it may have even enhanced it somewhat (Gibson 2007). Even highly controversial decisions need not necessarily subtract from the court's legitimacy.

A handful of studies of the state courts have addressed the question of whether judicial campaigns undermine legitimacy.[4] In chapter 2 I utilized an experimental vignette that exposes the respondents to different types of campaign activities, including "policy speech" (i.e., in the post–*Republican Party of Minnesota v. White* era). When citizens hear issue-based speech from candidates for judicial office, it appears that court legitimacy does not suffer. Of greater relevance is my finding that, for many citizens, contributions to candidates for judicial office imply a conflict of interest, even a quid pro quo relationship between the donor and the judge, which undermines perceived impartiality and legitimacy (see also Gibson and Caldeira 2012). Importantly, the judiciary is not distinctive on this score: as I reported in chapter 2, campaign contributions to candidates for the state legislature also imply a conflict of interest and therefore can detract from the legitimacy of legislatures as well. Little is unique about the judiciary on this score.

Research of this sort is limited, however, in several important ways. First, it is based on descriptions of hypothetical ads, and these ads do not necessarily contain the full sting of actual advertisements. For instance, the attack ads were modeled via the following manipulation read to the respondents: "Judge Anderson's campaign ads vigorously attack his opponent, claiming that his opponent is biased in favor of insurance companies and other such businesses, and would therefore not be able to make fair and impartial decisions if elected to the supreme court." Moreover, the experiment was highly constricted in time—conducted within a single interview with the respondents—and no evidence of an enduring effect of the ads was adduced. Finally, the vignette's dependent variable, while appropriate to the experiment, leaves some questions about whether the larger concept of institutional legitimacy is being validly measured. The indicators used in the experiment are stylized and related to the context presented in the vignettes. Thus, this research cannot be taken as the final word on whether and how campaigns affect citizens.

Finally, in the most directly relevant study, Gibson et al. (2011) investigate the effects of judicial campaign ads on the legitimacy of the Pennsylvania Supreme Court. Using an experiment embedded within a three-wave Internet panel survey, they found that exposure to attacking ads did in fact subtract from the legitimacy of the Pennsylvania Supreme Court, although so too did the conventional, nonattacking endorsement ads that have characterized judicial elections in the past (e.g., "AFL-CIO says vote for Judge X"). Importantly, the control group—those exposed to no ads—substantially *increased* their support for the Pennsylvania Supreme Court over the period from before the election to afterward. Most significant, the negative effect of the campaign ads was about one-half the size of the positive effect in the control group, leading to the conclusion that the net effect of the election was *beneficial* to the Pennsylvania Supreme Court.[5] This is an extremely important finding: despite the rough and tumble of hard-fought campaigns, which are indeed off-putting to some constituents, having the opportunity to hold judges accountable through elections generates sufficient goodwill to weather the storm of fierce campaigns.[6] Unfortunately, however, there remain some doubts about the external validity of the findings owing to some possible defects in their Internet sample of Pennsylvanians.

This finding from Pennsylvania fits with a handful of research studies showing (or suggesting) that elections, ipso facto, seem to boost citizen support for the political system and its institutions (see Rahn, Brehm, and Carlson 1999; Banducci and Karp 2003). For instance, Price and Romantan (2004, 953, emphasis added) draw the following conclusion from their research on the contested US presidential election of 2000: "On the whole our findings are consistent with the hypothesis that the election even with the vituperative disputes in its wake served to *boost* public attachment to American political institutions." Elections enhance support at least in part because citizens learn (or remember) from elections that political institutions are accountable to them. As Rahn, Brehm, and Carlson (1999, 112–13) assert, "People's feeling about authorities—in particular, whether these authorities can be trusted—depend in part on whether citizens believe they can exercise influence over them." Perhaps the legitimacy-enhancing effects of elections can under some conditions be entirely washed away by certain types of campaigns, but the legitimacy base from which campaigns subtract is elevated—perhaps substantially so—by the simple opportunity of citizens to vote for their judges.

Thus, the store of available research, while pointing to the conclusion that judicial campaigns are not an unmitigated disaster for courts, is too fragmentary to warrant the firm conclusion that the critics are raising false alarms. We simply have too little rigorous research on campaign effects to draw credible conclusions. More research is undoubtedly required.

EXPECTANCY THEORY

As I have noted, practically none of the literature on campaign effects addresses the possibility of individual differences in the ways in which citizens react to campaign material. With the assistance of a simple theory of expectancies— outlined in chapter 5—this deficiency can be remedied.

This theory begins by asserting that citizens most likely hold views of what constitutes appropriate campaign activity. For example, within the context of presidential politics, many American Democrats seem to believe it inappropriate for Democratic candidates to viciously attack their Democratic competitors, even though such attacks directed against Republicans are not deemed inappropriate. The judicial context in particular is likely to be highly susceptible to these sorts of normative expectancies, since courts are often said to be constrained not just by their activities, but also by the *appearances* created by the activities. We typically think of courts as subject to some defining sets of expectations, as for instance, that they be fair and impartial. It seems quite reasonable to assume that the vast majority of citizens in democratic polities expect their judges to make decisions in a fair and impartial way on the basis of the rule of law. Indeed, the judicial role is most likely more constrained by normative expectations than any other in American politics.

The expectations of judicial campaigns are undoubtedly evolving as judges are granted greater leeway in their activities (e.g., as in *Republican Party of Minnesota v. White*). Some evidence indicates that many citizens would prefer that judges discuss their positions on substantive legal issues (e.g., the breadth of the Second Amendment) as part of their bid for judicial office (see chapter 2). Some might even prefer that judges commit to ruling for a particular side on certain legal issues (e.g., abortion rights). There does appear to be a line that most expect judges not to cross (see chapter 3). More generally, some citizens subscribe to a relatively politicized view of judging, a view that renders many sorts of conventional campaign activity entirely appropriate. Others may embrace some form of mechanical jurisprudence and therefore expect that judges come to cases as a tabula rasa unsullied by policy discussions during the campaign. The essential points here are that expectations matter and that expectations vary across citizens.[7]

Do politicized judicial selection processes undermine judicial legitimacy, and, if so, how widely? To the extent that people expect and prefer a judiciary that is well insulated from the political process, politicization of selection processes may undermine the legitimacy of courts. But to the extent that citizens instead expect political accountability for their judges, politicized campaigning is unlikely to affect legitimacy. The effect of judges' activities in their pursuit of a judgeship depends mightily on what people want from their judges, not what legal elites think people should want from their judges. Thus, it is crucial to map the expectations people hold and to determine whether those expectations are connected to the willingness to extend legitimacy to judicial institutions.

Thus, the overriding hypothesis of the research presented in this chapter is that people vary in their expectations of judges, that perceived campaign activity is judged according to these normative expectations, and that dissatisfaction diminishes the legitimacy accorded to the court.

THE JUDICIAL ELECTIONS OF 2006

The central purpose of this research is to assess the impact of judicial campaigns on the legitimacy of the Kentucky Supreme Court in the eyes of the people of Kentucky. Thus, the most useful research design is a multiwave panel survey. The value of a panel design is that it allows the assessment of individual change over time (something not possible with repeated cross-sections), and the crucial dependent variable, the perceived legitimacy of the supreme court, is measured outside the election season and thus is not contaminated with variance properly assigned to the independent variables—the campaign stimuli. Since the central hypotheses of this research concern the effects of the electoral process on individual citizens, no other research design would produce more probative data. I have therefore designed this research around a representative sample interviewed three times in 2006. The respondents were interviewed before the fall elections, during the election season, and well after the elections.

The Races

The justices of the Kentucky Supreme Court are elected from one of seven judicial districts; no justices run at large. In 2006, no election was held for the supreme court in two judicial districts (districts 3 and 7). In addition, John Minton Jr. ran unopposed in the Second Judicial District. Thus, two-candidate elections were held in four of the seven districts. In terms of the survey respondents, 60.1% lived in one of these four districts. In the Seventh Judicial District, a competitive race for the intermediate court of appeal took place, a race that was particularly salient because one of the candidates (Janet Stumbo) was from a prominent Kentucky political family and had earlier served on the Kentucky Supreme Court (and had been defeated for reelection in 2004).

Of the five supreme court elections held in 2006, only a single race turned out to be competitive. In the Fourth Judicial District, the incumbent William E. McAnulty defeated Ann O'Malley Shake by a margin of 51.8% to 48.2%. John Minton Jr. running unopposed received 100% of the vote in the Second District, but the losers in the other three races garnered from 35.6% (Marcus Carey) to 40.4% (incumbent John Roach) of the vote.

The Ad Campaigns

Five media markets relevant to Kentucky are monitored by CMAG (Campaign Media Analysis Group): Lexington, Louisville, and Paducah, Kentucky; Cincinnati, Ohio; and Evansville, Indiana.[8] No supreme court ads were broadcast in the Cincinnati media market. These markets do not perfectly overlap judicial districts, with both the Lexington and Louisville media markets encompassing six judicial districts, and the Evansville market covering two districts. Only the Fourth Judicial District is confined to a single CMAG market. Consequently, many Kentuckians almost certainly saw ads for candidates for whom they could not vote.[9]

In 2006, 27 ads were broadcast in the CMAG markets by candidates for the Kentucky Supreme Court. These 27 ads were aired 3,850 times; 78.2% of the ads were 30 seconds in length, the remainder were shorter. In terms of the CMAG media markets, judicial advertising was heaviest in Lexington (2,250 spots), followed by Louisville (1,176 spots), Paducah (362 spots), and Evansville (62 spots).

In all three of the supreme court races covered by CMAG, both candidates broadcast advertisements in the general election. As a rough characterization, airings parity characterized the Cunningham/Johnson and the McAnulty/Shake races, but losing candidate Roach broadcast more than twice as many ads as candidate Noble. The candidates and their ad activities are

Cunningham, 8 ads, 208 airings,		Johnson, 3 ads, 216 airings,
5,400 seconds	vs.	6,480 seconds
McAnulty, 2 ads, 374 airings,		Shake, 5 ads, 802 airings,
11,220 seconds	vs.	12,120 seconds
Noble, 4 ads, 368 airings,		Roach, 5 ads, 1,882 airings,
11,040 seconds	vs.	56,460 seconds

Each of the ads broadcast was classified according to its content: (1) attack, (2) contrast, or (3) promote. Only a single ad posed any difficulty whatsoever ("Cunningham Don't Decide"). Nearly all of the ads were promotional: of the 27 ads broadcast, three were classified as attack ads and one as contrasting the candidates. In terms of airings, 84.8% of the ads broadcast were promotional ads; only 14.3% were attack ads. Nearly 40% of the respondents lived in a media market in which attack ads were broadcast. Candidates Cunningham, Johnson, and Roach employed attack ads; McAnulty, Noble, and Shake did not. Perhaps the most vapid of the ads is the "My Dad" ad broadcast by candidate Rick Johnson.[10]

Were the 2006 supreme court elections in Kentucky politicized? Most were and some were not. Recall that the constituencies of Kentucky Supreme Court judges are not the entire state, but rather supreme court judicial districts. In 2006, John Minton Jr. ran unopposed in the Second District, and no elections were held in the Third and Seventh Districts. In the other districts, however, the campaigns were to at least some degree rancorous.

In the Sixth District, candidate Marcus Carey sought to tell the voters about his views on abortion, the right to bear arms, and gay marriage (Cross and Fortune 2007, 646). Similarly, Rick Johnson, candidate for the high bench in the First District, campaigned on "disputed, legal, social, and political issues" (Cross and Fortune 2007, 646; see also Johnson 2003), and "at the Fancy Farm Picnic in 2006, Johnson gave public voice to his conservative views on abortion, marriage, gay rights, prayer in schools, and the death penalty" (Cross and Fortune 2007, 647, citation omitted). Johnson's race with Circuit Judge Bill Cunningham "turned nasty, with charges and counter-charges of unethical campaigning" (Cross and Fortune 2007, 648). Johnson was criticized for his campaigning by both the Kentucky Judicial Campaign Conduct Committee (KJCCC)[11] and the mainstream media. Cross and Fortune refer to Marcus Carey and Rick Johnson as "the two 'White' candidates" (649). At the court of appeals level, the KJCCC judged the race for the Seventh District between David Barber and Janet Stumbo to have been politicized.

Thus, there can be little doubt that politicized judicial races for the Kentucky Supreme Court took place in the First, Fifth, and Sixth Districts and in the Seventh District for the court of appeals. Indeed, given the overlap between media markets and electoral districts, it is reasonable to conclude that the ad environment experienced by most if not nearly all Kentucky residents was quite politicized.

Public Attentiveness to and Knowledge of the Elections

To what degree did Kentuckians pay attention to the judicial elections of 2006? We first asked the respondents to report how closely they followed the elections. (See appendix H for all question wordings.) Our questions focused on the highest judicial election taking place in the district in which the respondent lived. For 59.3% of the respondents, the questions referred to the supreme court race; we queried the remainder about the court of appeals contest in their district.

Overall, attention to the election was limited, with only 5.1% of the respondents claiming to follow the judicial race closely, and with 34.5% admitting to paying no attention to the election. The data reveal no tendency for supreme court races to attract more attention than court of appeals contests. Although I have no comparable data on attentiveness to state legislative elections, it seems reasonable to conclude that the judicial elections in Kentucky were relatively low salience affairs.

At the same time, however, the voters were not completely in the dark about the elections for judges in 2006. We asked the respondents whether they recognized the names of the candidates for high judicial office in their district. We asked about four individuals: the two actual candidates and two foils (names of individuals who were not candidates: Monica E. Kinsella and Doug Rush). For the two actual candidates for judicial office, 28.0% recognized the names of both candidates, 36.7% identified one or the other of the candidates, and only 28.0% recognized the name of neither candidate. Furthermore, when presented in the next question with the names of each of the actual candidates, identified as the candidates, 58.6% of the respondents claimed to have heard of the first candidate presented to them and 49.9% claimed to have heard of the second candidate, and fully 34.7% claimed to have heard of both individuals. As for the foils, only 3.1% of the respondents selected both foils as candidates for judicial office, another 17.8% identified one foil or the other, and *fully 79.1% selected neither of the foil names*.[12] That more than three-fourths of the respondents failed to be tricked by names of individuals who were not candidates for Kentucky judicial office and that roughly three-fourths correctly identified at least one name of a candidate for judicial office is an impressive and unexpected finding.[13]

The survey asked the t_2 respondents about their exposure to campaign ads "on TV, radio, in newspapers, or elsewhere."[14] Most respondents reported having seen an ad (53.6%), although only a handful claimed to have seen numerous ads. The self-reported frequency of exposure to the ads varies significantly by judicial district, as it should, inasmuch as the number of ads broadcast also varies greatly by district. In the race between Mary Noble and John Roach (the Fifth District), approximately 70% of the respondents claim to have seen some advertisements; in the Second District, where John Minton Jr. ran unopposed, only 40% of the respondents reported seeing an ad. I do find a statistically significant difference in ad exposure across the seven judicial districts, although the difference according to whether a supreme court election was held in the district is not statistically significant (and neither is the difference between respondents residing in a CMAG media market and those not).[15] In the analysis that follows, I will control for the number of ads viewed by the respondent.

This measure of ad exposure, however, most likely does not capture all of the ad viewing that took place during the 2006 election. For example, it should not be assumed that respondents residing in areas outside these media markets were exposed to no ads during the campaign since much of the campaign of 2006 spilled over beyond television broadcasts, into newspaper reports, radio talk shows, blogs, and other less formal elements of the mass media. Moreover, the respondents were, obviously, interviewed at different points in the run-up to the election, and in fact there is a slight relationship between reported ad viewing and the number of days between the interview and the election: $r = -.06$, $p = .058$. As the number of days between the election and the interview increases, the likelihood of reporting seeing advertisements decreases. Even though this relationship is weak, I will control for the proximity of the interview to election day in the multivariate analysis below.[16]

Thus, most Kentuckians were exposed to judicial advertisements during the campaigns of 2006, and those campaigns were to a considerable degree politicized. It remains to consider whether the exposure to these campaigns affected public attitudes toward the Kentucky high court.

CHANGE IN ATTITUDES TOWARD THE KENTUCKY SUPREME COURT

Gibson and his colleagues have written about how the legitimacy of courts ought to be measured (Gibson, Caldeira, and Spence 2003b).[17] In that article, alternative measures of attitudes toward courts are discussed, followed by recommendations as to the most useful indicators of loyalty toward (or institutional support for) high courts. This analysis follows those prescriptions closely.

Across all three waves of the survey, we included eight core indicators of institutional loyalty. As detailed in table 6.1 (which reports the data for those

TABLE 6.1. LOYALTY TOWARD THE KENTUCKY SUPREME COURT

		Level of diffuse support for the supreme court					
		Percentage					
Item	Interview	Not supportive	Undecided	Supportive	Mean	s.d.	N
Do away with the court	t_1	19.3	10.0	70.7	3.66	1.09	983
	t_3	14.1	9.5	76.4	3.82	1.02	985
Court can be trusted	t_1	13.2	21.3	65.5	3.57	.83	985
	t_3	8.4	14.7	76.9	3.76	.76	982
Limit the court's jurisdiction	t_1	35.8	22.4	41.8	3.07	1.07	979
	t_3	26.3	22.4	51.3	3.26	1.00	985
Remove judges who decide against majority	t_1	39.3	18.1	42.6	3.02	1.14	983
	t_3	36.0	16.3	47.7	3.12	1.15	985
Court gets too mixed up in politics	t_1	43.4	29.3	27.3	2.78	.97	984
	t_3	44.5	26.1	29.5	2.80	.97	985
Majority view of constitution is most important	t_1	51.6	15.7	32.7	2.78	1.15	982
	t_3	42.5	17.8	39.7	2.96	1.12	985
Must control the court	t_1	56.6	17.9	25.5	2.60	1.11	983
	t_3	53.8	19.6	26.5	2.69	1.05	985

Make the court less independent	t_1	60.7	13.2	26.1	2.59	1.07	984
	t_3	56.0	13.3	30.7	2.68	1.10	985
Index average	t_1				3.01	.64	976
	t_3				3.14	.64	985
Average number of supportive responses	t_1				3.32	2.14	976
	t_3				3.78	2.23	985

Note: The percentages are based on collapsing the five-point Likert response set (e.g., "agree strongly" and "agree" responses are combined). The means and standard deviations are calculated on the uncollapsed distributions. Higher mean scores indicate more institutional loyalty. The propositions are:

Do away with the court: If the Kentucky Supreme Court started making a lot of decisions that most people disagree with, it might be better to do away with the supreme court altogether.

Court can be trusted: The Kentucky Supreme Court can usually be trusted to make decisions that are right for the state as a whole.

Limit the court's jurisdiction: The right of the Kentucky Supreme Court to decide certain types of controversial issues should be reduced.

Remove judges who decide against majority: Judges of the Kentucky Supreme Court who consistently make decisions at odds with what a majority of the people in the state want should be removed from their position as judge.

Court gets too mixed up in politics: The Kentucky Supreme Court gets too mixed up in politics.

Majority view of constitution is most important: The Kentucky Supreme Court may have its ideas about what the constitution means, but more important is what the majority of people think the constitution means.

Must control the court: It is inevitable that the Kentucky Supreme Court gets mixed up in politics; therefore, we ought to have stronger means of controlling the actions of the Kentucky Supreme Court.

Make the court less independent: The Kentucky Supreme Court ought to be made less independent so that it listens a lot more to what the people want.

responding to all three waves of the survey and who were deemed part of the court's attentive public on the basis of the initial interview), at the aggregate level, these eight items seem to indicate reasonably high levels of support for the court.[18] The eight indicators are quite reliable measures of institutional support: at t_1, Cronbach's alpha = .73; for t_3, the coefficient is .78.

In the analysis that follows, I focus on change in the number of supportive answers given to these eight questions. The correlation of the support indices for the t_1- t_3 pair is .64. When the t_3 index is regressed on the t_1 measure, a great deal of the variance can be accounted for (R^2 = .40). The equation connecting the two scores is

$$\text{Support } t_3 = 1.218 + .637 \times \text{Support } t_1 \quad (\beta = .635)$$

In terms of the simple number of supportive replies given on the eight-item set, 66.1% of the respondents became more supportive of the court from the t_1 to the t_3 interview, 17.9% did not change in their level of support, and 16.0% became less supportive. Thus, the first important conclusion of this analysis is that it seems that the election had a positive impact on court support, a finding consistent with the research of Gibson et al. (2011) in Pennsylvania and other nonjudicial research. Judicial elections, perhaps even irrespective of the nature of the campaigning, result in an increase in the allegiance citizens give to their courts.

In the analysis that follows, I measure change in attitudes toward the Kentucky Supreme Court as the difference between the t_3 index of loyalty and the t_1 measure. The mean on this index is .13 (s.d. = .55), and it ranges from −2.38 to 2.50. In this statewide sample, there is no statistically significant difference in support change associated with whether there was a supreme court election in the respondent's district (p = .707), or even across the seven judicial districts (p = .519), or whether the respondent lived in a CMAG media market or not (p = .757). This no doubt reflects the fact that media markets cross district lines, and therefore Kentuckians were almost certainly exposed to campaign ads for candidates for judicial office for whom they could not vote.

ASSESSMENTS OF THE ADVERTISEMENTS

Among the majority of respondents reporting seeing an ad, we asked a number of follow-up questions about overall assessments of the ads (see appendix H). As to negativity, 43.1% characterized the ads they witnessed as at least somewhat negative; 50.1% described the ads as at least somewhat partisan; while at the same time, 78.7% thought the ads at least somewhat fair, and *84.1%*

rated the ads as at least somewhat appropriate for a Kentucky judicial election.
Thus, these simple univariate frequencies hint at the possibility that negativity and partisanship per se do not necessarily create perceptions of unfairness and inappropriateness.

When perceptions of ad fairness are regressed on the other three ad judgments, the best predictor of fairness turns out to be the assessment of ad appropriateness ($\beta = .44, p < .001$). More interesting is the finding that ad partisanship is unrelated to perceptions of fairness ($\beta = -.05$, n.s.), and ad negativity is only moderately related ($\beta = .29, p < .001$). Of course, both fairness and appropriateness are clearly normative judgments of the ads, whereas partisanship (especially) and negativity are more descriptive assessments. Thus, these data hint at the possibility that not all respondents view partisan and negative ads as inappropriate. I consider this possibility in the analysis later in this chapter.

Those who reported seeing no actual ads for the judicial elections were asked to evaluate real ads that had been broadcast (and that the respondent might have had a chance to observe). These ads were secured from CMAG.[19] Of course, the respondents were simply read the text of the ads; they were not shown any visuals inasmuch as the interviews were conducted over the telephone. The respondents were asked to make the same types of judgments about the specific ad they were read as the respondents who reported seeing some ads. Thus, the ad presented to the respondent was rated on negativity, partisanship, the tone of the ad, and appropriateness for a judicial election.

Nearly all of the respondents were presented with an ad promoting the candidates; only 9.2% were read an attack ad. Even with this imbalance, the attack ads were judged to be significantly more negative ($p < .001$) and less appropriate ($p < .001$), and slightly more partisan ($p = .018$). Interestingly, however, the attack ads were not rated as more unfair ($p = .751$). Fairness seems to be orthogonal to the other ad judgments, at least for these respondents.

On three of the four attribute ratings, there is a statistically significant difference between the self-reports of ads seen during the election and the evaluations of the specific ads read to the respondents on the telephone. The real ads were judged to be less negative, less partisan, but also less fair. They were not, however, seen as less appropriate for a judicial election. Indeed, although the difference is not statistically significant, those who heard ads presented during the interview were more likely to view them as appropriate. None of these relationships, however, is very strong: the strongest observed correlation is with ad negativity, where $r = .15$. In the analysis that follows, I will control for the respondent's type of ad exposure.

The overriding hypothesis of this research is that support for the Kentucky Supreme Court was eroded by exposure to the election of 2006 and especially by exposure to the politicized campaign ads broadcast during the election.

Table 6.2 reports four separate regression analyses.[20] The data are first divided by whether the respondent observed some real ads during the campaign or, among those who did not, the responses to the ads read to the respondents during the interview.[21] Within the groups defined by whether they observed real advertisements or not (i.e., the columns), the first part of the table reports the regression of change in institutional support on each of the four ad ratings; the second regression uses the index derived from the four ratings.[22]

The first conclusion from this table is that the impact of the ad ratings is greater among those read an ad during the interview. That the effect of ad exposure is somewhat stronger is in one sense expected inasmuch as *all respondents* undeniably heard the ads, whereas some respondents reporting hearing actual ads during the campaign were no doubt misremembering (thereby watering down the relationship).[23]

Some variability is also apparent in which specific ad attributes affect change in institutional support. Among those observing ads during the campaign, the strongest influence is from perceptions of ad partisanship and unfairness. Ads judged to be partisan and to be unfair subtracted from the legitimacy of the supreme court. These effects are not strong, but nor are they trivial. For instance, among those rating no ads as negative, partisan, unfair, or inappropriate (zero on each of the ad attributes), the predicted value for change in institutional support is .27 (the intercept), indicating an increase in institutional support. The maximum effect of ad partisanship (when $X = 3$) is to subtract .24 from this intercept, resulting in a change score of approximately zero. For ad unfairness, the effect is roughly the same ($-.27$). Thus, only when the ads were rated as extremely partisan *and* as not at all fair was the net effect of the election on change in institutional support negative. Ratings of extreme partisanship in the ads actually observed were quite uncommon (7.1%), as were ratings of great unfairness (6.6%), and only 0.7% of the respondents (three individuals) scored the ads they saw during the campaign at the most extreme score on both partisanship and unfairness. Ads can indeed "cross the line" (see chapter 3) and thereby injure the legitimacy of the institution, but at least in the election of 2006 in Kentucky, this happened with only a tiny proportion of the respondents.[24]

Those presented with a candidate promotion ad during the interview were

TABLE 6.2. THE IMPACT OF AD PERCEPTIONS ON CHANGE IN COURT LEGITIMACY

Ad perceptions	Ads observed during the election				Ads heard during the interview (promote ads)			
	r	b	s.e.	β	r	b	s.e.	β
Negativity	−.05	.04	.03	.07	−.20	−.09	.04	−.14*
Partisanship	−.12	−.08	.03	−.13**	−.17	−.06	.03	−.11*
Fairness	−.11	−.09	.04	−.12*	−.08	.03	.05	.04
Tone	−.07	.00	.05	.00	−.14	−.05	.04	−.07
Intercept		.27	.05			.31	.05	
Standard deviation— Dependent variable		.54				.57		
Standard error of estimate		.54				.55		
R^2				.02**				.05***
N		531				410		
Ad perceptions index	−.11	−.10	.04	−.11**	−.21	−.19	.05	−.21***
Intercept		.24	.05			.33	.05	
Standard deviation— Dependent variable		.54				.57		
Standard error of estimate		.54				.55		
R^2				.01**				.04***
N		532				410		

Significance of standardized regression coefficients: *** $p < .001$ ** $p < .01$ * $p < .05$

affected by it—indeed, even more so than those observing real ads during the campaign. Among this group, the characteristics most influential are negativity and partisanship. From the intercept of .31, the maximum effect of negativity is to subtract .27; the maximum effect of partisanship is to reduce positive change in support for the court by .18. Only 1.1% of this subgroup rated the ads they heard at the most extreme position on negativity and partisanship ($N = 5$ people). For the vast majority of the respondents, moderate levels of negativity and/or partisanship still resulted in a net change in institutional support that is positive.[25]

Perhaps it is useful to digress for a moment and consider further the ads read to those respondents who had not seen any actual campaign ads at the time of the interview. Owing in part to the timing of the fieldwork,[26] 75.4% of the respondents ($N = 363$) heard the same ad. However, their judgments of the ad varied substantially. The ad read,

We are interested in your opinion of the following ad broadcast by a candidate for the Kentucky Supreme Court in the race between John Roach and Mary Noble. I'll read you the ad and then ask your opinion of it. (AD BEGINS:)

> This ad is a series of screens on the TV that read as follows:
> Kentucky Supreme Court: Only Candidate with Supreme Court experience.
> Justice Roach: Over 1000 Supreme Court Cases.
> Justice Roach: A top graduate UK Law School.
> Justice Roach: Respected by Democrats.
> Justice Roach: Respected by Republicans.
> Justice Roach: Not Respected by Dancers to the Jailhouse Rock.
> A Judge of Good Character: Keep Justice Roach.
> Paid for by: The Committee to Keep Justice Roach.

Considerable disagreement characterizes the ad ratings. The percentages of respondents scoring at the mode of the rating are 43.8%, 31.8%, 59.6%, and 43.3%, for the negativity, partisanship, unfairness, and inappropriateness ratings. In terms of ad partisanship, 29.3% rated the ad as not at all partisan, whereas 8.2% rated it as extremely partisan (and another 31.8% as somewhat partisan). Thus, it is clear that Kentuckians do not judge ads similarly; Kentuckians differ. Furthermore, a substantial portion of the variance in ad judgments seems to stem from the individual, not from the ad itself.[27]

In order to consider the combined effect of the ad judgments in a way that is comparable across the two different types of ad consumption, an index of ad churlishness would be useful. Such an index is possible inasmuch as these ad assessments are fairly strongly intercorrelated. Among those seeing some real ads during the campaign, Cronbach's alpha for the set of four ad assessments is .76; among those hearing the ads during the interview, alpha is .70. For both groups, the ad judgments are strongly unidimensional (as revealed by common factor analyses). Consequently, for some analytical purposes, I have created an index that is the mean of the responses to the four ad attributes. This index varies from 0 to 3 and is of course strongly correlated with each of its components. I will refer to this as an index of ad churlishness. A statistically significant but not very strong relationship exists between whether the respondent was responding to ads heard during the election or ads they heard during the interview, with the former providing more negative judgments ($p < .001$; $\eta = .12$). This no doubt reflects the fact that those to whom we read ads during the interviews overwhelmingly heard ads promoting rather than attacking candidates.[28] The regressions for this index are shown in the bottom half of table 6.2.

In terms of the simple relationship between ad exposure and change in institutional support for the Kentucky Supreme Court among those witnessing actual ads during the campaign, a significant relationship is observed between ad churlishness and institutional support: those reporting hearing more disagreeable ads became less supportive of the court ($r = -.11$). The equation is

$$\text{Change in Institutional Support} = .235 - .097 \times \text{Ad Assessments}$$
$$(\text{s.e.} = .038)$$

Since the ad assessment index varies from 0 to 3, the predicted values of the change measure range from .235 ($X = 0$) to $-.032$ ($X = 3$). Thus, under the most extreme exposure to adverse ads, change in institutional support becomes negative (although very slightly and *not* significantly so). From this equation, expected change in institutional support becomes negative at a score of approximately 2.50 on the ad index. As it turns out, 98.8% of the respondents observing judicial ads during the campaign scored 2.50 or lower on the index. Thus, for the vast majority of respondents exposed to ads during the 2006 campaign—even ads thought to be highly disagreeable—the net effect of the election was either no change or an increase in support for the Kentucky Supreme Court. To put the finding starkly, among the few respondents who rated the ads at the most extremely negative point on each response set—the most negative, the most partisan, the most unfair, and the most inappropriate— change in institutional support from prior to the election to after it is expected to be $-.03$ on a scale that varies from -2.38 to 2.50.

For the respondents exposed to ads during the telephone interview, the effect of the ads on change in institutional support is somewhat stronger ($r = -.21$). The equation is

$$\text{Change in Institutional Support} = .334 - .193 \times \text{Ad Assessments}$$
$$(\text{s.e.} = .045)$$

Among these respondents, expected change in institutional support becomes negative with an ad assessment score of approximately 1.75. Based on the distribution of ad assessment scores, 91.7% of these respondents scored 1.75 or lower. For the vast majority of these respondents, the effect of exposure to even disagreeable ads was not to generate a net loss in the legitimacy of the supreme court.[29]

The data indicate that those judging ads they heard during the election were more negative in their assessments of the ads. This finding is interesting because among those perceiving ads to be more objectionable, the effects of the ads in terms of reducing institutional support were weaker, not stronger. This causes me to wonder whether the viewing of actual campaign ads, even those that were thought to be objectionable, also imparted other messages to the respondents—such as the candidate thought it important to try to convince them how to vote—that reinforced judicial legitimacy. If so, this suggests that campaign ads may be multidimensional in content—for example, disagreeable as to style, but informative as to substance—with different aspects of the ads leaving different residues on the citizen.

Endogeneity

For some time now (e.g., Ansolabehere, Iyengar, and Simon 1999), scholars have worried about the structure of the error in self-reports of exposures to ads. Such reports may be endogenous in the sense that the variation in the reports is determined at least in part by the attributes of the respondents, not the attributes of the external ad environment. The problem is particularly acute when both the independent variable (self-reported ad exposure) and the dependent variable (e.g., self-reported voting turnout) are characterizations of the respondent's own attributes, by the respondent (e.g., Vavreck 2007). Under such circumstances, it is easy to imagine a characteristic of the individual (e.g., responsiveness to social desirability) that strongly influences both of the variables, creating a spurious correlation between them. As Vavreck (2007) has shown, adding control variables can remedy this problem, but, at least in her case, a bevy of controls was required.

In the case of this research, it is difficult to imagine how the internal correlates of self-reported ad exposure are related to responses to propositions about the legitimacy of the Kentucky Supreme Court, especially when attitudes toward the institution were collected months before and months after the interview in which the self-reports of ad exposure were provided. In addition, the items in the support scale are not all focused in the same direction, and often a "disagree" response must be given to express support for the court. Only a very convoluted argument would connect the error terms in these two measures.

Moreover, Vavreck (2007) has shown that, when reported exposure and actual exposure are compared, reported exposure produces a much stronger impact on the dependent variable (in her case, voting turnout). This is not surprising because the observed relationship between the two reported behaviors is a function of the "true" impact of X on Y and the spurious contribution of attributes such as social desirability responsiveness and acquiescence bias.

Again, when factors related to these biases are controlled, less biased, and perhaps even unbiased, coefficients result.

In the case of this analysis, the correlations of attitude change with the variables indicating self-reported exposure and actual exposure during the interview do differ somewhat. However, the pattern is precisely the opposite of what would be expected: the correlation is *weaker* with the self-report variable. This finding is directly contrary to that of Vavreck, most likely indicating that the errors in the self-reported exposure variables are uncorrelated with my dependent variable. Instead, as I have noted, I understand the weakened relationship with self-reports to be due to measurement error of the type of misremembering ad exposure or being exposed to ads after the t_2 interview. Indeed, with what must be a nontrivial amount of measurement error in the ad exposure measures, that the observed correlations are unlikely to be attributable to chance is remarkable. Thus, it seems that I am entitled to at least some confidence in the conclusion that the observed effects of ad exposure on change in court support are relatively unbiased estimates.

Summary

At this point in the analysis, three conclusions emerge: elections tend to elevate institutional support, but being exposed to objectionable ads subtracts from support, even if, for the vast majority of respondents, the negative effect of the objectionable ads is smaller than the positive effect of the election.[30] And, these findings hold even when extensive control variables are added to the equation.

THE CONDITIONAL EFFECTS OF JUDICIAL EXPECTATIONS

The expectancy model advanced in this research posits that the effects of ad exposure differ according to the expectations the citizen holds of the judiciary. The conventional assumption is that everyone prefers a highly nonpoliticized judiciary and therefore any politicization of campaigns undermines legitimacy because it is judged objectionable. But if citizens vary in their expectations, and especially in the degree to which they view politicized campaigns negatively, then controlling for expectations is crucial. From the analysis above, it is clear that different people are judging the same ad differently. It is therefore useful to try to determine the basis of these judgments.

How one reacts to campaign activity is in part a function of what one judges as appropriate or inappropriate—one's normative expectations. When these expectations are paired with perceptions of reality, judgments result. For instance, it is often claimed that the American people abhor partisanship. This means that they hold expectations for nonpartisan behavior and that when they observe partisanship they are dissatisfied. Expectations in essence become a normative weight attached to perceptions. Especially in the context of an institution so thoroughly enveloped in normative theories of correct behavior (e.g., judicial ethics), expectations are likely to be influential in shaping the fundamental legitimacy of legal institutions.

In the context of this research, at least two of the ad ratings reflect the application of normative expectations. Judging a campaign activity as "unfair" or "inappropriate" is obviously a normative conclusion (even if the components of fairness and appropriateness are not necessarily revealed in these summary conclusions). With slightly less confidence I also believe assessments of ad negativity are normative inasmuch as few respondents are likely to view negativity positively. The fourth criterion, partisanship, however, is quite different. As previous research (Gibson and Caldeira 2009a) has revealed, the constituency for partisan judging is not trivial. Those who (normatively) expect judges to act as Democrats or as Republicans are unlikely to be put off by campaign activity stressing partisanship.

As a direct test of this theory of expectations, I consider a simple interactive model composed of perceptions of ad partisanship, expectations of partisanship, and the interaction of the two (the multiplicative term) as predictors of change in institutional support. In this model, the null hypothesis of interest is whether the slopes of the perceptions vary according to the levels of expectations, or, more specifically, whether the difference of slopes between units of expectations is indistinguishable from zero.

In fact, the difference of slopes is distinguishable from zero ($p = .035$), indicating that a conditional relationship exists.[31] The coefficient of the interaction term (which indicates the difference in slopes associated with a one-unit change in the conditional variable, the expectations) is .048 (s.e. = .017). The intercept is .228 (s.e. = .038). Consequently, the predicted values for change in institutional support across the entire range of values of perceived ad partisanship are

Not at all partisan .242 (s.e. = .041)
Extremely partisan .067 (s.e. = .053)

The predicted score for the lowest perceived partisanship is distinguishable from zero and positive; the predicted score for extremely partisan perceptions is indistinguishable from zero. Three conclusions emerge from this analysis: (1) ad partisanship subtracts from institutional legitimacy; (2) the most partisan ads still do not generate a net loss in legitimacy; and (3) the impact of ad partisanship varies significantly according to the expectations one holds of the judiciary.[32]

DISCUSSION AND CONCLUDING COMMENTS

Two notable theoretical conclusions stand out from this analysis. First, citizens vary in their expectations of judicial campaigns, and this variability must be considered when assessing how campaign activities affect the legitimacy of courts. The assumption that all of the courts' constituents expect strong judicial independence with nonpartisan and nonideological decision making is clearly wrong. Whether it is desirable or undesirable, a sizable portion of Americans expect a politicized judiciary and therefore are not put off by politicized campaigns.

Second, the effect of campaigns on citizens must be calculated as a net effect, after taking into consideration the many dimensions on which campaigns are perceived and evaluated. Experimental research examining campaign effects in isolation is certainly useful. But the oversight of most research lies in the failure to understand that elections, by themselves, provide a significant boost to the legitimacy of courts. Elections may be (and almost certainly are) a mixed bag, with some positive influences on citizens but with negative consequences as well. Only when we gauge whether the positive outweighs the negative can we draw proper verdicts about the institutional consequences of elections.

These conclusions have important policy implications, the most obvious of which is that those who base their criticisms of elections on unseemly campaign activity must consider as well that simply being able to vote for judges makes courts more legitimate. Presumably, we care most about whether elections add to or subtract from the legitimacy of courts in toto, not whether a particular ad campaign is churlish. Opponents of elections cannot in the future ignore the fact that the rough and tumble of judicial campaigns may be doing little more than denying courts the full benefits of elections, rather than creating a deficit in institutional legitimacy.

The increment in institutional support for any given election is undoubtedly small. This research has not established whether each election in a series of elections has the same consequences for institutional legitimacy. We know that most state high courts in the United States are elected and that state courts enjoy an unexpectedly high level of support/approval from their constituents. Perhaps this bountiful reservoir of goodwill has been swollen by a slow but steady trickle of legitimacy from a continuous stream of elections.

Whether the legitimacy-enhancing effects of elections attach to every form of judicial balloting is not at all clear from this research. One might easily hypothesize that retention elections provide no expansion of judicial legitimacy. And it may well be that for elections to affect legitimacy, a threshold level of public attention to the campaigns must take place. Elections that generate the greatest amount of candidate-to-voter communication may be the most effective at elevating court legitimacy. Elections to which people are oblivious are unlikely to enhance judicial legitimacy.

Elections are complicated, multidimensional events, and the lessons citizens learn from elections are no doubt similarly complex. Only through additional research that is sensitive to the mix of harmony and cacophony in the rumble of campaigns can their effects be more fully cataloged and understood. In the end, Bonneau and Hall were undoubtedly correct when they observed (2009, 2), "elections generally are one of the most powerful legitimacy-conferring institutions in American democracy and should serve to balance if not counteract other negative features associated with campaigns." And only with empirical evidence of the sort presented here can the normative debate over how we select judges reach a reasonable and rational conclusion.

CHAPTER SEVEN

JUDICIAL CAMPAIGNS, ELECTIONS FOR JUDGES, AND COURT LEGITIMACY: DO JUDICIAL ELECTIONS REALLY STINK?

How dangerous is campaign activity to the legitimacy of American courts? At least one of the most prominent analysts of campaigning and elections has predicted that

> the spread of negative campaigning in judicial races is likely to have adverse consequences for the court system. The motives of judicial candidates will be cast into doubt, and public esteem for the judiciary will suffer. Not only will candidates for judicial office be equated with ordinary politicians, but the impartiality, independence, and professionalism of the judiciary will also be called into question. Large-scale advertising in state judicial elections will further politicize state courts in the eyes of the public. (Iyengar 2002, 697)

If this scenario did indeed come to pass, the American state judiciaries—the workhorse of litigation in the United States—would be seriously undermined and compromised.

Because the empirical evidence necessary to substantiate these fears is so limited, this study was conceived and executed. My goal was to examine the consequences of electoral activity with a research design tailored to answer some of the key empirical questions about elections and legitimacy. In order to be able to make causal claims about campaign causes and legitimacy effects with a high degree of confidence, this project employed the two major cornerstones of causal inference: experiments with random assignment of respondents to treatments and dynamic analysis of change over time. In order to overcome the limits of nonrepresentative samples and unknown generalizability, the research design employed a representative sample of the adult residents of one of the American states. There are still limits to this project—only some of my results from Kentucky have been replicated with nationally representative data—but the empirical basis of the substantive conclusions I draw in this book is perhaps as strong or stronger than any prior study of judicial campaigns and elections.

The most important conclusion of this book is that judicial campaign activities do not seem to damage the legitimacy of those courts that select their judges through popular elections. This is an unexpected finding and a bold conclusion. A recap of the evidence supporting that conclusion is therefore in order.

From chapter 6, I learned that judicial elections directly contribute to the legitimacy of courts, most likely by reminding citizens that their courts are accountable to their constituents, the people. The American people generally prefer that the balance between accountability and judicial independence be tilted toward the accountability end of the continuum, so it is not at all surprising that elections would have this effect. In assessing the impact of campaign activity on judicial legitimacy, analysts must begin by recognizing that all such activity must be evaluated in relationship to the legitimacy-boosting effects of electoral accountability.

How much legitimacy do the elected high courts in the American states enjoy? Because the vast majority of judges in the United States are subject to some form of electoral accountability, it is therefore not surprising that state courts in this country are widely accepted as legitimate institutions. I readily admit that the evidence for this conclusion is perhaps not as strong as it might be, but it seems that somewhere around three-fourths of the American people extend legitimacy to their state judicial institutions. Indeed, state high courts seem to be as legitimate as the venerable US Supreme Court.

Critics of elections might view this figure as low—in comparison to 100%—and might argue that there has been a slow and steady erosion from unanimity over the course of years of judicial elections.

My own view is quite the contrary. Legitimacy is not the natural state of affairs in politics. The natural state of affairs more likely involves approving of institutions that generate benefits and disapproving of those that do not, perhaps even through some sort of simple running tally of likes and dislikes. Over time, however, relative satisfaction with the performance of an institution goes through a metamorphosis, changing into a more fundamental commitment to accept the decisions of institutions, even when those decisions are objectionable. It is this very quality that makes legitimacy so valuable as a form of political capital—legitimacy convinces losers in law and politics to accept their losses (e.g., Democrats in *Bush v. Gore*). That any institution acquires this power is wondrous. So, from this perspective, a percentage of three-fourths seems high, not low, and seems to reflect the accumulated result of additions to a base percentage much lower than three-fourths.

I therefore suggest that one mechanism responsible for the transformation of performance evaluations into the more obdurate institutional legitimacy is judicial elections (other mechanisms might be procedural fairness and principled decision making). When people know that they have the power to turn out judges who perform poorly, they are more willing to accept the decisions of those judges. From this perspective, elections slowly build the legitimacy of courts, rather than slowly eroding that legitimacy.

This research obviously cannot answer this much larger question of where legitimacy comes from and whether state courts start from a base figure of zero or one hundred. It does, however, provide some evidence that at least one election in at least one state has legitimacy-enhancing properties.[1] And I can conjure no logic to suggest that it would be otherwise in states other than Kentucky.[2]

This study also goes some distance toward understanding how elections work their magic. Contrary to the views of some (e.g., the dissenters in *Republican Party of Minnesota v. White*), citizens want to know the policy views of those who are candidates for state courts of last resort, and they are pleased when provided this sort of information. It seems clear that the American people recognize an appropriate policy-making role for courts—perhaps as an inevitable consequence of the common law system—and are not put off by this function.

It also seems clear that the American people do not view judges as mechanical jurisprudes, simply "interpreting" laws via syllogisms (see Gibson and Caldeira 2011). Thus, the logic of electoral legitimacy might go something like this:

(1) Inevitably, supreme court judges are exercising discretion in deciding cases and making public policy. (2) In making decisions, judges cannot but rely upon their own political and ideological values. (3) In a democratic political system, these value-based decisions should comport with the will of the majority. (4) For the majority to get its way on many (if not most) issues of public policy is not necessarily to trample upon the "inalienable" rights of the minority. (5) Thus, elections are desirable because they ensure that judicial public policy is accountable to the preferences of the people, at least on most substantive issues of law and politics.

If in fact judges are making decisions with no technically or legally "correct" answer (is the death penalty cruel and/or unusual?), then judges must side with the values of the majority or the minority. Obviously, in a democracy, minorities cannot expect to control public policy on all issues of the day. Where one draws the line may be subject to some debate—the voting rights of minorities, for example, should not be limited by the majority—but, in a democracy, many if not most ordinary public policy disputes ought to be resolved in favor of the preferences of the majority. When courts are responsive to the majority—or even perceived to be responsive—legitimacy accrues.

Such an argument may have a rebuttal, but I suspect the elemental logic of this position is attractive to many, if not most, Americans. If so, it follows that voters in judicial elections have the right to query candidates about their policy views on important socio-legal issues likely to come before the high court. In terms of the independence–accountability continuum, I suspect that most Americans favor getting more accountability from their judges rather than giving their judiciary more independence. Policy talk enhances accountability and thereby contributes to institutional legitimacy. It may well be that the American people accept this policy-making role of courts precisely because most judges are subject to the controlling force of elections.

Ultimately, the majority in *Republican Party of Minnesota v. White* was probably correct about at least one thing: if elections are employed as a means of selecting judges, then the elections must be legitimate, and all campaign activity that is allowed in elections for other offices must be tolerated in elections for judges. Critics complain that it is nearly impossible to do away with elected selection/retention systems because most Americans favor such processes for selecting their judges. Perhaps this is so. But to restrict policy talk among candidates for public office seems to strike at the very essence of elections and at the means of selecting policy makers in a democratic political system. Talking about legal policies may be a crucial element of the legitimacy-enhancing electoral process. My finding that stating one's policy position in judicial elections does not undermine judicial legitimacy will be surprising only to those analysts believing that the American people want more independence from their judges than accountability.

Many legal elites in the United States strongly disapprove of allowing judges to make policy pronouncements during their campaigns for seats on the high courts of the states. It seems to me that there are several possible reasons why this may be so.

First, some may sincerely believe that by announcing policy views, judges in fact compromise their actual impartiality and open-mindedness. It would surprise me, however, to learn that informed observers adopt such a naive view of the process of judicial decision making. The worry cannot be simply that judges are biased in their decision making, since to hold a policy view but not announce it should be of roughly equal concern to holding a policy view and announcing it. Obviously, judges, especially those with much judicial experience, have reached conclusions on myriad legal issues in their earlier decisions, so to expect that judges are tabulae rasae when they confront new cases is naive. Finally, informed observers surely recognize that the process of decision making is typically highly discretionary and that discretion is often little constrained by law (e.g., of conflicting precedents, which set should be "followed"?), and therefore that discretion must be controlled by the preferences of the decision maker. It would indeed be surprising to learn that observers believe that the simple event of making a policy statement somehow changes the processes of decision making that judges employ. Campaign talk, one way or other, is unlikely to change the *true* nature of the decision-making processes used by judges.

A second argument is that these pledges may actually cause ordinary people to lose faith in the judiciary, irrespective of actual processes of decision making. The evidence of this book is that some extreme forms of policy talk hurt courts; most talk does not. So the concerns of the critics of *Republican Party of Minnesota v. White* are not entirely discounted by the analysis presented here. The key issue, however, is to pinpoint exactly what sorts of speech are corrosive, instead of muzzling judges across the board.

A third argument is more complicated. Suppose that most legal elites hold at least moderately left-wing ideological positions. Further, assume that these elites generally perceive the American people as both ill informed and at least somewhat conservative. Therefore, anything that strengthens the connection between judges and ordinary people will necessarily increase the likelihood of conservative decisions by judges (e.g., the use of the death penalty—see Brace and Boyea 2008). When observers distrust and/or disagree with the constituents of courts, they are likely to want to minimize the influence of the constituents' preferences over the making of public policy.[3] Banning policy talk is one way to do this.

Finally, in the absence of policy cues from candidates, citizens generally have little guidance on how to cast their votes. To the extent that policy voting is more difficult, the influence of interest groups and political parties is likely to increase. If citizens cannot vote on the issues dear to them, they will either not vote or cast their votes on the basis of recommendations from bar and lawyer groups, media outlets, or other interest groups. Without policy cues, the influence of legal elites on the selection of judges is likely to increase. And if elections have no policy relevance to voters, then one of the most important rationales for holding judges accountable to their constituents is itself seriously weakened, thereby opening the door to the possibility of doing away with elections altogether.

The analysis of this book does not suggest that every form of campaigning talk is entirely innocuous. The equations I report in chapter 6 indicate that there are some circumstances under which the legitimacy benefits of elections can be negated. In my analysis, these circumstances are exceedingly rare. Perhaps some can imagine a judicial campaign that is so politicized—and is perceived as such by the citizenry—that the net effect of the election goes to zero or even into the negative territory. Such a campaign would likely be suicidal for a candidate, but perhaps a third-party group might mount such an effort. Since the evidence of chapter 6 is that citizens draw different judgments about the same ad, in order for a consensus to emerge that the line of propriety has been crossed the activity would have to be extreme. Still, I must acknowledge that this research has uncovered some evidence that extremely politicized campaign ads may have negative consequences.[4]

From the point of view of ordinary citizens, complaints about policy talk in judicial elections are generally unwarranted; complaints about scurrilous and churlish campaign activities, however, may not be entirely unfounded. The evidence of this book is that judicial campaigns can indeed "cross the line" of appropriateness, and when they do so, legitimacy suffers. I acknowledge that my evidence is not unequivocal (in part because this portion of the analysis used real campaign ads, which always convey a mix of messages to viewers), but it appears that the line that gets crossed is that between ordinary politicians and judicial politicians. It is not politics per se that is objectionable; the American people recognize and accept the inherently political nature of courts.

Instead, it is a particular type of politics—the politics associated with legislatures in particular—that threatens judicial legitimacy. To the extent that judges are perceived as principled, rather than self-interested, politics is not damaging to courts. Some ads, however, portray courts as "just another political institution," as indistinguishable from the other branches of government, and doing so seems to shift courts from being perceived as principled policy makers to self-interested and strategic makers of public policy. We have observed this effect in the case of confirmation hearings for appointments to the US Supreme Court (Gibson and Caldeira 2009a). I observe the same effect with highly politicized campaign ads in Kentucky. If I am right about this, then it is not the innuendo and half-truths that do the damage (characteristics that

FIGURE 7.1 AN EXAMPLE OF A VAPID JUDICIAL ADVERTISEMENT.

are so offensive to legal scholars and analysts) but rather the framing of courts as being little different from other political institutions (e.g., from chapter 3: "Is he a judge, or just another politician?"). Understanding better how citizens categorize various political institutions—and how they associate different attributes with different institutions—is a research problem of considerable importance for future investigations of courts.

At the same time, ads without content should also be carefully scrutinized. In a lower court judicial race in 2006 in Kentucky, a candidate for a circuit court judgeship ran the ad depicted in figure 7.1. It is difficult for me to imagine the logic of this ad. While opponents of politicized campaign activity are quick to criticize candidates and activities they believe cross the line of appropriate behavior, rarely, if ever, are they critical of the vapid ads broadcast by so many candidates for judicial office. Ads such as this seem to serve no legitimate purpose in an election in a democratic society.

My evidence on attack ads is that even moderately churlish ads have only minor consequences for judicial legitimacy. Campaign contributions, however, are another matter. Perhaps the two simplest findings of this research are that policy talk is good for judicial legitimacy but campaign contributions are decidedly not. The American people seem to accept serious debate about legal policy, even debate that is rough and not entirely fair. What they find objectionable is debate that is insincere and self-interested, especially when connected to campaign supporters and contributors.

This conclusion should be placed in cross-institutional context. The damage of campaign contributions is no greater in the judiciary than it is in the legislature. As a consequence, any proposed palliative ought to be applied to both institutions (and executives as well), not just to courts.

The findings of this book also demonstrate just how important it is to consider individual differences in the normative expectations citizens hold of campaign activity. The American people are not uniform in their conceptions of what constitutes a good judge, with a substantial minority willing to endorse a fairly politicized view of judging. Statements such as "policy X will cause the American people to lose confidence in their courts" ignore the fact that people differ on which policies are inappropriate and threatening to judicial legitimacy. We can only understand the consequences of campaign activity by comparing perceptions of those actions with normative expectations about how judges ought to behave. Failure to do so leads to gross misestimates of the consequences of campaigns and elections.

Perhaps the single expectation about which there is widespread agreement is that judicial elections ought to continue to be held. Elections boost legitimacy, and they do so even when we discount that boost by the effects of objectionable campaign activity. Undoubtedly, the most important conclusion of this book is that campaign activity must be considered within the context of the legitimacy-enhancing effects of elections and that, at least in Kentucky, the costs of untoward campaign activity were small in comparison to the benefits of electing judges. My bet is that this positive net effect of elections is commonplace, but certainly additional research on this question must be conducted.

Caveats and Limitations

As with all studies of a single election (e.g., Obama's presidential victory), legitimate questions arise as to the generalizability of the research findings. In the instance of the analysis reported in this book, one might reasonably wonder whether the findings are generalizable across time, space, and institutional structures. Although I have addressed these issues to some degree in each of the analyses above, it is useful to collect and summarize my positions in this concluding chapter of the book.

Temporal Generalizability. The nature of elections in the American states was in flux at the time of my surveys, and that characterization continues to pertain to the state judiciaries today. As judicial campaigns evolve, citizens' expectations of judges, courts, and campaigns are likely to evolve as well (see the findings I report in chapter 2 from the national survey, which distinguishes between states with elected judges and those without), making it risky to generalize too much beyond the time frame of this book.

So while this study is indeed fixed in time, as I note at several points above, this particular time point (the Goldilocks zone—near the beginning of politicized elections, neither too politicized, nor too sleepy) is one that can shed some important light on how campaign activities affect citizens' perceptions and judgments of courts—courts are not invisible to citizens, but nor are citizens jaded and disgusted. Moreover, our understanding of campaign effects would profit from studies in systems in which politicization is low, medium, and high, especially since the suggestion of this analysis is that citizens may change their expectations of campaigns as they become acclimated to various types of campaign activities. And as I reported above, in terms of campaign spending in the 2004 elections (the election immediately prior to the one analyzed here), spending in Kentucky defined the national median. So while I cannot claim that 2006 is representative of the past or the present, perhaps it is representative in some sense of the *future* of judicial elections in many of the American states.

Spatial Generalizability. But is Kentucky in some sense unique? Putting aside for a moment the question of the structure of Kentucky's judicial institutions, I can only repeat that many of the findings from the Kentucky survey mirror those from nationally representative surveys. The level of approval of Kentucky's court is similar to that of the other states, according to a JaS survey. According to my national replication on the campaign activity experiment, the Kentucky findings dovetail almost completely with the findings from states in which judges are elected (however "election" is defined). Kentuckians seem no more or less knowledgeable about the structure of their courts than their fellow Americans. A comparison of the nature of judicial expectations in Kentucky and the country at large reveals no systematic differences. As to the inherent legitimizing effect of elections, the Kentucky findings closely parallel findings from Pennsylvania (Gibson et al. 2011). In no sense is Kentucky a "microcosm" of the country—no single state can claim that attribute. But there is nothing in the findings of this book that points to Kentucky or Kentuckians as being unusual when it comes to how they evaluate the campaigns of judges.[5]

Institutional Generalizability. The limit about which I worry the most has to do with how Kentucky selects its judges. As indicated above, the system Kentucky uses to select its judges is nearly unique in the sense that Kentucky uses nonpartisan elections but with single-member districts (as opposed to the at-large, statewide elections used in most states). In an important piece of earlier research, Hall (1992) has shown that such a method of selection can make judges more attentive to the preferences of their constituents. Perhaps that attentiveness has something to do with the findings reported here.

The crucial issue is whether Kentucky's system of districts versus at-large nonpartisan elections has any obvious implications for the findings of this book.[6] Frankly, I can think of none. We know from earlier research that districts tend to connect the representative to the constituents more directly, but it is unclear how that might affect campaign strategies. A logic explaining how districts are more likely to produce policy talk or attack ads is not obvious to me. Smaller districts might involve less expensive campaigns, but, then again, one of the most expensive elections ever was from a supreme court district in Illinois. Most important, citizens most likely are not aware of the judicial districts system—and because media markets dramatically and haphazardly cross judicial district boundaries, they very well may have seen advertisements for judicial candidates for whom they could not vote—and therefore that structure has practically no implications for how they perceive or judge campaign activity. Judicial districts just do not seem to be politically or legally salient in Kentucky (and perhaps elsewhere as well).

I should also return to the point that in some sense virtually every state selection system is unique, either as to its formal or informal characteristics. Examples are easy to list. Ohio and Michigan use formally nonpartisan judicial elections, but the candidates are selected via partisan conventions, and most voters know which candidates are Democrats and which are Republicans. Pennsylvanian voters have recently faced a confusing ballot requiring them to vote yes or no for the retention of a sitting supreme court judge at the same time that a different portion of the ballot asked the voter to select two of four candidates (identified by partisan affiliation) for seats on the state supreme court. Some so-called merit selection systems use retention elections, but others do not. In some states, norms require that judges end their careers by retiring before the end of their term (thus allowing the governor an opportunity to name a replacement judge, who then has the advantage of running for "reelection" as an "incumbent"). It appears, at least in 2011, that Wisconsin is a somewhat unique case by virtue of one judge getting another in a choke hold during a fight over a legal issue! Most important, state judicial selection processes (including so-called merit selection plans) vary considerably in the degree to which they have been politicized. In some sense, then, every state is sui generis; in some very loose sense, all state selection systems are idiosyncratic to the state and its history. Kentucky is no exception.

Should State Selection Systems Be Judged Only by Their Popular Legitimacy?
After consuming the various arguments and analyses of this book, one could easily conclude that I believe that state judicial selection systems should be judged by only a single criterion: how much popular legitimacy they generate. That conclusion, although certainly understandable, would be wrong. I readily acknowledge that popular judgments of fairness, impartiality, and legitimacy may profit from judicial elections while other desirable qualities of judges and judging may suffer (or be unaffected). Institutional legitimacy is but one of many consequences that might flow from the methods by which judges are selected and retained.

For instance, this book is completely silent about the quality of judges produced by different selection systems. Some excellent research on this question exists—see especially Choi, Gulati, and Posner (2010), who conclude that nearly all conventional assumptions about selection systems and the quality of judges is empirically wrong. Although the available evidence does not seem to suggest it, it is possible that judicial elections tend to recruit lawyers of less judicial training and temperament (see also Bonneau and Hall 2009). From the analysis in this book, I simply cannot assess whether electing judges forces a trade off of legitimacy for judicial quality and, if so, how a common metric could be developed to assess the net value of legitimacy.

Perhaps more worrisome are the handful of findings suggesting that the proximity to elections influences how judicial actors behave (e.g., Huber and Gordon 2004; Brace and Boyea 2008). My analysis is not informative as to whether the behaviors of legal actors (judges and prosecutors) are (or should or should not be) altered as an election nears so as to please the actor's constituents.[7]

This book is *not* a comprehensive analysis of all that is desirable and undesirable about the American system of electing judges. Instead, it examines a single prominent critique of elections—that campaign activities undermine judicial legitimacy. Perhaps the next focus of research should be on whether other tawdry consequences of elections outweigh the legitimacy-giving effects of allowing citizens to vote for who will judge them.[8]

Summary

In the final analysis, observers are correct to worry about judicial legitimacy. As I have argued on many occasions (e.g., Gibson and Caldeira 2009a), no stock of political capital is more valuable than legitimacy. But policy talk does not undermine judicial legitimacy. The American people recognize that judges make public policy and therefore expect candidates for judicial office to announce where they stand on crucial issues of law and politics. In addition, attack ads in general are at least tolerated by the American people, in part because attack ads convey policy-based information (e.g., Geer 2006) that voters want to know. Candidates can alienate voters with attack ads, but, presumably, as those seeking judicial office become more sophisticated campaigners, they will recognize that some types of ads are efficacious and that others are not. And the general maxim that the antidote for bad speech is a flood of good speech seems to apply to the case of judicial campaign advertisements.

The problem for courts is campaign contributions, although it is no more of a problem in the judicial case than in the legislative or gubernatorial cases. Unfortunately, the American people do not seem to distinguish between contributions from those with direct, self-interested business before an institution and groups seeking to select like-minded representatives on either the courts or the legislature. A strong, consensual, and nearly indiscriminate revulsion to all forms of campaign contributions characterizes the American people, including the likely failure to distinguish between contributions to candidates and independent expenditures. Even if contributions could be dealt with via some system of public funding of campaigns, it is unclear to me how the current constitutional regime can do much to limit the efforts of independent groups to influence elections. Would anyone seriously advocate that the ACLU, the ABA, the NAACP Legal Defense Fund, the NRA, Planned Parenthood, the Right to Life committees, and so on, should be denied the right to try to influence the outcomes of elections?[9]

Finally, even with the effects of undesirable campaign activity, *the net effect of judicial elections is positive*. Many observers rue the evidence that American people side with Andrew Jackson in wanting to elect their judges. But even under this simple fact, a great deal could be done to make elections more rational and reasonable, as Bonneau and Hall have so ably taught us (2009). And the simple truth is that elections themselves build legitimacy in a democracy, for courts, as for other political institutions as well.

THE OLFACTORY THEORY OF COURTS: THE SMELL OF ELECTIONS
In his classic article entitled "Why Judicial Elections Stink," Professor Geyh wrote:

> To the extent the decision [*Republican Party v. White*] liberates judicial candidates to emulate their counterparts in political branch races by committing themselves to positions on issues they are likely to decide as judges, it will accelerate the downward spiral of politicization that can be arrested only if judicial elections are eliminated. (Geyh 2003, 9)

Do judicial elections really stink? From this analysis, it appears that elections are more complicated than the summary judgment issued by Professor Geyh against electing judges (and, of course, Professor Geyh drew his conclusion before much empirical work had been done on public reactions to elections). Elections seem to constitute a bouquet of scents, some on the putrid side, some smelling sweeter. The foul odors of innuendos and half-truths are offensive to many and have perhaps had undue influence over blanket conclusions about the value of elections. To some, attack ads also seem to poison the electoral atmosphere. But mixed with these malodorous elements are more fragrant ingredients, such as the life-giving breath of institutional legitimacy. One of the most pungent conclusions of this research is that "judicial campaigns and elections" cannot be treated as a single undifferentiated whole. Some aspects have salutary effects; some do not.

And the senses of smell of the constituents of courts are far from uniform. Just as an anchovy can turn the stomach of some Caesar salad lovers, while causing others to drool, citizens have different tastes for judicial elections. This research has shown the error of assuming that all of the constituents of courts hate anchovies. Because some understand judging as inherently discretionary and ideological, it makes sense that judges should be elected. At the same time, others see judging as some sort of neutral, deductive process grounded in jural postulates or other eternal verities; for these constituents, elections are unlikely to select the most learned logicians. Constituents vary in their taste and that variation has a great deal to do with how campaign activities are evaluated.

Still, for most constituents of courts, the predominant essence of judicial elections is not foul. Because it is not, holding judges accountable, with its messiness and fuss, stills serves to make courts more legitimate and hence more efficacious, which cannot help but bolster democracy and the rule of law.

APPENDIX A

LEGAL DEVELOPMENTS POST-*WHITE*

This book is not specifically about *Republican Party of Minnesota v. White*, even though that decision stimulated the design of this study. Nonetheless, an overview of the legal developments since the *White* decision demonstrates that the issue of the free-speech rights of judges continues to be politically significant.

On remand from the Supreme Court's decision in *White*, the Eighth Circuit, in an 11–3 vote, struck down Minnesota's limit on partisan conduct by judicial candidates (law, in one form or another, in 19 states) and narrowed the limit on candidates' personal solicitation of campaign funds (law in almost 30 states). Republican Party of Minnesota v. White, 416 F.3d 738, 754, 765–66 (8th Cir. 2005) (Caufield 2005).

Post-*White*, states can still place some restrictions on judicial candidate speech. First, several states have in place limits on judicial contributions. In addition, many states still prohibit judicial candidates from personally soliciting campaign contributions (Bopp and Neeley 2008). According to Bopp and Neeley (2008, 203), these bans may not work in practice, but "do, however, allow states to maintain the fiction that judges are not directly involved in the campaign fundraising process."

This limit on personal solicitations has subsequently been enjoined by four federal courts. First, the Eighth Circuit Court in the *White* remand: *Republican Party of Minnesota v. White*. In *Weaver v. Bonner*, the Eleventh Circuit Court, ruled that two canons of Georgia's Code of Judicial Conduct were unconstitutional, following a challenge by a judicial candidate. The canons prohibit candidates from making false and misleading statements and from personally soliciting campaign contributions. The circuit court based its opinion on *White* (Caufield 2005). District courts in Kentucky (*Family Trust Foundation of Ky., Inc. v. Wolnitzek*) and Kansas also enjoined bans on personal solicitations. However, the Tenth Circuit later overturned the injunction on issues of standing. Kansas Judicial Watch, 519 F.3d 1107 (10th Cir. 2008).

However, in *Siefert v. Alexander*, the Seventh Circuit broke this trend by upholding restrictions on the ability of judicial candidates to make political endorsements and personally solicit campaign contributions (Note 2011). Seifert, a judicial candidate, sought to keep his Democratic Party affiliation while running—the court ruled in favor of Seifert on this claim, using *White*. However, the court upheld Wisconsin restrictions on judicial candidates publicly endorsing other candidates; additionally, the court upheld Wisconsin's prohibition on personal solicitation of campaign funds, under the reasoning that it serves Wisconsin's interest in preventing judicial corruption. "Beyond creating a circuit split, *Siefert* is notable as the first circuit decision to subject a judicial speech restriction not to strict scrutiny, but rather to a more deferential balancing test designed to evaluate the constitutionality of restrictions on the speech of public employees" (Note 2011, 1090).

In addition, two state courts have upheld the constitutional challenges of solicitation prohibitions. *In re Dunleavy* upheld Maine's solicitation clause against First Amendment challenge by potential contributors, but did not consider whether the provision violated judicial candidates' First Amendment rights (Bopp and Neeley 2008). Additionally, *Dunleavy's* holding was explicitly made contingent on the fact that judges in Maine were not elected. Second, the Arkansas Supreme Court also upheld the state's solicitation clause in Simes v. Arkansas Judicial Discipline and Disability Commission, 247 S.W.3d 876 (Ark. 2007). The court noted, "attorneys ought not feel pressured to support certain judicial candidates in order to represent their clients." To Bopp and Neeley (2008, 206), "this reasoning is out of step with the *White* decision and its progeny, as it attempts to justify the solicitation clause not because of the effect such solicited contributions might have on candidates, but rather because of concern about the subjective feelings of those solicited."

According to Schotland (2007), federal courts in Alaska, Kansas, Kentucky, and North Dakota have also rejected the widespread limits on candidates making "pledges or promises" and/or "commitments." These cases are *Kansas Judicial Watch v. Stout*; *Alaska Right to Life Political Action Comm. v. Feldman*; *Family Trust Foundation of Ky., Inc. v. Wolnitzek*; and *North Dakota Family Alliance, Inc. v. Bader*.

Caufield (2005) notes three important post-*White* cases, as well. First, in *In re Kinsey*, a candidate for judge was accused of encouraging the impression that she was tough on crime and would support the police in criminal proceedings. The Florida Supreme Court ruled that her campaign statements did violate Canon 7 of the Florida Ethics Code, and that Florida's "pledges or promises" clause and "commit" clause were narrowly tailored enough to stand up against constitutional challenge. However, in two cases from New York—*In re Raab*, 100 N.Y.2d 305 (N.Y. 2003), and *In re Watson*, 100 N.Y.2d 290, 302 (N.Y. 2003)—the New York Court of Appeals held that the "pledges or promises" clause and restrictions that bar judicial candidates from inappropriate political activities in New York's Code of Judicial Conduct were acceptable because they were narrow enough to serve a compelling governmental interest.

Public funding of judicial campaigns has also met some judicial resistance. In *Day v. Holahan*, the Eighth Circuit struck down Minnesota's public funding scheme because it penalized First Amendment rights. The rescue funds provision turned independent expenditures over the trigger amount into de facto contributions to an opponent's campaign and was, therefore, a burden on First Amendment rights the court judged to be impermissible. However, in *Daggett v. Commission on Governmental Ethics and Election Practices*, the First Circuit upheld the rescue funds provision of Maine's public funding scheme. Finally, in *Gable v. Patton* the Sixth Circuit upheld a Kentucky plan in which publicly funded candidates were allowed to raise up to $600,000 in private contributions and were given two dollars in government funding for every privately raised dollar up to that amount.

THE SURVEYS

THE KENTUCKY PANEL SURVEY DESIGN

t_1—The Initial Interview

This survey is the initial wave in a three-wave panel survey of the residents of Kentucky. The questionnaire was subjected to a formal test and, on the basis of the results of the pretest, was significantly revised. The survey was conducted by Schulman, Ronca, and Bucuvalas Inc. (SRBI) during the early summer of 2006. Computer-assisted telephone interviewing was used. Within households, the respondents were selected randomly. One adult age 18 or older was selected as the designated respondent in each eligible household.[1] No respondent substitution was allowed. The interviews averaged just over 20 minutes. The selected respondent was offered $10 for completing the interview. A total of 20,078 telephone numbers were used in the survey, with a resulting AAPOR (American Association for Public Opinion Research) Cooperation Rate #3 of 38.7% and an AAPOR Response Rate #3 of 28.7% (see AAPOR 2000). The final data set was subjected to some relatively minor post-stratification and was also weighted by the size of the respondent's household.

t_2—The Second Interview

In the month before the general election, the survey firm attempted to reinterview all of the respondents interviewed earlier as part of the t_1 survey. Of the 2,048 respondents from the first survey, interviews were completed with 1,438 individuals. The AAPOR Response Rate #3 is 78.7%, and the Cooperation Rate #3 is 89.4%.

I have carefully investigated the t_2 sample to determine whether any evidence of unrepresentativeness can be found. One way in which the representativeness of the t_2 sample can be assessed is to determine whether those who were interviewed in the second survey differ from those who were not interviewed. The null hypothesis (H_0) is that no difference exists between the two subgroups.

With over 1,400 completed interviews at t_2 and over 2,000 at t_1, tests of statistical significance are not very useful (i.e., even trivial differences are statistically significant given this large number of cases). Therefore, I focus on the degree to which the dichotomous variable indicating a successful t_2 interview predicts responses to a number of important t_1 variables. The only interesting relationship discovered in this analysis (using as a criterion an eta of greater than or equal to .10 as an indication of a notable difference) has to do with the age of the respondent: eta = .15.[2] The average age of those interviewed at t_2 is 51.3 years old; for those not interviewed, the age is 46.1. This finding is typical of panel surveys, with young people being difficult to track down for subsequent interviews.

In terms of substantive variables, however, I find practically no interesting differences. For instance, in terms of knowledge of courts, I find statistically significant but trivial differences between those interviewed at t_2 and those not, with those interviewed having only slightly greater knowledge of courts than those not interviewed (30.5% versus 26.4%, respectively, with relatively high knowledge). Awareness of the Kentucky Supreme Court is similarly distributed (79.2% versus 74.1%, with at least some awareness). In terms of support for the court, the correlation between the feeling thermometer responses and whether a t_2 interview was conducted is .06; for the institutional loyalty factor score (measured, of course, at t_1), the correlation is .07. In general, the analy-

TABLE B.1. ATTRIBUTES OF THE SAMPLE

Attribute	Sample characteristic
% female	52.5
Party identification	
% Democrat	42.1
% Republican	32.5
Ideological identification	
% liberal	25.4
% conservative	54
% owning their home	72.6
Race	
% white	91.8
% black	5.7
% rural	47.6
Religious affiliation	
% Protestant	71.8
% Catholic	12
% Born again	50.3
% Attending church at least once a week	47.4
Average age	46.5 years old
Level of education	
% less than high school	19.1
% high school degree	35.7
% college graduate and/or postgraduate work	18.9

sis reveals that the t_2 sample is biased in favor of higher levels of information and awareness, but the bias is slight indeed. Moreover, when post-stratification weights are applied to the t_2 data, even this minimal bias becomes entirely trivial.

t_3—The Final Interview

The final interview in the three-wave panel was conducted several months after the end of the 2006 election process. Only those respondents interviewed at t_2 ($N = 1,438$) were eligible for the t_3 interview. Using the AAPOR standards (Response Rate #3), the t_3 response rate is 76.6%, with a cooperation rate of 93.6% (#3). Of course, with such high rates of interviewing, practically no issues of representativeness emerge.

The question of how to weight the panel data is somewhat complicated. The t_1 survey was subjected to some slight post-stratification so as to improve its representativeness (see table B.1). Weights were then developed for the t_2 and t_3 surveys to improve the representativeness of these subsamples. The target for the t_2 and t_3 weighting was the characteristics of the t_1 survey. As a consequence, when I analyze the panel data, I use the t_3 weight, but when I consider only the t_1 data, I use the original weight variable. Since virtually all of the analysis reported in this paper is based on questions asked in the third interview, the data are weighted by the t_3 weight.

THE NATIONAL SURVEY DESIGN

This survey is based on a nationally representative sample. The survey was fielded during the summer of 2007. Computer-assisted telephone interviewing was used. Within households, the respondents were selected randomly. The interviews averaged around 25 minutes in length. The AAPOR Cooperation Rate #3 was 43.8%, and the AAPOR Response Rate #3 was 29.5% (see AAPOR 2000), which is about the average of telephone surveys these days (Holbrook, Krosnick, and Pfent 2007). The final data set was subjected to some relatively minor post-stratification and was also weighted to accommodate variability in the sizes of the respondents' households. The initial questionnaire was subjected to a formal test, and, on the basis of the results of the pretest, was significantly revised.

APPENDIX C

EXPERIMENTAL VIGNETTES

VIGNETTE—KENTUCKY SUPREME COURT

1. AAAA

1A. Now we would like to tell you a story about a judge whom we will call Judge Anderson. We would like you to imagine that Judge Anderson is running for reelection to his position on the Kentucky Supreme Court. This is the court that sits in Frankfort.

2A-C. Judge Anderson receives campaign contributions—that is, money—from corporations and public interest groups that regularly try cases before his court, the Kentucky Supreme Court.

3A-C. Judge Anderson's campaign refuses to talk about issues of public policy, saying that a judge should not discuss issues that his court may have to decide some day. Instead, his television ads focus mainly on his qualifications to be a judge—things like what his background is and where he went to law school.

4A-C. Judge Anderson's campaign ads rarely mention his opponent, instead focusing on providing voters information about himself, and claiming that, if elected, he will make fair and impartial decisions on cases before the court.

2. AAAB

1A. Now we would like to tell you a story about a judge whom we will call Judge Anderson. We would like you to imagine that Judge Anderson is running for reelection to his position on the Kentucky Supreme Court. This is the court that sits in Frankfort.

2A-C. Judge Anderson receives campaign contributions—that is, money—from corporations and public interest groups that regularly try cases before his court, the Kentucky Supreme Court.

3A-C. Judge Anderson's campaign refuses to talk about issues of public policy, saying that a judge should not discuss issues that his court may have to decide some day. Instead, his television ads focus mainly on his qualifications to be a judge—things like what his background is and where he went to law school.

4B-C. Judge Anderson's campaign ads vigorously attack his opponent, claiming that his opponent is biased in favor of insurance companies and other such businesses, and would therefore not be able to make fair and impartial decisions if elected to the supreme court.

3. AABA

1A.   Now we would like to tell you a story about a judge whom we will call Judge Anderson. We would like you to imagine that Judge Anderson is running for reelection to his position on the Kentucky Supreme Court. This is the court that sits in Frankfort.

2A-C.   Judge Anderson receives campaign contributions—that is, money— from corporations and public interest groups that regularly try cases before his court, the Kentucky Supreme Court.

3B-C.   Judge Anderson's campaign broadcasts some ads on television which focus mainly on his views and positions on important legal issues like abortion, lawsuit abuse, and the use of the death penalty in Kentucky.

4A-C.   Judge Anderson's campaign ads rarely mention his opponent, instead focusing on providing voters information about himself, and claiming that, if elected, he will make fair and impartial decisions on cases before the court.

4. AABB

1A.   Now we would like to tell you a story about a judge whom we will call Judge Anderson. We would like you to imagine that Judge Anderson is running for reelection to his position on the Kentucky Supreme Court. This is the court that sits in Frankfort.

2A-C.   Judge Anderson receives campaign contributions—that is, money— from corporations and public interest groups that regularly try cases before his court, the Kentucky Supreme Court.

3B-C.   Judge Anderson's campaign broadcasts some ads on television which focus mainly on his views and positions on important legal issues like abortion, lawsuit abuse, and the use of the death penalty in Kentucky.

4B-C.   Judge Anderson's campaign ads vigorously attack his opponent, claiming that his opponent is biased in favor of insurance companies and other such businesses, and would therefore not be able to make fair and impartial decisions if elected to the supreme court.

5. AACA

1A.   Now we would like to tell you a story about a judge whom we will call Judge Anderson. We would like you to imagine that Judge

Anderson is running for reelection to his position on the Kentucky Supreme Court. This is the court that sits in Frankfort.

2A-C. Judge Anderson receives campaign contributions—that is, money—from corporations and public interest groups that regularly try cases before his court, the Kentucky Supreme Court.

3C-C. Judge Anderson's campaign broadcasts some ads on television which focus mainly on his views and positions on important legal issues like abortion, lawsuit abuse, and the use of the death penalty in Kentucky. He promises that, if reelected, he will decide these kinds of cases in the way that most people in Kentucky want them decided.

4A-C. Judge Anderson's campaign ads rarely mention his opponent, instead focusing on providing voters information about himself, and claiming that, if elected, he will make fair and impartial decisions on cases before the court.

6. AACB

1A. Now we would like to tell you a story about a judge whom we will call Judge Anderson. We would like you to imagine that Judge Anderson is running for reelection to his position on the Kentucky Supreme Court. This is the court that sits in Frankfort.

2A-C. Judge Anderson receives campaign contributions—that is, money—from corporations and public interest groups that regularly try cases before his court, the Kentucky Supreme Court.

3C-C. Judge Anderson's campaign broadcasts some ads on television which focus mainly on his views and positions on important legal issues like abortion, lawsuit abuse, and the use of the death penalty in Kentucky. He promises that, if reelected, he will decide these kinds of cases in the way that most people in Kentucky want them decided.

4B-C. Judge Anderson's campaign ads vigorously attack his opponent, claiming that his opponent is biased in favor of insurance companies and other such businesses, and would therefore not be able to make fair and impartial decisions if elected to the supreme court.

7. ABAA

1A. Now we would like to tell you a story about a judge whom we will call Judge Anderson. We would like you to imagine that Judge Anderson is running for reelection to his position on the Kentucky Supreme Court. This is the court that sits in Frankfort.

2B-C. Judge Anderson receives campaign contributions—that is, money—

from corporations and public interest groups that are interested in influencing legal decisions, but which do not try cases before Judge Anderson's court, the Kentucky Supreme Court.

3A-C. Judge Anderson's campaign refuses to talk about issues of public policy, saying that a judge should not discuss issues that his court may have to decide some day. Instead, his television ads focus mainly on his qualifications to be a judge—things like what his background is and where he went to law school.

4A-C. Judge Anderson's campaign ads rarely mention his opponent, instead focusing on providing voters information about himself, and claiming that, if elected, he will make fair and impartial decisions on cases before the court.

8. ABAB

1A. Now we would like to tell you a story about a judge whom we will call Judge Anderson. We would like you to imagine that Judge Anderson is running for reelection to his position on the Kentucky Supreme Court. This is the court that sits in Frankfort.

2B-C. Judge Anderson receives campaign contributions—that is, money— from corporations and public interest groups that are interested in influencing legal decisions, but which do not try cases before Judge Anderson's court, the Kentucky Supreme Court.

3A-C. Judge Anderson's campaign refuses to talk about issues of public policy, saying that a judge should not discuss issues that his court may have to decide some day. Instead, his television ads focus mainly on his qualifications to be a judge—things like what his background is and where he went to law school.

4B-C. Judge Anderson's campaign ads vigorously attack his opponent, claiming that his opponent is biased in favor of insurance companies and other such businesses, and would therefore not be able to make fair and impartial decisions if elected to the supreme court.

9. ABBA

1A. Now we would like to tell you a story about a judge whom we will call Judge Anderson. We would like you to imagine that Judge Anderson is running for reelection to his position on the Kentucky Supreme Court. This is the court that sits in Frankfort.

2B-C. Judge Anderson receives campaign contributions—that is, money— from corporations and public interest groups that are interested in influencing legal decisions, but which do not try cases before Judge Anderson's court, the Kentucky Supreme Court.

3B-C.   Judge Anderson's campaign broadcasts some ads on television which focus mainly on his views and positions on important legal issues like abortion, lawsuit abuse, and the use of the death penalty in Kentucky.

4A-C.   Judge Anderson's campaign ads rarely mention his opponent, instead focusing on providing voters information about himself, and claiming that, if elected, he will make fair and impartial decisions on cases before the court.

10. ABBB

1A.   Now we would like to tell you a story about a judge whom we will call Judge Anderson. We would like you to imagine that Judge Anderson is running for reelection to his position on the Kentucky Supreme Court. This is the court that sits in Frankfort.

2B-C.   Judge Anderson receives campaign contributions—that is, money— from corporations and public interest groups that are interested in influencing legal decisions, but which do not try cases before Judge Anderson's court, the Kentucky Supreme Court.

3B-C.   Judge Anderson's campaign broadcasts some ads on television which focus mainly on his views and positions on important legal issues like abortion, lawsuit abuse, and the use of the death penalty in Kentucky.

4B-C.   Judge Anderson's campaign ads vigorously attack his opponent, claiming that his opponent is biased in favor of insurance companies and other such businesses, and would therefore not be able to make fair and impartial decisions if elected to the supreme court.

11. ABCA

1A.   Now we would like to tell you a story about a judge whom we will call Judge Anderson. We would like you to imagine that Judge Anderson is running for reelection to his position on the Kentucky Supreme Court. This is the court that sits in Frankfort.

2B-C.   Judge Anderson receives campaign contributions—that is, money— from corporations and public interest groups that are interested in influencing legal decisions, but which do not try cases before Judge Anderson's court, the Kentucky Supreme Court.

3C-C.   Judge Anderson's campaign broadcasts some ads on television which focus mainly on his views and positions on important legal issues like abortion, lawsuit abuse, and the use of the death penalty in Kentucky. He promises that, if reelected, he will decide these kinds of cases in the way that most people in Kentucky want them decided.

4A-C. Judge Anderson's campaign ads rarely mention his opponent, instead focusing on providing voters information about himself, and claiming that, if elected, he will make fair and impartial decisions on cases before the court.

12. ABCB

1A. Now we would like to tell you a story about a judge whom we will call Judge Anderson. We would like you to imagine that Judge Anderson is running for reelection to his position on the Kentucky Supreme Court. This is the court that sits in Frankfort.

2B-C. Judge Anderson receives campaign contributions—that is, money—from corporations and public interest groups that are interested in influencing legal decisions, but which do not try cases before Judge Anderson's court, the Kentucky Supreme Court.

3C-C. Judge Anderson's campaign broadcasts some ads on television which focus mainly on his views and positions on important legal issues like abortion, lawsuit abuse, and the use of the death penalty in Kentucky. He promises that, if reelected, he will decide these kinds of cases in the way that most people in Kentucky want them decided.

4B-C. Judge Anderson's campaign ads vigorously attack his opponent, claiming that his opponent is biased in favor of insurance companies and other such businesses, and would therefore not be able to make fair and impartial decisions if elected to the supreme court.

13. ACAA

1A. Now we would like to tell you a story about a judge whom we will call Judge Anderson. We would like you to imagine that Judge Anderson is running for reelection to his position on the Kentucky Supreme Court. This is the court that sits in Frankfort.

2C-C. Judge Anderson has been offered campaign contributions—that is, money—from corporations and public interest groups, but he declines to accept any contributions whatsoever, saying that he wants to avoid any threats to his impartiality when deciding cases before the Kentucky Supreme Court.

3A-C. Judge Anderson's campaign refuses to talk about issues of public policy, saying that a judge should not discuss issues that his court may have to decide some day. Instead, his television ads focus mainly on his qualifications to be a judge—things like what his background is and where he went to law school.

4A-C.   Judge Anderson's campaign ads rarely mention his opponent, instead focusing on providing voters information about himself, and claiming that, if elected, he will make fair and impartial decisions on cases before the court.

14. ACAB

1A.   Now we would like to tell you a story about a judge whom we will call Judge Anderson. We would like you to imagine that Judge Anderson is running for reelection to his position on the Kentucky Supreme Court. This is the court that sits in Frankfort.

2C-C.   Judge Anderson has been offered campaign contributions—that is, money—from corporations and public interest groups, but he declines to accept any contributions whatsoever, saying that he wants to avoid any threats to his impartiality when deciding cases before the Kentucky Supreme Court.

3A-C.   Judge Anderson's campaign refuses to talk about issues of public policy, saying that a judge should not discuss issues that his court may have to decide some day. Instead, his television ads focus mainly on his qualifications to be a judge—things like what his background is and where he went to law school.

4B-C.   Judge Anderson's campaign ads vigorously attack his opponent, claiming that his opponent is biased in favor of insurance companies and other such businesses, and would therefore not be able to make fair and impartial decisions if elected to the supreme court.

15. ACBA

1A.   Now we would like to tell you a story about a judge whom we will call Judge Anderson. We would like you to imagine that Judge Anderson is running for reelection to his position on the Kentucky Supreme Court. This is the court that sits in Frankfort.

2C-C.   Judge Anderson has been offered campaign contributions—that is, money—from corporations and public interest groups, but he declines to accept any contributions whatsoever, saying that he wants to avoid any threats to his impartiality when deciding cases before the Kentucky Supreme Court.

3B-C.   Judge Anderson's campaign broadcasts some ads on television which focus mainly on his views and positions on important legal issues like abortion, lawsuit abuse, and the use of the death penalty in Kentucky.

4A-C.   Judge Anderson's campaign ads rarely mention his opponent, instead focusing on providing voters information about himself, and claiming that, if elected, he will make fair and impartial decisions on cases before the court.

16. ACBB

1A.   Now we would like to tell you a story about a judge whom we will call Judge Anderson. We would like you to imagine that Judge Anderson is running for reelection to his position on the Kentucky Supreme Court. This is the court that sits in Frankfort.

2C-C.   Judge Anderson has been offered campaign contributions—that is, money—from corporations and public interest groups, but he declines to accept any contributions whatsoever, saying that he wants to avoid any threats to his impartiality when deciding cases before the Kentucky Supreme Court.

3B-C.   Judge Anderson's campaign broadcasts some ads on television which focus mainly on his views and positions on important legal issues like abortion, lawsuit abuse, and the use of the death penalty in Kentucky.

4B-C.   Judge Anderson's campaign ads vigorously attack his opponent, claiming that his opponent is biased in favor of insurance companies and other such businesses, and would therefore not be able to make fair and impartial decisions if elected to the supreme court.

17. ACCA

1A.   Now we would like to tell you a story about a judge whom we will call Judge Anderson. We would like you to imagine that Judge Anderson is running for reelection to his position on the Kentucky Supreme Court. This is the court that sits in Frankfort.

2C-C.   Judge Anderson has been offered campaign contributions—that is, money—from corporations and public interest groups, but he declines to accept any contributions whatsoever, saying that he wants to avoid any threats to his impartiality when deciding cases before the Kentucky Supreme Court.

3C-C.   Judge Anderson's campaign broadcasts some ads on television which focus mainly on his views and positions on important legal issues like abortion, lawsuit abuse, and the use of the death penalty in Kentucky. He promises that, if reelected, he will decide these kinds of cases in the way that most people in Kentucky want them decided.

4A-C. Judge Anderson's campaign ads rarely mention his opponent, instead focusing on providing voters information about himself, and claiming that, if elected, he will make fair and impartial decisions on cases before the court.

18. ACCB

1A. Now we would like to tell you a story about a judge whom we will call Judge Anderson. We would like you to imagine that Judge Anderson is running for reelection to his position on the Kentucky Supreme Court. This is the court that sits in Frankfort.

2C-C. Judge Anderson has been offered campaign contributions—that is, money—from corporations and public interest groups, but he declines to accept any contributions whatsoever, saying that he wants to avoid any threats to his impartiality when deciding cases before the Kentucky Supreme Court.

3C-C. Judge Anderson's campaign broadcasts some ads on television which focus mainly on his views and positions on important legal issues like abortion, lawsuit abuse, and the use of the death penalty in Kentucky. He promises that, if reelected, he will decide these kinds of cases in the way that most people in Kentucky want them decided.

4B-C. Judge Anderson's campaign ads vigorously attack his opponent, claiming that his opponent is biased in favor of insurance companies and other such businesses, and would therefore not be able to make fair and impartial decisions if elected to the supreme court.

LEGISLATURE VIGNETTE

19. BAAA

1B. Now we would like to tell you a story about a member of the Kentucky State Legislature, which sits in Frankfort. We will refer to this person as Senator Anderson. We would like you to imagine that Senator Anderson is running for reelection to his position in the Kentucky Senate.

2A-L. Senator Anderson receives campaign contributions—that is, money—from corporations and public interest groups that regularly receive contracts and public spending approved by the Kentucky Senate.

3A-L.   Senator Anderson's campaign refuses to talk about issues of public policy, saying that a legislator should not discuss issues that the senate may have to vote on some day. Instead, his television ads focus mainly on his qualifications to be a senator—things like what his background is and where he went to school.

4A-L.   Senator Anderson's campaign ads rarely mention his opponent, instead focusing on providing voters information about himself, and claiming that, if elected, he will make fair and impartial decisions on legislation before the senate.

20. BAAB

1B.   Now we would like to tell you a story about a member of the Kentucky State Legislature, which sits in Frankfort. We will refer to this person as Senator Anderson. We would like you to imagine that Senator Anderson is running for reelection to his position in the Kentucky Senate.

2A-L.   Senator Anderson receives campaign contributions—that is, money—from corporations and public interest groups that regularly receive contracts and public spending approved by the Kentucky Senate.

3A-L.   Senator Anderson's campaign refuses to talk about issues of public policy, saying that a legislator should not discuss issues that the senate may have to vote on some day. Instead, his television ads focus mainly on his qualifications to be a senator—things like what his background is and where he went to school.

4B-L.   Senator Anderson's campaign ads vigorously attack his opponent, claiming that his opponent is biased in favor of insurance companies and other such businesses, and would therefore not be able to make fair and impartial decisions if elected to the senate.

21. BABA

1B.   Now we would like to tell you a story about a member of the Kentucky State Legislature, which sits in Frankfort. We will refer to this person as Senator Anderson. We would like you to imagine that Senator Anderson is running for reelection to his position in the Kentucky Senate.

2A-L.   Senator Anderson receives campaign contributions—that is, money—from corporations and public interest groups that regularly receive contracts and public spending approved by the Kentucky Senate.

3B-L.   Senator Anderson's campaign broadcasts some ads on television which focus mainly on his views and positions on important policies like abortion, lawsuit abuse, and the use of the death penalty in Kentucky.

4A-L.   Senator Anderson's campaign ads rarely mention his opponent, instead focusing on providing voters information about himself, and claiming that, if elected, he will make fair and impartial decisions on legislation before the senate.

22. BABB

1B.   Now we would like to tell you a story about a member of the Kentucky State Legislature, which sits in Frankfort. We will refer to this person as Senator Anderson. We would like you to imagine that Senator Anderson is running for reelection to his position in the Kentucky Senate.

2A-L.   Senator Anderson receives campaign contributions—that is, money—from corporations and public interest groups that regularly receive contracts and public spending approved by the Kentucky Senate.

3B-L.   Senator Anderson's campaign broadcasts some ads on television which focus mainly on his views and positions on important policies like abortion, lawsuit abuse, and the use of the death penalty in Kentucky.

4B-L.   Senator Anderson's campaign ads vigorously attack his opponent, claiming that his opponent is biased in favor of insurance companies and other such businesses, and would therefore not be able to make fair and impartial decisions if elected to the senate.

23. BACA

1B.   Now we would like to tell you a story about a member of the Kentucky State Legislature, which sits in Frankfort. We will refer to this person as Senator Anderson. We would like you to imagine that Senator Anderson is running for reelection to his position in the Kentucky Senate.

2A-L.   Senator Anderson receives campaign contributions—that is, money—from corporations and public interest groups that regularly receive contracts and public spending approved by the Kentucky Senate.

3C-L. Senator Anderson's campaign broadcasts some ads on television which focus mainly on his views and positions on important policies like abortion, lawsuit abuse, and the use of the death penalty in Kentucky. He promises that, if reelected, he will vote on these kinds of issues in the way that most people in Kentucky want them decided.

4A-L. Senator Anderson's campaign ads rarely mention his opponent, instead focusing on providing voters information about himself, and claiming that, if elected, he will make fair and impartial decisions on legislation before the Senate.

24. BACB

1B. Now we would like to tell you a story about a member of the Kentucky State Legislature, which sits in Frankfort. We will refer to this person as Senator Anderson. We would like you to imagine that Senator Anderson is running for reelection to his position in the Kentucky Senate.

2A-L. Senator Anderson receives campaign contributions—that is, money—from corporations and public interest groups that regularly receive contracts and public spending approved by the Kentucky Senate.

3C-L. Senator Anderson's campaign broadcasts some ads on television which focus mainly on his views and positions on important policies like abortion, lawsuit abuse, and the use of the death penalty in Kentucky. He promises that, if reelected, he will vote on these kinds of issues in the way that most people in Kentucky want them decided.

4B-L. Senator Anderson's campaign ads vigorously attack his opponent, claiming that his opponent is biased in favor of insurance companies and other such businesses, and would therefore not be able to make fair and impartial decisions if elected to the senate.

25. BBAA

1B. Now we would like to tell you a story about a member of the Kentucky State Legislature, which sits in Frankfort. We will refer to this person as Senator Anderson. We would like you to imagine that

Senator Anderson is running for reelection to his position in the Kentucky Senate.

2B-L. Senator Anderson receives campaign contributions—that is, money—from corporations and public interest groups that are interested in influencing legislation, but which do not receive any contracts or public spending approved by the Kentucky Senate.

3A-L. Senator Anderson's campaign refuses to talk about issues of public policy, saying that a legislator should not discuss issues that the senate may have to vote on some day. Instead, his television ads focus mainly on his qualifications to be a senator—things like what his background is and where he went to school.

4A-L. Senator Anderson's campaign ads rarely mention his opponent, instead focusing on providing voters information about himself, and claiming that, if elected, he will make fair and impartial decisions on legislation before the senate.

26. BBAB

1B. Now we would like to tell you a story about a member of the Kentucky State Legislature, which sits in Frankfort. We will refer to this person as Senator Anderson. We would like you to imagine that Senator Anderson is running for reelection to his position in the Kentucky Senate.

2B-L. Senator Anderson receives campaign contributions—that is, money—from corporations and public interest groups that are interested in influencing legislation, but which do not receive any contracts or public spending approved by the Kentucky Senate.

3A-L. Senator Anderson's campaign refuses to talk about issues of public policy, saying that a legislator should not discuss issues that the senate may have to vote on some day. Instead, his television ads focus mainly on his qualifications to be a senator—things like what his background is and where he went to school.

4B-L. Senator Anderson's campaign ads vigorously attack his opponent, claiming that his opponent is biased in favor of insurance companies and other such businesses, and would therefore not be able to make fair and impartial decisions if elected to the senate.

27. BBBA

1B. Now we would like to tell you a story about a member of the Kentucky State Legislature, which sits in Frankfort. We will refer to this person as Senator Anderson. We would like you to imagine that Senator Anderson is running for reelection to his position in the Kentucky Senate.

2B-L. Senator Anderson receives campaign contributions—that is, money—from corporations and public interest groups that are interested in influencing legislation, but which do not receive any contracts or public spending approved by the Kentucky Senate.

3B-L. Senator Anderson's campaign broadcasts some ads on television which focus mainly on his views and positions on important policies like abortion, lawsuit abuse, and the use of the death penalty in Kentucky.

4A-L. Senator Anderson's campaign ads rarely mention his opponent, instead focusing on providing voters information about himself, and claiming that, if elected, he will make fair and impartial decisions on legislation before the senate.

28. BBBB

1B. Now we would like to tell you a story about a member of the Kentucky State Legislature, which sits in Frankfort. We will refer to this person as Senator Anderson. We would like you to imagine that Senator Anderson is running for reelection to his position in the Kentucky Senate.

2B-L. Senator Anderson receives campaign contributions—that is, money—from corporations and public interest groups that are interested in influencing legislation, but which do not receive any contracts or public spending approved by the Kentucky Senate.

3B-L. Senator Anderson's campaign broadcasts some ads on television which focus mainly on his views and positions on important policies like abortion, lawsuit abuse, and the use of the death penalty in Kentucky.

4B-L. Senator Anderson's campaign ads vigorously attack his opponent, claiming that his opponent is biased in favor of insurance companies and other such businesses, and would therefore not be able to make fair and impartial decisions if elected to the senate.

29. BBCA

1B. Now we would like to tell you a story about a member of the Kentucky State Legislature, which sits in Frankfort. We will refer to this person as Senator Anderson. We would like you to imagine that Senator Anderson is running for reelection to his position in the Kentucky Senate.

2B-L.   Senator Anderson receives campaign contributions—that is, money—from corporations and public interest groups that are interested in influencing legislation, but which do not receive any contracts or public spending approved by the Kentucky Senate.

3C-L.   Senator Anderson's campaign broadcasts some ads on television which focus mainly on his views and positions on important policies like abortion, lawsuit abuse, and the use of the death penalty in Kentucky. He promises that, if reelected, he will vote on these kinds of issues in the way that most people in Kentucky want them decided.

4A-L.   Senator Anderson's campaign ads rarely mention his opponent, instead focusing on providing voters information about himself, and claiming that, if elected, he will make fair and impartial decisions on legislation before the senate.

30. BBCB

1B.   Now we would like to tell you a story about a member of the Kentucky State Legislature, which sits in Frankfort. We will refer to this person as Senator Anderson. We would like you to imagine that Senator Anderson is running for reelection to his position in the Kentucky Senate.

2B-L.   Senator Anderson receives campaign contributions—that is, money—from corporations and public interest groups that are interested in influencing legislation, but which do not receive any contracts or public spending approved by the Kentucky Senate.

3C-L.   Senator Anderson's campaign broadcasts some ads on television which focus mainly on his views and positions on important policies like abortion, lawsuit abuse, and the use of the death penalty in Kentucky. He promises that, if reelected, he will vote on these kinds of issues in the way that most people in Kentucky want them decided.

4B-L.   Senator Anderson's campaign ads vigorously attack his opponent, claiming that his opponent is biased in favor of insurance companies and other such businesses, and would therefore not be able to make fair and impartial decisions if elected to the senate.

31. BCAA

1B.   Now we would like to tell you a story about a member of the Kentucky State Legislature, which sits in Frankfort. We will refer to this person as Senator Anderson. We would like you to imagine that Senator Anderson is running for reelection to his position in the Kentucky Senate.

2C-L.   Senator Anderson has been offered campaign contributions—that is, money—from corporations and public interest groups, but he declines to accept any contributions whatsoever, saying he wants to avoid any threats to his impartiality when voting on legislation in the Kentucky Senate.

3A-L.   Senator Anderson's campaign refuses to talk about issues of public policy, saying that a legislator should not discuss issues that the senate may have to vote on some day. Instead, his television ads focus mainly on his qualifications to be a senator—things like what his background is and where he went to school.

4A-L.   Senator Anderson's campaign ads rarely mention his opponent, instead focusing on providing voters information about himself, and claiming that, if elected, he will make fair and impartial decisions on legislation before the senate.

32. BCAB

1B.   Now we would like to tell you a story about a member of the Kentucky State Legislature, which sits in Frankfort. We will refer to this person as Senator Anderson. We would like you to imagine that Senator Anderson is running for reelection to his position in the Kentucky Senate.

2C-L.   Senator Anderson has been offered campaign contributions—that is, money—from corporations and public interest groups, but he declines to accept any contributions whatsoever, saying he wants to avoid any threats to his impartiality when voting on legislation in the Kentucky Senate.

3A-L.   Senator Anderson's campaign refuses to talk about issues of public policy, saying that a legislator should not discuss issues that the senate may have to vote on some day. Instead, his television ads focus mainly on his qualifications to be a senator—things like what his background is and where he went to school.

4B-L.   Senator Anderson's campaign ads vigorously attack his opponent, claiming that his opponent is biased in favor of insurance companies and other such businesses, and would therefore not be able to make fair and impartial decisions if elected to the senate.

33. BCBA

1B.   Now we would like to tell you a story about a member of the Kentucky State Legislature, which sits in Frankfort. We will refer to this person as Senator Anderson. We would like you to imagine that Senator Anderson is running for reelection to his position in the Kentucky Senate.

2C-L.   Senator Anderson has been offered campaign contributions—that is, money—from corporations and public interest groups, but he declines to accept any contributions whatsoever, saying he wants to avoid any threats to his impartiality when voting on legislation in the Kentucky Senate.

3B-L.   Senator Anderson's campaign broadcasts some ads on television which focus mainly on his views and positions on important policies like abortion, lawsuit abuse, and the use of the death penalty in Kentucky.

4A-L.   Senator Anderson's campaign ads rarely mention his opponent, instead focusing on providing voters information about himself, and claiming that, if elected, he will make fair and impartial decisions on legislation before the senate.

34. BCBB

1B.   Now we would like to tell you a story about a member of the Kentucky State Legislature, which sits in Frankfort. We will refer to this person as Senator Anderson. We would like you to imagine that Senator Anderson is running for reelection to his position in the Kentucky Senate.

2C-L.   Senator Anderson has been offered campaign contributions—that is, money—from corporations and public interest groups, but he declines to accept any contributions whatsoever, saying he wants to avoid any threats to his impartiality when voting on legislation in the Kentucky Senate.

3B-L.   Senator Anderson's campaign broadcasts some ads on television which focus mainly on his views and positions on important policies like abortion, lawsuit abuse, and the use of the death penalty in Kentucky.

4B-L.   Senator Anderson's campaign ads vigorously attack his opponent, claiming that his opponent is biased in favor of insurance companies and other such businesses, and would therefore not be able to make fair and impartial decisions if elected to the senate.

35. BCCA

1B.   Now we would like to tell you a story about a member of the Kentucky State Legislature, which sits in Frankfort. We will refer to this person as Senator Anderson. We would like you to imagine that Senator Anderson is running for reelection to his position in the Kentucky Senate.

2C-L.   Senator Anderson has been offered campaign contributions—that is, money—from corporations and public interest groups, but he declines to accept any contributions whatsoever, saying he wants to avoid any threats to his impartiality when voting on legislation in the Kentucky Senate.

3C-L.   Senator Anderson's campaign broadcasts some ads on television which focus mainly on his views and positions on important policies like abortion, lawsuit abuse, and the use of the death penalty in Kentucky. He promises that, if reelected, he will vote on these kinds of issues in the way that most people in Kentucky want them decided.

4A-L.   Senator Anderson's campaign ads rarely mention his opponent, instead focusing on providing voters information about himself, and claiming that, if elected, he will make fair and impartial decisions on legislation before the senate.

36. BCCB

1B.   Now we would like to tell you a story about a member of the Kentucky State Legislature, which sits in Frankfort. We will refer to this person as Senator Anderson. We would like you to imagine that Senator Anderson is running for reelection to his position in the Kentucky Senate.

2C-L.   Senator Anderson has been offered campaign contributions—that is, money—from corporations and public interest groups, but he declines to accept any contributions whatsoever, saying he wants to avoid any threats to his impartiality when voting on legislation in the Kentucky Senate.

3C-L.   Senator Anderson's campaign broadcasts some ads on television which focus mainly on his views and positions on important policies like abortion, lawsuit abuse, and the use of the death penalty in Kentucky. He promises that, if reelected, he will vote on these kinds of issues in the way that most people in Kentucky want them decided.

4B-L.   Senator Anderson's campaign ads vigorously attack his opponent, claiming that his opponent is biased in favor of insurance companies and other such businesses, and would therefore not be able to make fair and impartial decisions if elected to the senate.

APPENDIX D

QUESTION WORDING

Because the supreme court and state senate questions differed in entirely minor ways, and because my primary focus in this chapter is on the legitimacy of state courts of last resort, I report here only the questions used in the supreme court version of the vignette.

MEASURES OF LEGITIMACY

Do you strongly believe Judge Anderson can serve as a fair and impartial judge for Kentucky, somewhat believe he can be fair and impartial, somewhat believe he *cannot* be fair and impartial, or strongly believe he *cannot* be fair and impartial?

Assume for the moment that all judges on the Kentucky Supreme Court were selected in the same way as Judge Anderson. Would you consider the Kentucky Supreme Court as a very legitimate institution, a somewhat legitimate institution, not a very legitimate institution, or not legitimate at all?

How likely are you to accept decisions made by Judge Anderson as impartial, fair, and legitimate? Are you very likely, somewhat likely, not too likely, or not at all likely?

MANIPULATION CHECKS

Judge Anderson accepted financial contributions to his election campaign?
    1. Not certain at all → 10. Very certain

Judge Anderson received campaign contributions—that is, money—from corporations and public interest groups that regularly try cases before the Kentucky Supreme Court.
    1. Not certain at all → 10. Very certain

Judge Anderson received campaign contributions—that is, money—from corporations and public interest groups, who do not have cases that will come before the Kentucky Supreme Court but who seek to influence legal policies.
    1. Not certain at all → 10. Very certain

Judge Anderson made his policy positions known to people through his campaign ads.

1. Not certain at all → 10. Very certain

Judge Anderson made promises about how he would decide cases if elected to the Kentucky Supreme Court.

1. Not certain at all → 10. Very certain

Judge Anderson attacked his opponent during the campaign with charges of bias and inability to make fair and impartial decisions.

1. Not certain at all → 10. Very certain

INSTITUTIONAL LOYALTY[1]

I measured loyalty toward the Kentucky Supreme Court with reactions (collected on a five-point Likert response set) to the following statements:

If the Kentucky Supreme Court started making a lot of decisions that most people disagree with, it might be better to do away with the supreme court altogether.

The right of the Kentucky Supreme Court to decide certain types of controversial issues should be reduced.

The Kentucky Supreme Court can usually be trusted to make decisions that are right for the state as a whole.

Judges of the Kentucky Supreme Court who consistently make decisions at odds with what a majority of the people in the state want should be removed from their position as judge.

It is inevitable that the Kentucky Supreme Court gets mixed up in politics; therefore, we ought to have stronger means of controlling the actions of the Kentucky Supreme Court.

The Kentucky Supreme Court may have its ideas about what the constitution means, but more important is what the majority of people think the constitution means.

The Kentucky Supreme Court gets too mixed up in politics.

The Kentucky Supreme Court ought to be made less independent so that it listens a lot more to what the people want.

The index of court support is simply the number of statements to which the respondents gave supportive replies.

KNOWLEDGE OF THE KENTUCKY SUPREME COURT

The questions we asked and the percentages of respondents answering correctly are

- Whether the justices are elected or not—24.0% correct
- Whether the justices serve a life or fixed term—32.9% correct
- Whether the justices have the "last say" on the meaning of the constitution—45.6% correct

Across all three items, the average number of correct answers is 1.0, with fully one-third of the respondents getting none of the test items correct and only 7.3% answering accurately to all three.

APPENDIX E

THE DISTRIBUTIONS OF THE ANALYTICAL VARIABLES

TABLE E.1. THE DISTRIBUTIONS OF THE KEY ANALYTICAL VARIABLES

Variable	Coding	Range	Mean	s.d.	N
Judicial vignette					
Campaign contributions from litigants	0. No 1. Yes	0→1	.34	.47	330
Campaign contributions from interest groups	0. No 1. Yes	0→1	.33	.47	330
Policy commitment: Policy views	0. No 1. Yes	0→1	.33	.47	330
Policy commitment: Promises	0. No 1. Yes	0→1	.33	.47	330
Use of attack ads	0. No 1. Yes	0→1	.50	.50	330
Judgment of impartiality/Legitimacy	Continuous index score	0→1	.57	.29	327
Legislative vignette					
Campaign contributions from contractors	0. No 1. Yes	0→1	.32	.47	348
Campaign contributions from interest groups	0. No 1. Yes	0→1	.34	.47	348
Policy commitment: Policy views	0. No 1. Yes	0→1	.38	.49	348
Policy commitment: Promises	0. No 1. Yes	0→1	.32	.47	348
Use of attack ads	0. No 1. Yes	0→1	.48	.50	348
Judgment of impartiality/Legitimacy	Continuous index score	0→1	.55	.29	344

APPENDIX F

INTERACTIVE ANALYSIS

TABLE F.1. INTERACTIVE ANALYSIS OF THE CONSEQUENCES OF CAMPAIGNING FOR INSTITUTIONAL LEGITIMACY

Manipulation/Value	Model I			Model II		
	b	s.e.	β	b	s.e.	β
Campaign contributions						
From litigants/contributors	−.18	.04	−.29***	−.17	.04	−.28***
From interest groups	−.15	.04	−.25***	−.14	.04	−.23***
Policy commitments						
Policy views	−.01	.04	−.02	−.15	.07	−.24*
Promises	.04	.04	.06	−.10	.08	−.16
Attack ads						
Uses ads	.01	.03	.02	.00	.03	.01
Whether judges are elected	−.00	.04	−.01	−.12	.06	−.19*
Elected judges × Policy views	—	—	—	.19	.09	.27*
Elected judges × Policy promises	—	—	—	.18	.98	.27*
Equation statistics						
Intercept	.67	.05		.75	.06	
Standard deviation—						
Dependent variable	.29			.29		
Standard error of estimate	.28			.28		
R^2			.08***			.09***
N	327			327		

Note: All the independent variables are dichotomies, scored at 0 or 1. The dependent variables also vary from 0 to 1.

Standardized regression coefficients (β): *** $p < .001$ ** $p < .01$ * $p < .05$

APPENDIX G

MEASURING SUPPORT FOR DEMOCRATIC INSTITUTIONS AND PROCESSES

Following earlier research (e.g., Gibson 2007), support for democratic institutions and processes is conceptualized as a multidimensional syndrome of attitudes. Three subdimensions of democratic values are included in this analysis.

SUPPORT FOR THE RULE OF LAW

This survey asked people to agree or disagree (on a five-point Likert scale, ranging from agree strongly to disagree strongly) with statements pitting the rule of law against another value. In two questions, the other value was expediency. The statements are

> *The government should have some ability to bend the law in order to solve pressing social and political problems. (32.4% agree)*
> *Sometimes it might be better to ignore the law and solve problems immediately rather than wait for a legal solution. (23.6% agree)*

Another statement paired the rule of law with fairness:

> *It is not necessary to obey a law you consider unjust. (15.8% agree)*

Finally, many believe that elections provide legitimacy to governments and the laws they make. Conversely, law made by a government one opposes and did not vote for may not be deemed worthy of support. We tested this idea with the following statement:

> *It is not necessary to obey the laws of a government that I did not vote for. (8.0% agree)*

Common Factor Analysis reveals that these items are unidimensional (the eigenvalue of the second extracted factor is .94). The best indicator of the concept is the statement about obeying unjust laws. The average interitem correlation is, however, only .19, and Cronbach's alpha for the set of items is low ($\alpha = .47$). This relatively low level of reliability has been observed in earlier research and most likely reflects the fact that some measures refer to individual adherence to law while others refer to the state. Without an adequate number of indicators of these subcomponents of the concept, high reliability is difficult to achieve.

SUPPORT FOR LIBERTY OVER ORDER

The respondents were asked to assign relative valuations to order and liberty under the premise that the two are in conflict. The items read

> *Society shouldn't have to put up with those who have political ideas that are extremely different from the majority. (24.6% agree)*
>
> *It is better to live in an orderly society than to allow people so much freedom that they can become disruptive. (58.9% agree)*
>
> *Free speech is just not worth it if it means that we have to put up with the danger to society of extremist political views. (26.9% agree)*

Common Factor Analysis reveals that these items are unidimensional (the eigenvalue of the second extracted factor is .86). The best indicator of the concept is the statement that free speech is not worth the danger of extremist views. The average interitem correlation is, however, only .24, and Cronbach's alpha for the set of items is low ($\alpha = .49$). This relatively low level of reliability has not been observed in earlier research. This likely reflects the fact that two of the measures were relatively difficult for the respondents (only roughly 25 agreed with the first and last items), and none of the stimuli presented pose a strong test of commitments to individual liberty.

DEMOCRATIC VALUES

Following Sullivan, Piereson, and Marcus (1982), measures of support for due process aspects of democracy were also put to the respondents.

> *When the country is in great danger, we may have to force people to testify against themselves in court even if it violates their rights. (24.8% agree)*
>
> *If someone is suspected of treason or other serious crimes, he should not be entitled to be released on bail. (72.3% agree)*
>
> *Any person who hides behind the laws when he is questioned about his activities doesn't deserve much consideration. (46.7 % agree)*

Common Factor Analysis reveals that these items are unidimensional (the eigenvalue of the second extracted factor is .82). The best indicator of the concept is the statement about hiding behind the law. The average interitem correlation is, however, only .26, and Cronbach's alpha for the set of items is inexplicably low ($\alpha = .52$).

Were the entire nine-item set considered as a single measure of support for democratic institutions and processes, Cronbach's alpha would attain a more reasonable figure of .63.

APPENDIX H

QUESTION WORDING

QZ6.[1] Have you happened to have followed the elections for the [INSTITU-TION] this fall? Would you say you have

1. Followed the elections very closely
2. Paid some attention to them
3. Paid only a little attention to them
4. Haven't followed the judicial elections at all
8. (VOL) DON'T KNOW
9. (VOL) REFUSED

QZ7. In terms of the upcoming elections in November for the [INSTITUTION], can you tell me whether you recognize any of the following people as candidates for a judgeship on the court?

   a. CANDIDATE X
      1. Bill Cunningham
      2. Kelly Thompson
      3. Michael L. Henry
      4. William E. McAnulty
      5. John Roach
      6. Marcus Carey
      7. Janet L. Stumbo
         1. Recognize as a candidate
         2. Does not recognize as a candidate
         8. (VOL) DON'T KNOW
         9. (VOL) REFUSED

   b. CANDIDATE Y
      1. Rick Johnson
      2. Dwight T. Lovan
      3. James H. Lambert
      4. Ann O'Malley Shake
      5. Mary Noble
      6. Wil Schroder
      7. David A. Barber
         1. Recognize as a candidate
         2. Does not recognize as a candidate

8. (VOL) DON'T KNOW

9. (VOL) REFUSED

c. Monica E. Kinsella

1. Recognize as a candidate

2. Does not recognize as a candidate

8. (VOL) DON'T KNOW

9. (VOL) REFUSED

d. Doug Rush

1. Recognize as a candidate

2. Does not recognize as a candidate

8. (VOL) DON'T KNOW

9. (VOL) REFUSED

In the November election, in Judicial District [INSERT DISTRICT #], where you live, the candidates for the [INSTITUTION] are

CANDIDATE X

CANDIDATE Y

Z8a. Have you ever heard of CANDIDATE X?

1. Have heard of CANDIDATE X

2. Have not heard of CANDIDATE X

8. (VOL) DON'T KNOW

9. (VOL) REFUSED

Z8b. Have you ever heard of CANDIDATE Y

1. Have heard of CANDIDATE Y

2. Have not heard of CANDIDATE Y

8. (VOL) DON'T KNOW

9. (VOL) REFUSED

25. Do you recall if you have seen any advertisements, on TV, radio, in newspapers, or elsewhere, about candidates for the [INSTITUTION]? Would you say you (READ RESPONSE OPTIONS)?

1   Have seen many

2   Have seen some

3   Have seen a few, or

4   Have seen none

8   (DO NOT READ) Don't Know

9   (DO NOT READ) Refused

NOTE: FOR Q.25 EQUALS CODES 4, 8, OR 9, GO TO PART B, OTHERWISE CONTINUE TO PART A

PART A
(ASK Q.27 IF Q.25 EQUALS CODES 1, 2 OR 3)
27. In general, how would you rate the advertisements you saw in terms of negativity? Would you say the ads were (READ RESPONSE OPTIONS)?

1 Extremely negative
2 Somewhat negative
3 Not very negative, or
4 Not negative at all
8 (DO NOT READ) Don't know
9 (DO NOT READ) Refused

(ASK Q.28 IF Q.25 EQUALS CODES 1, 2, OR 3)
28. How would you rate the advertisements you saw in terms of partisanship? Would you say the ads were (READ RESPONSE OPTIONS)?

1 Extremely partisan
2 Somewhat partisan
3 Not very partisan or
4 Not at all partisan
8 (DO NOT READ) Don't know
9 (DO NOT READ) Refused

(ASK Q.29 IF Q.25 EQUALS CODES 1, 2, OR 3)
29. How would you rate the advertisements you saw in terms of fairness? Would you say the ads were (READ RESPONSE OPTIONS)?

1 Extremely fair
2 Somewhat fair
3 Not very fair or
4 Not at all fair
8 (DO NOT READ) Don't know
9 (DO NOT READ) Refused

30. And finally, how would you rate the tone of the ads—would you say

1 The ads were entirely appropriate for a [INSTITUTION] election
2 Somewhat appropriate for a [INSTITUTION] election
3 Not very appropriate for a [INSTITUTION] election

4 Not at all appropriate for a [INSTITUTION] election
8 (DO NOT READ) Don't know
9 (DO NOT READ) Refused

PART B: FOR THOSE WHO HAVE SEEN NO ACTUAL ADVERTISEMENTS (Q.25 = 4, 8, OR 9)

We are interested in your opinion of the following ad broadcast by a candidate for the [Kentucky Supreme Court in the race between John Roach and Mary Noble].[2] I'll read you the ad and then ask your opinion of it

> (AD BEGINS:)
> This ad is a series of screens on the TV that read as follows:
> Kentucky Supreme Court: Only Candidate with Supreme Court experience.
> Justice Roach: Over 1,000 Supreme Court Cases.
> Justice Roach: A top graduate UK Law School.
> Justice Roach: Respected by Democrats.
> Justice Roach: Respected by Republicans.
> Justice Roach: Not Respected by Dancers to the Jailhouse Rock.
> A Judge of Good Character: Keep Justice Roach.
> Paid for by: The Committee to Keep Justice Roach.

GO TO Q.27

27. In general, how would you rate this advertisement in terms of negativity? Would you say the ad is (READ RESPONSE OPTIONS)?

1 Extremely negative
2 Somewhat negative
3 Not very negative, or
4 Not negative at all
8 (DO NOT READ) Don't know
9 (DO NOT READ) Refused

28. How would you rate the advertisement in terms of partisanship? Would you say the ad is (READ RESPONSE OPTIONS)?

1 Extremely partisan
2 Somewhat partisan
3 Not very partisan or
4 Not at all partisan
8 (DO NOT READ) Don't know
9 (DO NOT READ) Refused

29. How would you rate the advertisement in terms of fairness? Would you say the ad is (READ RESPONSE OPTIONS)?

1 Extremely fair
2 Somewhat fair
3 Not very fair or
4 Not at all fair
8 (DO NOT READ) Don't know
9 (DO NOT READ) Refused

30a. And how would you rate the tone of the ad—would you say

1 The ad is entirely appropriate for a Kentucky Supreme Court election
2 Somewhat appropriate for a Kentucky Supreme Court election
3 Not very appropriate for a Kentucky Supreme Court election
4 Not at all appropriate for a Kentucky Supreme Court election
8 (DO NOT READ) Don't know
9 (DO NOT READ) Refused

Q.17. Now I would like you to focus on thinking about the characteristics of a good supreme court judge, that is, what a good judge ought to be like. First, how important would you say it is for a good Kentucky Supreme Court judge to (INSERT ITEM)? How important is it to (INSERT NEXT ITEM)?

. . . Base their decisions on whether they are a Republican or a Democrat

1 Very important
2 Somewhat important
3 Not very important, or
4 Not important at all
8 (DO NOT READ) Don't know
9 (DO NOT READ) Refused

APPENDIX I

ADDING CONTROL VARIABLES

The analysis in the text reports essentially bivariate analyses. In order to add credibility to a causal claim, a host of control variables must be considered.

Change in attitudes toward the Kentucky Supreme Court can be modeled as a function of the attributes of the individual and the court attitudes held prior to the election, objective characteristics of the electoral environment, perceptions of that environment, and expectations about the judiciary, judicial elections, and campaign activity. Consequently, I include in the fully specified model of change in institutional support a number of variables: (1) the amount of exposure to campaign ads; (2) the degree to which the ads are perceived as disagreeable; (3) a control for whether the ad measure is based on real or presented ads; (4) number of days between the interview and the election; (5) the degree of attention paid to the judicial elections in 2006; (6) whether a competitive supreme court election was held in the respondent's district; (7) general knowledge about the Kentucky judiciary; (8) specific knowledge about the candidates for judicial office; (9) awareness of the Kentucky Supreme Court; (10) general political involvement; (11) support for democratic institutions and processes; and (12) a number of mainly demographic control variables. Table I.1 reports the analysis in which change in institutional support is the dependent variable.

The first thing to note about the data in this table is that only a limited amount of the variability in change in institutional support can be accounted for by the model: $R^2 = .05$. This coefficient is statistically significant, but still fairly small.

One conclusion that might be drawn from the coefficients in table I.1 is that the dependent variable has so much error variance in it that none of the independent variables can exert much of an influence. If this is so, it is *not* because the measures of institutional support are packed with error variance. When I regress institutional support at t_1 using the independent variables reported in table I.1, an R^2 of .31 results. For institutional support at t_3, the R^2 is .35. By the standards of survey research, these are both impressive levels of explained variance. I use this evidence merely to demonstrate that the components of the change measure—support at t_1 and at t_3—are not themselves unreliable and therefore inexplicable statistically.[1]

Virtually all of this explained variance can be attributed to the respondents'

**TABLE I.1. A FULLY SPECIFIED MODEL OF
CHANGE IN INSTITUTIONAL SUPPORT**

Type of predictor/indicator	r	b	s.e.	β
Ad indicators				
Amount of ad exposure	−.03	−.03	.04	−.04
Degree objectionable	−.15	−.14	.03	−.16***
Type of ad rated	−.01	.06	.07	.05
Judicial election				
Days to election	.00	.00	.00	−.00
Attentiveness to election	−.04	−.03	.02	−.05
Whether supreme court election in district	−.01	−.03	.04	−.02
Knowledge and information				
Judicial knowledge	.07	.04	.02	.06
Candidate knowledge	.01	−.00	.02	−.01
Awareness of the court	.04	.02	.03	.03
Political involvement	.03	.05	.06	.03
Support for democratic institutions and processes				
Democratic values	−.01	−.05	.10	−.02
Order v. liberty	−.04	−.12	.10	−.05
Rule of law	−.04	−.09	.11	−.03
Control variables				
Level of education	.02	.02	.07	.01
Gender	.05	.05	.04	.04
Age	.02	.00	.00	.04
Whether own home	.00	−.01	.05	−.00
Whether African American	.06	.14	.08	.06
Party identification	.02	.06	.05	.04
Ideological identification	−.04	−.12	.07	−.06
Equation statistics				
Intercept		.29	.16	
Standard deviation—Dependent variable		.55		
Standard error of estimate		.55		
R^2				.05***
N		953		

Significance of standardized regression coefficient (β): *** $p < .001$ ** $p < .01$ * $p < .05$

evaluations of the ads to which they were exposed. By far the best predictor of change in institutional support is the index of exposure to churlish ads, for which the negative consequences (*b*) of being exposed to churlish ads range from 0 (no exposure) to −.426. This finding is all the more important because of the heavy controls included in the equation. Exposure to objectionable ads detracts from institutional support even when controlling for overall ad exposure, attention to the election, judicial knowledge, level of education, etc. Indeed, the effect of being exposed to the largest quantity of negative, partisan, unfair, and inappropriate ads $(3 \times -.143)$ is to eliminate entirely the positive effect of the election itself $(.287 - .426)$, driving the change predicted score into negative territory, ceteris paribus, that is. Although practically no respondents $(N = 2)$ score at the highest level of exposure to objectionable ads, were the electorate to be presented with unremittingly and uniformly churlish ads, judicial legitimacy would not decline, but nor would it reap the benefits that seem to attach, almost automatically, from the process of electing judges.

The most important conclusion from this portion of the analysis is quite simple. Judicial elections seem to boost the institutional legitimacy of courts, but extraordinarily objectionable campaign activity—in the eyes of the citizenry—can wipe out the salutary effects of elections.

NOTES

CHAPTER ONE

1. See also the subsequent court of appeals decision: *Republican Party of Minnesota v. White*, 416 F.3d 738 (8th Cir. 2005).

2. Sandra Day O'Connor, who voted with the majority to strike down the Minnesota restriction of free judicial speech, is reported to have said after she left the bench that the "*White* case, I confess, does give me pause." O'Connor was reacting to what she apparently sees as the increasing politicization of state judicial elections. See http://www.law.com/jsp/article.jsp?id=1162893919695 (accessed May 1, 2011).

3. Appendix A provides an analysis of court rulings subsequent to the *White* decision.

4. For a quite useful review of the relevant literature on judicial campaigns, see Baum (2003). For an excellent collection of essays on judicial elections, see Streb (2007).

5. I realize, of course, that not all state courts of last resort are actually named "supreme courts." Nonetheless, for simplicity, I will use that term to refer to these institutions.

6. Through the Campaign Media Analysis Group (CMAG), all advertisements for candidates running for office are captured from the public airwaves and made available for analysis.

7. As early as 1992, Hojnacki and Baum (1992) wrote of the "new style" of judicial campaigns. Ohio has indeed long been a state with politicized judicial elections, in part owing to the strength of unions in that state. What makes present judicial elections even more "new style" is the Supreme Court's ruling allowing candidates to discuss judicial policy issues and the dramatic increase in spending in these contests. One interest group claims, "If 2000 was the turning point for special interest influence on judicial elections, 2004 was the tipping point. *The problem is no longer limited to a few perennial battleground states: it's spreading across the country, and no state that elects judges is safe.*" Justice at Stake Campaign (2004, emphasis in original).

8. "Authority" is sometimes used as a synonym for legitimacy. Institutions perceived to be legitimate are those with a widely accepted mandate to render judgments for a political community. "Basically, when people say that laws are 'legitimate,' they mean that there is something rightful about the way the laws came about . . . the legitimacy of law rests on the way it comes to be: if that is legitimate, then so are the results, at least most of the time" (Friedman 1998, 256).

9. I equate several terms in this book: institutional legitimacy, diffuse support, and institutional loyalty. This is the same concept Caldeira and Gibson (1992) refer to as "institutional support." For a full explication of the conceptual and theoretical meaning of this concept, see the discussion in Caldeira and Gibson (1992, 636–42). For a recent review, see Gibson (2008a).

10. Comparativists (e.g., Tsebelis 2000) often focus on courts as "veto players" and have acknowledged that legitimacy is a necessary resource if courts are to play this role. See also Clark 2011.

11. For useful studies of efforts to punish the court, see Whittington (2003); Geyh (2006); and Clark (2011). In the European context, see Schwartz (2000).

12. For a discussion of earlier court-curbing efforts in the American case, see Friedman (2005, 314–15).

13. That paper provides full citations to support this claim.

14. On the other hand, Kritzer (2005, 173) analyzes multiple opinion surveys and concludes: "What is perhaps most striking about the analysis presented above is that one is likely to draw different conclusions about trends in support for the Supreme Court depending upon which survey series one looks at." See also Gibson 2007.

15. The court packing plan would have allowed Roosevelt to appoint six new justices, which would have shifted the balance of votes on the Supreme Court, allowing Roosevelt to get his New Deal policies implemented. Packing the court became unnecessary after one of the justices of the court changed his votes to favor FDR's legislation.

16. This of course means that citizens acquire information about courts that they may subsequently forget. If so, this has important implications for the timing of surveys about public knowledge of law and courts.

17. As will be discussed in later chapters, political scientists have devoted considerable effort to examining the political consequences of campaign activity. Excellent research exists—for example, on the use of attack ads (e.g., Brader 2006; Brooks 2006; Geer 2006; Mark 2006; Franz et al. 2008)—but none of those studies addresses courts, and none directly considers consequences such as perceived impartiality and institutional legitimacy.

18. A few points from this literature bear emphasis. First, the literature on the consequences of negative campaigns is certainly mixed, although it seems transparently obvious that candidates for political office *believe* such campaigns to be effective (as do the critics of negative advertising). Ansolabehere and Iyengar (1995) (and other studies) document a significant drop in voter turnout associated with negative ads (presumably due to "tuning out" of the electoral process). However, in a very important meta-analysis of the research literature, Lau et al. (1999; see also Lau, Sigelman, and Rovner 2007) conclude that negative campaign ads have little effect, although they acknowledge that virtually no research examines the long-term implications of such ads (1999, 860), as in the consequences for institutional legitimacy. Furthermore, judicial campaigns have several attributes that render them different from other campaigns for public office. Thus, beyond contributing to the literature on judicial elections, this research may well add an important dimension to ongoing efforts in other subfields to assess the impact of negative campaigning on citizen attitudes and behaviors.

19. In her analysis of public attitudes toward state courts and court systems, Benesh (2006, 700) argues that Americans prefer independence over accountability, citing evidence from Heagarty (2003, 1305). My reading of that and other evidence, however, is that this conclusion is far from solid (and certainly Heagarty's data are far from dispositive). For some research supportive of my view, see Wenzel, Bowler, and Lanoue (2003). More generally, judicial independence is most likely a multidimensional concept, with citizens supporting some types of independence (e.g., from the executive) but not others (e.g., from the preferences of the majority of the citizenry).

20. The questions read:

In many states, the justices of the state Supreme Court are elected and they therefore have to campaign to get people to vote for them. Do you agree strongly, agree, are uncertain, disagree or disagree strongly with the following statement: When state supreme court judges run for election they should make their views known about controversial issues, such as abortion, gun control, the death penalty, and gay marriage.

Do you agree strongly, agree, are uncertain, disagree or disagree strongly with the following statement: When state supreme court judges run for election they should be allowed to attack their opponents' positions on issues that might come before the court.

Please tell me if you agree strongly, agree, are uncertain, disagree or disagree strongly with the following statement: When state supreme court judges run for election, they should NOT accept campaign contributions from any lawyer or law firm.

21. See Persily and Lammie (2004) for what is perhaps the definitive study of American attitudes toward campaign contributions.

22. Some of these ideas were reported in an earlier paper advocating a theory of expectations (see Gibson 1997). That paper reports the results from a survey in Western Europe in which both expectations and perceptions of courts were measured. Enormous cross-national variability exists in how people think courts ought to function. For instance, a small minority of residents of the former East Germany (26.6%) thought that law should trump majority preferences; the comparable figure for Danes was 75.5%.

23. Of course, expectations and perceptions may not be independent of one another. In general, I attempt to force the variables apart by measuring expectations in the initial interview, prior to the campaign season, and perceptions in the midst of the election campaigns.

24. Pozen (2008, 11) claims that judges make more policy now than ever before in American history.

25. See, e.g., Walker 1977; Lehne and Reynolds 1978; Fagan 1981; Flanagan, McGarrell, and Brown 1985; Olson and Huth 1998; Wenzel, Bowler, and Lanoue 2003; Overby et al. 2004.

26. For recent examples, see Wenzel, Bowler, and Lanoue (2003); Benesh (2006). On the measurement of various attitudes toward courts, see Gibson, Caldeira, and Spence (2003b).

27. So, e.g., Benesh (2006, 701–2) uses the following measure as her dependent variable: "What is your level of confidence in the courts in your community?" Even notwithstanding the critique of confidence measures by Gibson, Caldeira, and Spence (2003b), it is not clear to me how the respondents understood "courts in your community." For a related analysis of confidence in state political institutions, see Kelleher and Wolak (2008).

28. Among the many virtues of their analysis is the effort to use multiple indicators of the dependent variable. Single-item indicators pose extraordinary challenges for mea-

surement and statistical analysis, most of which are simply impossible to overcome (e.g., reliability cannot be estimated).

29. Of course, I recognize that scholars are doing the best they can with secondary analysis of data sets collected by interest groups such as JaS. I have no doubt that, were resources provided to conduct original research, more valid and reliable measures of court attitudes would be produced.

30. A theory of change must include two components. First, a theory of cross-sectional differences is necessary. Such a theory provides an explanation of why citizens differ in their attitudes at any given point in time. For instance, Caldeira and Gibson (1995) have shown that the tendency to extend legitimacy to courts is in part a function of support for democratic values more generally. That theory has proven to be quite valuable in understanding and predicting individual difference in attitudes toward courts. Second, a theory of *change* must also be grafted onto the cross-sectional theory. For instance, it is unlikely that changes in levels of legitimacy are due to alterations in support for democratic values inasmuch as the latter is usually thought to be formed early in life and resistant to change (e.g., Gibson 1995). The cross-sectional theory must identify causal factors that are themselves subject to exogenous influences.

31. Kentucky is unusual in how it structures its elections for judges on its supreme court. The judges run within single-member districts instead of running in statewide elections. There are seven judicial districts (for a discussion of the candidates running in each of the districts, see chapter 6). In addition, Kentucky uses nonpartisan judicial elections, meaning of course that the ballot does not identify candidates as either Democrats or Republicans (or members of some other party). In the concluding chapter of this book, I offer some speculation about whether this institutional structure might affect the substantive findings of my analysis. In short, I argue that the implications are small, at most.

32. The Family Trust Foundation sued to overturn Canon 5B(1)(c) of Kentucky's Code of Judicial Conduct after failing in its effort to survey all candidates for judicial office in Kentucky in 2004 on a variety of contentious legal issues. The foundation succeeded in getting the Canon declared to be in violation of the First Amendment to the US Constitution (*Family Trust Foundation of Kentucky v. Wolnitzek*, 345 F. Supp. 2d 672 [E.D. Ky. 2004]). For a discussion of campaign speech by candidates for judicial office, see Bopp and Woudenberg (2007a and 2007b). Bopp successfully argued *Republican Party of Minnesota v. White* before the US Supreme Court.

33. Note that Kentucky selects its high court judges via nonpartisan elections held within seven judicial districts. This is a fairly rare combination of institutions, which I discuss more fully below. In some sense, no single state can ever be "representative" of some larger population or subpopulation of states, especially on matters of judicial selection and retention. Each state has its own somewhat idiosyncratic history with judicial campaigns (especially since politicized campaigns are relatively new). And indeed, if one looks closely at the traditional five-category description of methods of selecting judges in the United States, one finds a great deal of *within-category* variability, so states we often collapse together are in fact heterogeneous. Consequently, I have tried in this analysis to be cautious about overclaiming in the ability to generalize from Kentucky.

34. The tendency to study judicial institutions in isolation, without comparison to other comparable political institutions, has long impeded our understanding of courts. Exceptions exist (e.g., Bonneau 2005), and no one has shown us better than Hall (2001) the value of cross-institutional analysis in thinking about judicial elections and politics (see also Gibson and Caldeira 1998).

CHAPTER TWO

1. O'Connor voted with the majority in extending free-speech rights to candidates for judicial office.

2. For an excellent collections of essays on various aspects of judicial elections, see Streb (2007).

3. For the purposes of this analysis, I equate perceived impartiality and institutional legitimacy. Both terms were used in the questions associated with the empirical analysis (see below). And conceptually, impartiality is a bedrock of judicial legitimacy, even if legitimacy might be considered to be grounded in factors in addition to fair and impartial decision making by judges.

4. Panel studies of attitudes toward judicial institutions are as rare as they are important. For one of the few such studies, see Hoekstra (2003).

5. In the past, judicial controversies were not especially harmful to legitimacy because the controversies were enveloped in legitimacy-conferring symbols (e.g., on the effect of the court's decision in *Bush v. Gore*, see Gibson, Caldeira, and Spence [2003a]; see also Gibson et al. [2011]). Today, however, campaigns reinforce the view that courts are just like any other political institution, and that therefore their claims to impartiality, independence, and fairness are not prima facie valid.

6. Mark (2006, 2) defines "negative campaigning" as "actions a candidate takes to win an election by attacking an opponent, rather than emphasizing his or her own positive attributes or policies."

7. Perhaps the most important exception to this claim is the research of Mutz and Reeves (2005), who find that uncivil debate undermines trust. Still, the conceptual distance between trust and institutional legitimacy is not small. Moreover, Hall and Bonneau (2011) examine the consequences of campaign activity for voting in judicial elections (which is discussed more fully in the concluding chapter of this book).

8. On the value of campaign ads for democratic citizenship, see Freedman, Franz, and Goldstein (2004).

9. Perhaps the most useful (and most rigorous, focusing as it does on all partisan and nonpartisan elections for state courts of last resort from 1990 to 2000) study of campaign spending is that produced by Bonneau (2005), who finds that, in many important respects (e.g., the influence of open seats), judicial campaigns look quite similar to legislative races (see also Bonneau 2004). Bonneau also demonstrates that partisan and nonpartisan elections differ little (an increasingly familiar finding within the literature on state courts— e.g., Hall 2001). On electoral politics and state court policy making, see Hall (1992). On state judicial elections more generally, see Bonneau and Hall (2009).

10. The interest group JaS conducted a national survey in 2001 on various issues of

judicial campaigns. In response to the question, "How much influence do you think campaign contributions made to judges have on their decisions?" 36% replied "a great deal of influence" and another 40% selected the "some influence" response option. Only 5% of the respondents judged there to be "no influence at all." Justice at Stake Campaign (2001).

11. For instance the 2001 JaS survey found that 25% of the American people have a great deal of confidence in their state courts and judges, while another 52% express some confidence. Only 5% claim to have no confidence at all. It is also interesting to note that when the same question was put to the respondents toward the end of the interview, after being pummeled with questions about excessive influence of campaign contributors and special interest groups, confidence in the state judiciaries actually increased, albeit ever so slightly.

12. Some research suggests that the type of selection system has something to do with confidence in state courts (e.g., Benesh 2006; Cann and Yates 2008). The conventional finding is that partisan elections undermine confidence. However, this research suffers from some important limitations, not the least of which is the use of a flawed measure of institutional legitimacy (see Gibson, Caldeira, and Spence 2003b). Moreover, even if we accept the correlational findings at face value, questions of causality abound, as do questions about what exactly about partisan elections drags confidence down. Given the state of extant literature, it seems prudent to draw no conclusion as yet about the impact of selection systems on the legitimacy of state judiciaries.

13. Persily and Lammie argue, "The state has an interest in combating the appearance of corruption, then, not because such appearances are inherently bad, but because such appearances result in second-order effects: public cynicism, alienation, lack of trust, and lack of confidence in government. . . . Under this view, government loses legitimacy when the public perceives campaign contributions as having a greater effect than do constituent preferences or a representative's conscience on a representative's behavior" (2004, 128).

14. See also Coleman and Manna (2000), who find no effect on trust or efficacy from campaign spending in the 1994 and 1996 US House elections.

15. These contributions also raise important ethical issues connected to judicial recusals. See, e.g., http://www.al.com/news/independent/index.ssf?/base/news/1162234574216310 .xml&coll=4 (accessed November 21, 2006). For an empirical analysis, see Gibson and Caldeira (2012).

16. Brace and Boyea (2008) report that before the Supreme Court ruled in 2002, 27 states placed speech restrictions on candidates for judicial office. Moreover, they found that in states with elective systems of selecting judges in the 1990s, the presence of campaign speech restrictions made it more likely that a judge would vote to overturn a capital verdict. They reason that speech restrictions provide protection to incumbents, allowing them to implement their own preferences rather than the preferences of their constituents. Such an effect was not found in systems using appointment or retention to select their judges.

17. For an interesting discussion of this issue, see Friedland (2004, 564), who analyzes how the following three campaign statements by a judge differ with regard to the due process rights of litigants.

I don't think there is any constitutional right to same-sex marriage.

If elected, I promise to interpret our state constitution as protecting a right to physician-assisted suicide.

We can't let terrorists and the fear they create tear our society apart. We need to elect judges, like me, who will worry less about the Constitution and more about locking up suspected terrorists. We must put our safety first.

18. The distinction between internal and external validity was first made by Cook and Campbell (see Cook and Campbell 1979).

19. Robinson and Darley assert (1998, 417) that we cannot ask people directly about their mental processes "because psychologists have discovered that subjects often do not have mental access to the principles and processes they use to make decisions, and thus cannot accurately articulate those principles. Instead, researchers present subjects with various cases to judge, and infer their judging principles from the resulting patterning of responses between the different cases."

20. Aronson et al. (1990) distinguish between experimental realism (the content of the experiment being realistic to the subjects so that they take the task seriously) and mundane realism (the similarity of the experimental context and stimuli to events likely to occur in the real world—in short, verisimilitude). This experiment has a great deal of both types of realism, since the issue of campaign finance is quite salient to the American people.

21. The policy commitment was framed in this general fashion so as not to imply the adoption of any particular position that might or might not be attractive to the respondent (and indeed, with the well-known "false consensus" effect, the vast majority of people consider their own views to be similar to those of the majority). Additional research is reported in chapter 3 focusing on whether more direct assertions of a policy position (e.g., "If elected, I will work to eliminate women's right to have abortions") have a more detrimental effect on institutional legitimacy than the somewhat amorphous policy commitment expressed in this version of the vignette.

22. For the supreme court, the first two eigenvalues are 2.15 and .47, respectively, and the first extracted factor accounts for 71.7% of the common variance. For the state senate, the eigenvalues are 2.09 and .51, with the first factor accounting for 69.7% of the common variance.

23. The dependent variable is continuous. For purposes of illustration *only*, I have created a categorical variable, dividing the scale at its center point.

24. Measures of the effectiveness of manipulations are never perfect, in part because different elements of the vignette can influence responses to the manipulation check questions. For instance, respondents may be suspicious of the scenario in which no contributions are said to have been received, but in which the candidate used attack ads and made policy promises, and this may account for some of the variance in their responses to the questions. And of course the various manipulation check variables are certainly not themselves orthogonal.

25. I present this analysis in a regression format because ordinary least squares (OLS)

includes all information typically found in analysis of variance (mainly inferential statistics) as well as measures of the degree of association between the variables. Because the number of cases is large, and because measures of statistical significance are extremely sensitive to sample size, my substantive conclusions are grounded more in the assessment of regression coefficients than in tests of statistical significance. Note as well that the dependent variable (and of course the dummy variables) ranges from 0 to 1.

To the extent that there are different degrees of variability in the variables of interest here, comparing standardized coefficients can be misleading. However, as reported in table 2.3, the variability in the dependent variable (the legitimacy factor scores) is often quite similar across the two institutions, so standardized coefficients can provide useful information in this sample. In any event, unstandardized coefficients are also reported in table 2.3 and are the most appropriate for cross-institutional comparisons.

26. This basic equation models the direct, linear effects of the variables on institutional legitimacy. I also considered interactive effects, beginning by assessing the eight two-way interactions among the manipulation dummy variables. The appropriate statistical test is of the significance of the change in R^2 with the addition of the variable set (see Cohen et al. 2003; Kam and Franzese 2007). In the case of the legislative vignette, the change in R^2 is trivial and insignificant, and not a single interaction term is statistically significant. In the court vignette, R^2 significantly increases with the full set of interaction terms ($p = .048$), but only a single interaction achieves statistical significance: that between the expression of policy views and the use of attack ads. I have carefully scrutinized this relationship in an attempt to understand it. Of the four cells (the results of the 2×2 interaction), institutional legitimacy is highest when no attack ads are used and when policy views are not given (remember that "not given" means that either no policy statements are made or specific promises are given—this is a dummy variable). In terms of the influence of attack ads, their impact is to some degree dependent on whether policy statements are made. When they are not, attack ads are considerably more detrimental than when they are made. Perhaps this means that if there is a policy debate, many more tactics are deemed legitimate, but if debate is more "gentlemanly," then attacking one's opponent is particularly glaring and upsetting. The converse (but still the same finding) is that when attack ads are used, it matters not at all whether policy pronouncements are made; when they are not used, the impact of policy statements is larger, but still small. Given the complexity of these relationships—and especially the fact that no such interactive effect was observed for the even more extreme case of explicit policy *commitments*—I have decided not to pursue these relationships further. I also ignore the higher order interactions, given the difficulty of providing substantive interpretations of any such effects. Thus, I conclude that the most important influences of these variables can be captured in their linear manifestations.

27. See Kam and Franzese (2007) for a discussion of the methodology of assessing interactive effects.

28. The equation reported in table 2.3 is not misspecified owing to the random assignment of individuals to the vignettes (which renders the manipulation variables uncorrelated with each other and with the equation's error term). However, when court sup-

port and knowledge are included in the interactive equations (both in their linear and conditional manifestations), the possibility of model misspecification does arise. Consequently, I considered a number of control variables, including the respondent's (1) gender, (2) age, (3) race, (4) home ownership, (5) religiosity, (6) ideological self-identification, (7) party identification, (8) level of education, (9) frequency of talking about politics, and (10) specific support for the supreme court (approval of the court's policy outputs). When these variables are added to the diffuse support interactive equation, the coefficient of the support–policy promises interaction is only slightly and nonsignificantly reduced (from $b = -.043$ to $b = -.036$). However, the addition of these control variables to the equation modeling the knowledge interactions does render the single significant interactive effect insignificant (with a change in the regression coefficient of the interaction term from .055 to .036). Thus, this analysis indicates that the findings from the support interaction analysis are fairly robust, whereas the suggestion of a knowledge interaction is not.

29. I also considered whether ideological or partisan intensity played any role in moderating these relationships, based on "folded" ideological and partisan self-identification questions. No evidence whatsoever was discovered of any interactive effects with the experimental manipulations.

30. For the supreme court, the first two eigenvalues are 2.10 and .56, respectively, and the first extracted factor accounts for 70.1% of the common variance. For the state senate, the eigenvalues are 2.10 and .53, with the first factor accounting for 70.0% of the common variance.

31. See appendix D for the text of the items used to check the manipulations.

32. The dependent variable is continuous. For purposes of illustration *only*, I have created a categorical variable, dividing the scale at its center point.

33. This analysis is confined to states using any form of election. The results, however, are the same if confined to only those states using partisan or nonpartisan elections. See also note 39 in this chapter.

34. I have conducted this analysis using OLS so as to be able to make direct comparisons to my Kentucky findings. Of course, the regression analysis includes all information typically found in analysis of variance (mainly inferential statistics) as well as measures of the degree of association between the variables. For the details of the distributions of the variables, see table E.1 in appendix E.

35. Note that owing to random assignment of respondents to treatment conditions, the independent variables are uncorrelated (and uncorrelated with the equation's error term) and, as a consequence, the estimates of bivariate and multivariate coefficients are the same. When independent variables are uncorrelated with all other causes of a dependent variable, the bivariate equation is *not* misspecified.

36. This cross-level analytical strategy follows that adopted by Benesh (2006) and others.

37. For the full results of the interactive regressions, see table F.1 in appendix F.

38. Following Benesh (2006, 704), I also controlled for a number of institutional factors such as level of professionalism, dissent rates, and the rate of the exercise of judicial

review (see Benesh 2006, 700n8). The addition of these variables to the interactive equation has no effect whatsoever, largely because, as in Benesh's analysis, these variables have no relationship with the dependent variable of this analysis.

39. I have re-run all of this analysis with a more restricted indicator of type of selection/retention system: partisan and nonpartisan elections versus all other systems. The results are extremely similar to those reported in table F.1 and discussed in the text above, with no modifications whatsoever required in the substantive conclusions.

40. Since national surveys are virtually never constructed to be representative of individual states, it is unwise to pursue further analysis of interstate differences in public opinion. This is particularly so since the number of respondents living in states without elections is small. On the basis of the limited analysis reported here, one can most likely have considerable confidence in the conclusion that policy talk has few consequences for legitimacy in states using elections to select or retain their judges, but less confidence in the conclusion that the process is different in states not relying upon elections.

CHAPTER THREE

1. The question read, "Next, I would like you to think about a lawsuit concerning whether a woman has the right to have an abortion. Imagine if you will that the judge deciding the case made some statements about abortion during his last election campaign—the one back in November. If the judge said during the campaign that 'I believe the constitution gives women the right to have abortions' would you think that this alone would mean that the judge cannot be fair and impartial in deciding the case, or would you think that irrespective of the statement the judge could be fair and impartial?" The two additional questions were, "If during the campaign the judge accepted campaign contributions from groups seeking to change Kentucky's law on abortion, would you think that this alone would mean that the judge cannot be fair and impartial in deciding the case, or would you think that irrespective of the statement the judge could be fair and impartial?" "And what if the judge said during the campaign 'If elected, I will change Kentucky's law on abortion.' Would you think that this alone would mean that the judge cannot be fair and impartial in deciding the case, or would you think that irrespective of the statement the judge could be fair and impartial?"

2. Since these activities were presented to the respondents in a random sequence, I have carefully considered whether the order of presentation has any influence on the responses. For the question about campaign contributions and the direct assertion that the candidate would change the law, there is no evidence whatsoever of order effects. Neither a chi-square test nor a difference of means t-test is statistically significant. However, for the statement about the candidate's interpretation of the constitution, a very slight order effect is observed. While the chi-square test of the trichotomous responses (impartial, not impartial, don't know) is *not statistically significant*, the t-test of the responses weighted by attitude strength is significant at .039, and eta = .08. When this activity is presented last it is least likely to produce a response that the judge can be fair and impartial. However, this effect is weak: the percentages believing the judge can be fair range from 58.7% when the statement is offered first, to 56.1% when it is second, and 51.4% when it is last. When

the respondent hears the statement last, it is in the context of the candidate already having said that he or she would change the law and after hearing that campaign contributions had been given. However, this effect is quite marginal, it only influences the intensity (not direction) of responses, and the other two statements are entirely unaffected by order effects, so I have therefore decided to reject the null hypothesis that these responses are influenced by presentation order, and therefore to ignore this factor in the analysis that follows. Note, however, that this decision has absolutely no consequences for the substantive conclusions one draws from the data reported in table 3.1.

3. Because some portion of the respondents was unable to judge these activities, the percentages believing the judge cannot be fair are not equal to 100% minus the percentages shown in this table. However, "don't know" responses to these questions were rare, ranging from only 4.2% to 5.6%.

4. The findings reported here are nearly identical were I to use the variables indicating affect toward "anti-abortion activists." For instance, the correlation between the direct assertion that the candidate would change the law and (unrecoded) affect toward anti-abortionists is .06; for affect toward pro-abortion activists, the correlation is −.01.

5. When experiments are embedded within representative surveys, not only are findings generalizable to the larger population from which the sample is drawn (external validity), but great confidence can also be placed in causal inferences (internal validity). With random assignment of respondents to vignette versions, the proverbial "all else" can indeed be considered equal. Cook and Campbell (1979) first made the distinction between internal and external validity.

6. It is also possible that the results reflect something of an interview artifact, but one with substantive implications. The interviews were conducted by telephone. These statements are fairly lengthy and complicated (especially statement 3). Under these conditions, perhaps the material at the end of the advertisement has disproportionate influence on the respondents. The respondents may not listen carefully to the text of the ads, but they know a question will be asked at the conclusion of the ad, so they are especially attentive to the material at the close of statement. The first two ads close with statements about judges (even if the Roach ad refers obliquely to "a real judge"). But the Stumbo ad directly implicates politics in closing, saying, "Is he a judge, or just another politician?" With this sentence, much of the ambiguity and clutter from the earlier statements in the ad may get washed away, and this last assertion may therefore have more influence on the responses. Still, I consider this a substantive effect because, given the inherent complexity of this ad, its influence on the telephone respondents is likely similar to its influence on voters who viewed the ad during Stumbo's campaign.

7. With random assignment of respondents to ad versions, it is not necessary to implement any control variables in order to estimate without bias the effect of the treatment (exposure to the ad). But because the ads differed in terms of a quite obvious characteristic of the candidates—gender—I considered whether reactions to the ads varied by the respondent's gender. In none of the three ad versions is there a statistically significant difference in the judgments of the male and female respondents in the sample. And within gender, the effects of the different advertisements were virtually identical. Because this

experiment was implemented in the third-wave interview, conducted several months after the election, I did not measure candidate preferences and therefore cannot ascertain whether such preferences were influential. But to reiterate, the estimates of the ad effects are unbiased even in the bivariate analysis.

8. During the second interview, the respondents were asked about six political/legal issues on which the Kentucky Supreme Court might rule in the next several years. After rating each on importance, the respondent was asked to designate the issue he or she thought most important. Nearly all respondents were able to respond to this query, and therefore the experiment referred to the individual respondent's most important issue. Only 2.5% of the respondents could not specify an issue as most important (and another 0.3% refused to do so). This small group of respondents was randomly assigned an issue.

9. I must acknowledge that this finding may be an artifact of the specific context of the interviews. Although this experiment preceded any mention of campaign contributions in the third-wave interview, the earlier interviews asked a variety of questions about campaign contributions. The earlier interviews may therefore have contributed to priming the respondents to think about contributions whenever they heard words like "promises." Unfortunately, I have no means of assessing this hypothesis. It should be noted, however, that with random assignment of respondents to treatment conditions, the statistical estimates of the effects of the treatments are unbiased.

10. This is why the number of cases drops in table 3.2 in the "Position: Most important issue" sections of the table. As I have noted, two-thirds of the respondents were assigned to the most important issue condition, and then that subsample was split evenly between agreeable and disagreeable policy promises.

11. To what degree is the impact of issue agreement/disagreement contingent upon the specific issue under consideration? Recall that the respondents were asked to indicate the most important issue to them and that two-thirds were then asked about that issue, varying the campaign promise from agreeing to disagreeing with the respondent's own position. Within each issue, is the effect of agreement/disagreement the same? It is not. On the death penalty and the tort issues, agreeable or disagreeable promises make little difference to the respondents; on the other four issues, it does. The strongest relationship is found on the issue of homosexuality and gay marriage, with weaker associations for abortion, religious displays on government property, and whether people should be allowed to burn the American flag in protest. Because I know of little theoretical basis for understanding cross-issue differences—all of these issues have the status of "most important" to the respondent—I do not pursue this matter further.

CHAPTER FOUR

1. A few scholars have examined public attitudes toward state and lower courts (e.g., Benesh 2006). See, e.g., Walker 1977; Lehne and Reynolds 1978; Fagan 1981; Flanagan, McGarrell, and Brown 1985; Olson and Huth 1998; Wenzel, Bowler, and Lanoue 2003; Overby et al. 2004.

2. Kritzer and Voelker note that court systems in a number of states have commissioned public opinion polls "with an eye toward finding ways to improve the quality of service

delivery and public support" (1998, 59). So obviously the court systems themselves believe that the views of their constituents are important and not entirely void of content.

3. State courts are not unique on this score; the very same assertion could be made about citizen attitudes toward state legislatures. Exceptions exist: see, e.g., Patterson, Ripley, and Quinlan 1992.

4. Note that the question explicitly invited "don't know" responses.

5. The correlation between feelings toward pro- and anti-abortion activists is surprisingly weak: $r = -.28$, indicating a lesser degree of opinion polarization than might be expected.

6. The correlation of affect toward the Kentucky Supreme Court and the Kentucky court system in general is .66, the strongest of any intercorrelation.

7. Among those who rated these institutions similarly (10 degrees or less apart), we asked which institution the respondent had more confidence in. A majority (54.9%) chose the supreme court, while 31.6% selected the state legislature (with the remainder unable to decide). About one-half of the sample rated the two institutions similarly on the feeling thermometers and therefore received the follow-up question.

8. The differences in the feeling thermometer responses to the court and the legislature were categorized as follows: substantially more positive toward the institution—a difference of more than 10 degrees on the thermometer; somewhat more positive—a difference between -1 and -10 or $+1$ and $+10$ degrees on the thermometer; and the same—the same rating.

9. Even a majority of those giving slightly more positive replies about the legislature selected the supreme court when asked to indicate which institution they have more confidence in.

10. Items such as these are routinely used in surveys measuring the levels of judicial knowledge of ordinary members of the mass public because they are simple enough that most respondents will either possess the information or not possess it. I acknowledge, however, that for highly sophisticated respondents, the questions might be understood to be simplistic, making it difficult to give a "correct" answer. For example, as to how judges are selected in Kentucky, one answer is that the normal pattern is for judges to retire near the end of their term, allowing the governor to appoint a replacement to the bench. Thus, "gubernatorial appointment" might be the correct answer to the question on selection if one were using de facto criteria to reach a conclusion. Similarly, as to the correct answer to the "last say" question, some respondents—especially those subscribing to popular constitutionalism (see Kramer 2004)—might believe that the people of Kentucky have the last say on the meaning of the state's constitution. Such respondents would find it difficult to answer the question as it was posed to them. There might also be some slight confusion as to the difference between a normative answer to this question (the people should have the last say) and an empirical one (the supreme court does have the last say). Few knowledge questions are ever unequivocally right or wrong—should a respondent who identifies John Roberts as the "chief justice of the US Supreme Court" be scored as answering wrongly to the question of what position Roberts holds because his actual title is "chief justice of the United States"? In my view, the amount of measurement error that

these indicators elicit due to overly sophisticated respondents is most likely minuscule and of no practical consequence.

11. Recall that the survey fieldwork was conducted well outside the general election season in 2006.

12. These findings contrast strongly with those of Gibson and Caldeira (2009b) on public knowledge of the US Supreme Court. For instance, more than two-thirds of Americans know that the justices of the Supreme Court are appointed, and significant majorities know that the justices are appointed to life terms.

13. In a nationally representative survey I conducted in 2008, I asked the respondents two questions about their state courts of last resort—whether the judges on the court are elected or appointed to the bench and whether they serve for a set number of years or whether they serve a life term. About 45% of the respondents replied that they did not know the answer to these questions. "Don't know" replies were most common in states using merit selection, with retention elections. A "don't know" reply in those states might reflect some degree of confusion about how to answer the question inasmuch as their judges are selected via appointments to the bench but retained by elections.

The different types of selection systems vary somewhat on the proportions of respondents who correctly identify the method of selection. If I score both appointment and election as correct for merit systems with retention elections, then I find that 44.8% of the respondents living in those states gave the correct answer. The percentage correct for legislative appointments ($N = 31$) is 45.2%; but for gubernatorial appointments only 27.4% ($N = 117$) answered the question correctly. Notably, those in partisan and nonpartisan elections were about equally likely to answer the question accurately (34.3% and 33.1%, respectively). About the same percentage (34.6%) correctly identified their merit system without retention election as being an appointed system. If I simply classify each system by whether the judges of the state court of last resort are selected or retained by elections, then I find that 31.1% of the respondents correctly asserted that their justices are elected, compared to 32.2% of those living in appointed systems correctly saying that their judges are appointed to the bench.

Regarding the length of the terms of the justices of the state court of last resort, only the justices in Rhode Island serve a life term. In Massachusetts and New Hampshire, the term terminates when the justice turns 70 years old. Thus, the correct answer to our question for nearly all of the respondents is "a set number of years."

A plurality of respondents (47.0%) asserted that they did not know the nature of the term of the justices. At the same time, only 13.7% claimed that the term was a life term, with 39.4% saying the terms are fixed. The data set is insufficient to support state-by-state analysis (Rhode Island $N = 5$).

Generally, then, a couple of conclusions emerge from this analysis. First, the percentage of people correctly identifying their selection system is fairly small—35.8%, overall. Second, knowledge of the selection system varies little by type of selection system, although the ambiguity of hybrid merit selection with retention elections (and the relatively small numbers of respondents for some selection systems) clouds this conclusion slightly. Finally, very few Americans believe that the justices of their state court of last resort serve life terms.

14. As a reminder, I equate several terms in this book: institutional legitimacy, diffuse support, and institutional loyalty. This is the same concept Caldeira and Gibson (1992) refer to as "institutional support." For a full explication of the conceptual and theoretical foundations of this concept, see the discussion in Caldeira and Gibson (1992, 636–42). For a recent review, see Gibson (2010). See also Gibson and Caldeira 2009a.

15. This follows the convention established in our earlier work on institutional legitimacy. See, e.g., Gibson, Caldeira, and Baird 1998; Gibson and Caldeira 2003. As we asserted: "The replies of those who claimed little or no awareness are most likely dominated by random variation. Excluding them may restrict somewhat the theoretical variation in the correlation coefficients (although not the empirical variance in the items, since these respondents tended overwhelmingly to give 'don't know' responses to our substantive questions), but we believe their exclusion is necessary when analyzing attitudes toward the national high courts" (Gibson, Caldeira, and Baird 1998, 348).

16. The eigenvalue of the second factor is 1.07, which is only marginally greater than the conventional standard of 1.0 for assigning a substantive interpretation to a factor.

17. An obvious possible explanation for this finding is that the trust item is scored in the opposite direction as compared to the other statements. Some of the "glue" that binds the responses to the seven questions together (response set) is randomized with this variable, resulting in lower interitem correlations. For a substantive analysis of the meaning of "trust" in the US Supreme Court, see Gibson (2011).

18. The correlation between the trust item and the factor score is .26.

19. With such a large number of cases, even relationships that are entirely trivial from a substantive point of view can fairly easily achieve statistical significance.

20. Note that education and level of court knowledge are not strongly correlated: $r = .15$.

21. I do not mean to make a bright-line distinction between cognition and emotion since practically no political psychologists subscribe to a rigid distinction. When I refer to symbols and emotion, I am closer to what is sometimes termed "hot cognition"—cognitive understandings of reality tinged with evaluative content.

CHAPTER FIVE

1. No better illustration of the way in which change in cultural values affects judges and law can be found than in Jacob's analysis of the postwar evolution of family law in the United States. See Jacob 1988.

2. From the text of the question (from the bottom of table 5.1) it might be assumed that the respondents were limited to only a single attribute that could be scored at "10." In fact, 30.6% of the respondents assigned no "10's"; 4.1% scored each of the responsibilities at "10." The average number of "10's" assigned is 3.9.

3. A strongly unidimensional structure emerged from this analysis, with eigenvalues of 5.64 and .85 for the first two factors extracted. Cronbach's alpha for the item set is .91, indicating very high reliability.

4. It is perhaps noteworthy that the JaS questions ask nothing about judicial campaign activity even though the survey was conducted in 2001. This is a testament to how rapidly the judicial landscape has changed.

5. To compare these Kentucky findings with similar questions in a national survey, see Gibson and Caldeira (2009a).

6. The eigenvalues of the first two extracted factors are 2.173 and .985.

7. I note that the correlations between the index of politicized judicial expectations and the responses to the relatively nonpolitical expectation are not quite as might be hypothesized: One might have expected them to be significantly negative in the sense that the antonym of the politicized model of judging is the legalistic model. The correlation between the index and the expectation that judges strictly follow the law is −.04, indicating no relationship whatsoever. The correlation of the index with the item on refusing to accept campaign contributions is .02. I understand this coefficient as suggesting that the idea of rejecting campaign contributions is a platitude, a symbolic value (like apple pie), that holds relatively little meaning for respondents. For instance, of those asserting that it is very important to refuse campaign contributions, 42.6% also said it is very important for judicial candidates to use campaign contributions to get their views on important issues out to the people. Questions about campaign contributions are most likely only useful when they force people to evaluate contributions in relationship to other, perhaps conflicting, values.

At the same time, however, the correlation of the index and the item on protecting people without power is .17, while the correlation with the item on respecting existing decisions is .22. These relationships are not easy to understand; but the most important conclusion is that, in the minds of the people of Kentucky, politicized judging is compatible with respecting existing decisions and is not incompatible with strictly following the law.

8. A substantial empirical literature exists regarding citizens' attitudes toward courts. For a recent example, see Gibson and Caldeira (2009a).

9. This correlation is based on measuring court attitudes at t_1, prior to the measurement of expectations. The identical set of questions was put to the respondents at t_2 (after the expectations questions) and at t_3. The correlation between expectations and support at t_2 is −.48; for support at t_3 and expectations, the coefficient is −.41. Irrespective of what index is used, support and expectations are strongly intercorrelated.

10. When the index is regressed on court knowledge at t_1, court knowledge at t_2, and candidate knowledge at t_2, all three predictors are significantly related to rejecting the politicized view of judging, with each of the regression coefficients achieving statistical significance. The cumulative effect of the three variables is an R^2 of .04 ($p < .000$).

11. The survey did not allocate many questions to exploring differences across institutions. We did, however, use a feeling thermometer to collect opinions toward the state legislature and the state supreme court. The correlation between holding politicized expectations of courts and the difference in the thermometer scores (a measure of the distinctiveness of judicial attitudes) is −.16: As politicized expectations increase, the two institutions are judged more similarly.

12. Bybee (2011) is undoubtedly correct when he refers to this view as a "half-law-half-politics understanding of the courts."

CHAPTER SIX

1. Legitimacy theory argues that courts must be able to persuade people to accept outcomes with which they strongly disagree, and most scholars acknowledge that legitimacy is a crucial component of that process. The relationship between perceptions of institutional legitimacy and willingness to accept unfavorable court decisions has been investigated in several contexts. See Gibson 1991, 2004; Gibson and Caldeira 1995, 2003; Gibson, Caldeira, and Spence 2003a, 2005.

2. See, e.g., Iyengar (2002, 697); Persily and Lammie (2004, 128).

3. Not much has been learned about campaigning and judicial legitimacy from research on campaign activity in other subfields of political science inasmuch as few of those studies address courts and none directly considers consequences such as perceived impartiality and institutional legitimacy (for a partial exception, focusing on trust in government, see Geer [2006], chapter 7). Lau et al. (1999; see also Lau, Sigelman, and Rovner 2007) conclude from a meta-analysis of the research findings that negative campaign ads have little effect, although they acknowledge that virtually no research examines the long-term implications of such ads (1999, 860), as in the consequences for institutional legitimacy. Thus, extant research is of only limited relevance for this inquiry into the effects of campaign activities on the legitimacy of courts. Note, however, that Hall and Bonneau (2011) have studied the effect of campaign activities (e.g., the use of attack ads) on rates of voting in state high court races and have discovered that attacks seem to mobilize, not discourage, voter turnout (i.e., attack ads are negatively related to roll off). This is a very important finding; future research may well wish to consider how turnout is related to institutional legitimacy.

4. Although scholars typically recognize the importance of state courts as makers of public policy, few studies of the legitimacy of these courts exists. See, e.g., Benesh 2006; Cann and Yates 2008; Gibson et al. 2011. For an excellent recent collection of essays on judicial elections, see Streb (2007).

5. Few analysts have considered the possible positive effects of campaigns and elections. The most important exception is Bonneau and Hall (2009), who argue that campaign spending provides voters more information about candidates, thereby increasing the number of voters who actually cast their ballots in judicial races (e.g., roll off is reduced). They further speculate that institutional legitimacy may be enhanced because elections create in voters "a greater sense of ownership in the outcomes of these races." See also Choi, Gulati, and Posner (2010) for some favorable views on the consequences of campaign expenditures.

6. The American people clearly prefer that their state judges be elected—see, e.g., Bonneau and Hall 2009. In light of this preference, it is reasonable that judicial elections might enhance court legitimacy. Elections satisfy the normative expectations of the constituents.

7. Few studies have seriously considered the expectations citizens hold of judges and courts. Notable exceptions include Baird's (2001) research on public attitudes toward the German Federal Constitutional Court. She shows that the nature of the expectations citizens hold of the FCC, and especially expectations of legalistic styles of decision making,

is related to the willingness to attribute legitimacy to the institution (see also Baird and Gangl 2006).

8. CMAG captures from the public airwaves all campaign ads and makes available the actual video, storyboards (television images and transcripts captured every few seconds), as well as analysis of the cost of the ads and their market penetration.

9. Furthermore, to assume citizens watched television only in their place of residence during the entire campaign season is almost certainly erroneous.

10. See http://www.judicialcampaignconduct.org/committees/Electronic%20Commit tee%20Files/KY%20misc/kjcchome.pdf (accessed May 16, 2011).

11. See http://www.loubar.org/JCCC/KJCCCHOME.HTM (accessed May 16, 2011). On Campaign Oversight Committees more generally, see Rottman (2007).

12. The order of presentation of the four name stimuli in this question was randomly varied. For the two foils, order made no difference for the percentage of respondents selecting the name (chi-square tests with the order of presentation indicator did not achieve statistical significance) for the female foil, but the order was significant for the male foil, with the respondents somewhat less likely to select the name when it was presented second and third. For the names of the actual candidates, responses to one name varied significantly by order but the other did not. For the test that was statistically significant, accurately selecting the name occurred slightly less frequently when the name was presented first and last. For the other name (the test that was not statistically significant), the name was selected least often when it was offered to the respondent as the third name. In light of the inconsistent results, and the weakness of the single observed difference, I have decided to ignore variation in the order of presentation in this analysis.

13. I computed an index of candidate awareness from these various questions. The index awards a score of 1 to the ability to recognize a candidate's name, subtracts .50 for each selection of a name used as a foil, and then adds .25 for each name that the respondent claims to recognize when told who the candidates are. The index varies from -1.00 to $+2.50$ and has a mean of 1.08 (and a standard deviation of .96). A total of 20.5% of the sample scored at the highest point on this scale. Index scores are moderately related to self-proclaimed attention to the judicial elections ($r = .21$).

14. Of those respondents interviewed at both t_1 and t_3, roughly two-thirds resided in one of the four media markets in which ads were broadcast.

15. Recall that judicial districts and media markets overlap and that respondents in districts in which no supreme court election was being held might well have seen ads pertinent to other judicial races.

16. Considerable cross-district variability is observed in the correlation between exposure to ads and the proximity of the interview to the election, with the correlations ranging from $-.18$ (Sixth District) to $+.13$ (Seventh District). This variability is difficult to understand, although it also indicates the need for a proximity control in the analysis below.

17. See their earlier work on measuring and analyzing institutional legitimacy—e.g., Gibson 1991, 2004; Gibson, Caldeira, and Baird 1998; Gibson and Caldeira 2003; Gibson, Caldeira, and Spence 2003a, 2003b, 2005.

18. For a cross-national perspective on the relative legitimacy of the US Supreme Court, see Gibson, Caldeira, and Baird (1998).

19. As CMAG reported a new ad being shown in a district, that ad was incorporated into the interview. Because the interview was always asking about the most recently shown ad (according to CMAG), and because the ads are district specific, the numbers of respondents viewing any given ad vary greatly and are in some instances quite small.

20. In analysis reported later in this chapter, I consider the question of the endogeneity of ad perceptions. This issue is best addressed once the structure of the data analysis is clear.

21. A very small number of the latter group—too few to analyze with any confidence—was presented with an attack ad. Since their responses differ from the remainder of the respondents who were presented with a promotional ad, they have been excluded from analysis. See also note 28 below.

22. As detailed further in appendix I, all of the findings considered in this section survive very extensive controls. Because few of those control variables are of much substantive interest, I have reported these results in the appendix.

23. As discussed further in appendix I, cross-sectional equations at t_1 and t_3 provide very strong ability to predict the variation in institutional support: at t_1, a well-specified model can account for 31% of the variance in institutional support; at t_3, the model explains 35% of the variance. This indicates that the measures of support attitudes contain a great deal of reliable variance (and concomitantly, that the error variance is relatively small). The relatively small amount of variance explained by the campaign perceptions reflects the fact that the dependent variable is change in support, that as a difference variable $(t_3 - t_1)$ a great deal of the reliable variance has in effect been allocated to the t_1 measure, that attitudes were reasonably stable from before to after the election, and that the independent variables no doubt include nontrivial measurement error.

24. This may be an explanation for the negative effect on US Supreme Court legitimacy of the Alito ad campaigns. For many citizens, the ads "crossed the line"—they violated the normative expectations held of the court and confirmation campaigns.

25. I acknowledge that one might reach somewhat different conclusions were one to include in these predicted score calculations the ad attributes that do not achieve statistical significance. My inclination is to accept the hypothesis test conclusion that these coefficients are indistinguishable from zero and therefore (implicitly) treat these coefficients as zero in calculating predicted scores. To treat these as nonzero and therefore to assign a *positive* influence to ad negativity among those observing ads during the election or a *positive* influence to unfairness among those hearing ads during the interview does not make a great deal of sense to me. On the basis of the coefficients in table 6.2, and the knowledge that all of the ad perceptions independent variables vary from 0 to 3, one can calculate any predicted value one wishes.

26. It was necessary to start the fieldwork before many ads had appeared in order to complete the t_2 interviews by the time of the election.

27. I should note in passing that the ad these respondents judged is hardly contentious. Perhaps some misunderstood the "Jailhouse Rock" comments, but this is the sort of ad

that belongs to historical judicial campaigns, not one of the "new style" type of ads. This finding is similar to that of Gibson et al. (2011), who found conventional endorsement ads just as damaging to judicial legitimacy as hard-core attack ads.

28. In fact the difference on this index between those read promote ads compared to those read attack ads is statistically significant ($p < .001$; $\eta = .21$).

29. To test further for the effects among those read an ad during the interview, I added those respondents exposed to an attack ad during the interview ($N = 40$) to a subset of respondents who observed no actual ads. Including a control for the type of ad shown, the following equation results:

Change in Institutional Support = .304 −.161 × Ad Assessment −.137
× Type of Ad Shown   (s.e. = .042)   (s.e. = .092)

The predicted scores for change in support range as follows (with the standard errors in parentheses):

Shown promotion ads	+.146 (.036)
Shown attack ad	−.065 (.091)
No churlish perceptions	+.296 (.052)
Complete churlish perceptions	−.213 (.094)

Among those scoring highest on the churlish ad perceptions index:

Shown promotion ads	−.179 (.089)
Shown attack ad	−.316 (.108)

This analysis supports the same conclusion as discussed in the text: Under most circumstances, churlish ads do not result in a negative net effect of the campaign on support for the court. However, under the most extreme circumstances—which are rare—the net effect can be negative. In many respects, this is similar to my finding in chapter 3 that most ads are not legitimacy threatening, but in the extreme, ads can indeed "cross a line" and result in harm to the legitimacy of courts.

30. Note that when I estimate an equation including perceptions of objectionable ads, the type of ads judged, and the interaction of type of ad with ad perceptions, neither the dummy variable for ad type nor the interaction term for type and ratings achieves statistical significance. This indicates that the difference between the effect of the ratings of the real ads and the ad presented during the interview is not statistically significant (the difference is not distinguishable from zero). I have decided to include a dummy variable for ad types in the fully specified model analyzed below because, on their faces, the bivariate correlations between ad ratings and institutional support seem to differ somewhat by type of ad judgments, even if the difference is not statistically significant.

31. See Kam and Franzese (2007) on how to analyze interaction hypotheses.

32. Note that additional support for this last conclusion is also provided by the findings (in table 6.2) that change in support is related to the normative judgments of unfairness and negativity. As normative conclusions, these ad judgments do not require conditional analysis to be modeled correctly.

CHAPTER SEVEN

1. Note that Gibson et al. (2011) report that judicial elections in Pennsylvania seem also to enhance the legitimacy of the Pennsylvania Supreme Court.

2. The exception to this conjecture, however, is retention elections, which may be viewed by many as sham elections and which therefore may possess little legitimizing capacity.

3. Of course, with different assumptions about ideological preferences, such an argument could easily be recast by simply reversing the words "liberal" and "conservative."

4. Recall that Gibson and Caldeira (2009a) discovered a negative effect of the ad campaigns associated with the Alito nomination on the institutional legitimacy of the US Supreme Court. But it must also be noted that nominations to the court are not elections and therefore that the court's legitimacy does not automatically profit from the selection process, as the state high courts seem to.

5. I should note as well that, regarding empirical findings on the issue of whether recusals can rehabilitate judges who experience conflicts of interest from campaign contributions, West Virginia survey results (Gibson and Caldeira 2012) have been replicated through a TESS national sample (Gibson and Caldeira 2010). I make no claim that Kentucky and West Virginia are the same (nor that they are not the same), but just as with my Kentucky/national findings from chapter 2, these two West Virginia papers point to nothing distinctive about West Virginian's perceptions and evaluations of their courts.

6. In the most comprehensive analysis reported to date, Hall and Bonneau (2011) examine the factors that affected voting in state high court elections during the period from 2002 to 2006. They discovered that in the seven states using district constituencies, "district elections increase ballot roll-off, by about 5%" (2011, 19). However, in one of their equations reported in table 2 (model 3), the coefficient for districts is not statistically significant, so perhaps the proper conclusion about the use of districts is that its effect on voting is small to insignificant. At the same time, however, their analysis shows a consistent and more substantial negative effect of nonpartisan elections on voting rates.

7. It is not clear to me that earlier research on this topic reaches unequivocal conclusions. Let me assume for a moment, for example, that a trial judge's sentences become more severe as an election approaches. The empirical fact is that her sentences differ depending upon whether her reelection period is close by or not.

It is easy to focus on the sentences becoming more severe and to condemn this as judicial or prosecutorial "pandering." But what if the more lenient sentences issued out of view from the electorate were more lenient solely because prosecutors and judges would do virtually anything to avoid the effort of going to trial and therefore they offer excessively lenient sentences in their plea bargains? That is, most seem to assume that more *severe* sentences are due to illicit factors, but I believe an argument can be made that the more *lenient* sentences might be due to illicit factors. Indeed, one might applaud the findings of differing sentence patterns by saying that judges and prosecutors can get away with murder when not scrutinized, and therefore that scrutiny brings their behaviors back into alignment with the law.

The same could be said for a judge who fails to reverse more death penalties as an election approaches. Might it be possible that outside the accountability of the election period, the judge believes he can implement his own anti–death penalty ideology in his decisions, but, as the election draws near, he fears getting caught by his constituents? Some scholars clearly believe that California's Chief Justice Rose Bird voted 58 times in 58 cases to overturn death penalty sentences not because she was strictly adhering to the rule of law, but rather because of her strong ideological beliefs about the wrongness of the death penalty. The point these illustrations make is simple—a difference in behavior between the electoral season and the off-season is not by itself evidence to condemn judicial behavior and to justify the elimination of the system of voting for judges (or prosecutors).

8. There are many directions such inquiry might take, including following up on the very important finding of Hall and Bonneau (2011, 18) that participation in elections for state high judges is enhanced by "campaign spending, narrowly decided races, broad interpretations of *White*, experience with competitive elections, and partisan ballots."

9. Some interest groups (e.g., the Brennan Center) are addressing the issue of conflicts of interest and perceptions of partiality with efforts to strengthen recusal norms and perhaps even with policies mandating recusals under certain circumstances. Many of the proposals lack details, but the theory seems to go as follows. Campaign contributions create conflicts of interest (or the appearance thereof) with individual judges; if those judges who are conflicted stand aside in individual cases, citizens will judge the case outcomes as impartial; and such recusals have few ancillary consequences for courts themselves. On administrative or efficiency grounds, no one likes recusals, but many see them as a palliative for the corrosive effects of campaign contributions on institutional loyalty. Unfortunately, very little is known about how citizens judge judicial impartiality and whether schemes such as recusals can rescue courts from illegitimacy. For an initial inquiry into whether recusals rehabilitate judicial legitimacy, see Gibson and Caldeira (2012).

APPENDIX B

1. The method is that devised by Rizzo, Brick, and Park (2004).

2. In all of this analysis, I have used unweighted data.

APPENDIX D

1. For a complete discussion of institutional loyalty, see chapter 4.

APPENDIX H

1. Because some pretest questions were not included in the final instrument, the question numbering is not necessarily sequential.

2. As noted, different ads were used at different points in the fieldwork. I report here the ad that was most commonly used.

APPENDIX I

1. Moreover, in a lagged equation in which t_3 support is the dependent variable and a t_1 control is included, I find that (a) a very strong relationship exists between court support at the two points in time, (b) nonetheless, the addition of the ad perception variable to

the lagged equation increases the explained variance by 3.7%, which is quite significant ($p < .001$), and (c) the impact of ad perceptions remains quite significant ($p < .001$) even when all of the control variables are then added. Adding the control variables increases the explained variance by a highly significant 5.6%, but the regression coefficient for ad perceptions declines only very slightly (from $-.200$ [s.e. $= .025$] to $-.164$ [s.e. $= .025$]). These findings contribute to confidence in the conclusion that perceptions of ad churlishness do indeed subtract from institutional legitimacy.

REFERENCES

American Association for Public Opinion Research. 2000. *Standard Definitions: Final Dispositions of Case Codes and Outcome Rates for Surveys.* Ann Arbor, MI: AAPOR.

Ansolabehere, Stephen, and Shanto Iyengar. 1995. *Going Negative: How Political Advertisements Shrink and Polarize the Electorate.* New York: Free Press.

Ansolabehere, Stephen D., Shanto Iyengar, and Adam Simon. 1999. "Replicating Experiments Using Aggregate and Survey Data: The Case of Negative Advertising and Turnout." *American Political Science Review* 93, no. 4 (December): 901–9.

Aronson, Elliot, Phoebe C. Ellsworth, J. Merrill Carlsmith, and Marti Hope Gonzales. 1990. *Methods of Research in Social Psychology.* 2nd ed. New York: McGraw-Hill Publishing Company.

Baird, Vanessa A. 2001. "Building Institutional Legitimacy: The Role of Procedural Justice." *Political Research Quarterly* 54, no. 2 (June): 333–54.

Baird, Vanessa A., and Amy Gangl. 2006. "Shattering the Myth of Legality: The Impact of the Media's Framing of Supreme Court Procedures on Perceptions of Fairness." *Political Psychology* 27, no. 4: 597–614.

Banducci, Susan A., and Jeffrey A. Karp. 2003. "How Elections Change the Way Citizens View the Political System: Campaigns, Media Effects and Electoral Outcomes in Comparative Perspective." *British Journal of Political Science* 33 (July): 443–67.

Banner, Stephen. 1988. "Disqualifying Elected Judges from Cases Involving Campaign Contributors." *Stanford Law Review* 40: 449–90.

Barnhizer, David. 2001. "'On the Make': Campaign Funding and the Corrupting of the American Judiciary." *Catholic University Law Review* 50, no. 2 (Winter): 361–427.

Baum, Lawrence. 1988–89. "Voters' Information in Judicial Contests: The 1986 Contests for the Ohio Supreme Court." *Kentucky Law Journal* 77: 645–70.

———. 2003. "Judicial Elections and Judicial Independence: The Voter's Perspective." In "Perspectives on Judicial Independence," special issue, *Ohio State Law Journal* 64: 13–41.

Baum, Lawrence, and Marie Hojnacki. 1992. "Choosing Judicial Candidates: How Voters Explain Their Decisions." *Judicature* 75: 300–9.

Benesh, Sara C. 2006. "Understanding Public Confidence in American Courts." *Journal of Politics* 68, no. 3 (August): 697–707.

Benesh, Sara C., Nancy Scherer, and Amy Steigerwalt. 2009. "Public Perceptions of the Lower Federal Courts." Paper presented at the 2009 Annual Meeting of the Midwest Political Science Association, Chicago.

Bonneau, Chris W. 2004. "Patterns of Campaign Spending and Electoral Competition in State Supreme Court Elections." *Justice System Journal* 25: 21–38.

———. 2005. "What Price Justice(s)? Understanding Campaign Spending in State Supreme Court Elections." *State Politics and Policy Quarterly* 5, no. 2 (Summer): 107–25.

Bonneau, Chris W., and Melinda Gann Hall. 2009. *In Defense of Judicial Elections*. New York: Routledge.

Bopp, James, Jr., and Josiah Neeley. 2008. "How Not to Reform Judicial Elections: Davis, White, and the Future of Judicial Campaign Financing." *Denver Law Review* 68: 195–233.

Bopp, James, Jr., and Anita Y. Woudenberg. 2007a. "An Announce Clause by Any Other Name: The Unconstitutionality of Disciplining Judges Who Fail to Disqualify Themselves for Exercising Their Freedom to Speak." *Drake Law Review* 55: 723–61.

———. 2007b. "To Speak or Not to Speak: Unconstitutional Regulation in the Wake of *White*." *Justice System Journal* 28, no. 3: 329–34.

Brace, Paul, and Brent D. Boyea. 2008. "State Public Opinion, the Death Penalty, and the Practice of Electing Judges." *American Journal of Political Science* 52, no. 2 (April): 360–72.

Brace, Paul, Melinda Gann Hall, and Laura Langer. 1999. "Judicial Choice and the Politics of Abortion: Institutions, Context, and the Autonomy of Courts." *Albany Law Review* 62, no. 4: 1265–1304.

Brader, Ted. 2006. *Campaigning for Hearts and Minds: How Emotional Appeals in Political Ads Work*. Chicago: University of Chicago Press.

Brandenburg, Bert, and Roy A. Schotland. 2008. "Keeping Courts Impartial amid Changing Judicial Elections." *Dædalus* 137, no. 4 (Fall): 102–9.

Brennan Center for Justice. 2006. "Alabama's Supreme Court Primary Campaigns Highlight Radical Transformation of State Judicial Elections," press release, June 2.

Brooks, Deborah Jordan. 2006. "The Resilient Voter: Moving toward Closure in the Debate over Negative Campaigning and Turnout." *Journal of Politics* 68, no. 3 (August): 684–96.

Bybee, Keith J. 2011. "The Rule of Law Is Dead! Long Live the Rule of Law!" In *What's Law Got To Do With It? What Judges Do, Why They Do It, and What's at Stake*, edited by Charles Gardner Geyh, 306–27. Stanford, CA: Stanford University Press.

Caldarone, Richard P., Brandice Canes-Wrone, and Tom S. Clark. 2009. "Partisan Labels and Democratic Accountability: An Analysis of State Supreme Court Abortion Decisions." *Journal of Politics* 71, no. 2 (April): 560–73.

Caldeira, Gregory A. 1986. "Neither the Purse nor the Sword: Dynamics of Confidence in the U.S. Supreme Court." *American Political Science Review* 80 (December): 1209–26.

———. 1987. "Public Opinion and the U.S. Supreme Court: FDR's Court-Packing Plan." *American Political Science Review* 81, no. 4 (November): 1139–53.

Caldeira, Gregory A., and James L. Gibson. 1992. "The Etiology of Public Support for the Supreme Court." *American Journal of Political Science* 36, no. 3 (August): 635–64.

———. 1995. "The Legitimacy of the Court of Justice in the European Union: Models of Institutional Support." *American Political Science Review* 89, no 2 (June): 356–76.

Cann, Damon M. 2002. "Campaign Contributions and Judicial Behavior." *American Review of Politics* 23 (Fall): 261–74.

Cann, Damon M., and Jeff Yates. 2008. "Homegrown Institutional Legitimacy: Assessing

Citizens' Diffuse Support for State Courts." *American Politics Research* 36, no. 2: 297–329.

Caufield, Rachel Paine. 2005. "In the Wake of White: How States Are Responding to *Republican Party of Minnesota v. White* and How Judicial Elections Are Changing."*Akron Law Review* 38: 625–47.

———. 2007. "Judicial Elections: Today's Trends and Tomorrow's Forecast." *Judges' Journal* 46 (Winter): 6–11.

Champagne, Anthony. 1986. "Judicial Selection: What Fits Texas?" *Southwestern Law Journal* 40: 53–117.

———. 1988. "Judicial Reform in Texas." *Judicature* 72: 146–59.

Cheek, Kyle, and Anthony Champagne. 2004. *Judicial Politics in Texas: Partisanship, Money, and Politics in State Courts.* New York: Peter Lang Publishing.

Choi, Stephen, Mitu Gulati, and Eric Posner. 2010. "Professionals or Politicians: The Uncertain Empirical Case for an Elected Rather Than Appointed Judiciary." *Journal of Law, Economics & Organization* 26, no. 2: 290–336.

Clark, Tom S. 2011. *The Limits of Judicial Independence.* New York: Cambridge University Press.

Cohen, Jacob, Patricia Cohen, Stephen G. West, and Leona S. Aiken. 2003. *Applied Multiple Regression/Correlation Analysis for the Behavioral Sciences.* 3rd ed. Mahwah, NJ: Lawrence Erlbaum Associates.

Coleman, John J., and Paul F. Manna. 2000. "Congressional Campaign Spending and the Quality of Democracy." *Journal of Politics* 62 (August): 757–89.

Cook, Thomas D., and Donald T. Campbell. 1979. *Quasi-Experimentation: Design and Analysis Issues for Field Settings.* Chicago: Rand McNally.

Cross, Al, and William H. Fortune. 2007. "Kentucky 2006 Judicial Elections." *Drake Law Review* 55 (Spring): 637–51.

Dahl, Robert A. 1971. *Polyarchy.* New Haven, CT: Yale University Press.

Dimino, Michael R. 2003. "Pay No Attention to That Man behind the Robe: Judicial Elections, the First Amendment, and Judges as Politicians." *Yale Law and Policy Review* 21 (Spring): 301–82.

Dubois, Philip L. 1986. "Penny for Your Thoughts? Campaign Spending in California Trial Court Elections, 1976–1982." *Western Political Quarterly* 38 (June): 265–84.

Duch, Raymond M., and Harvey D. Palmer. 2004. "It's Not Whether You Win or Lose, but How You Play the Game: Self-Interest, Social Justice, and Mass Attitudes toward Market Transition." *American Political Science Review* 98, no. 3 (August): 437–52.

Easton, David. 1965. *A Systems Analysis of Political Life.* New York: John Wiley & Son.

Echeverria, John D. 2001. "Changing the Rules by Changing the Players: The Environmental Issue in State Judicial Elections." *New York University Environmental Law Journal* 9: 217–303.

Fagan, R. W. 1981. "Public Support for the Courts: An Explanation of Alternative Explanations." *Journal of Criminal Justice* 9, no. 6: 403–17.

Farnsworth, Ward. 2004. "The Regulation of Turnover on the Supreme Court." Public

Law & Legal Theory, Working Paper No. 04-18, Boston University School of Law, Boston.

Finkel, Steven, and John Geer. 1998. "A Spot Check: Casting Doubt on the Demobilizing Effect of Attack Advertising." *American Journal of Political Science* 42 (April): 573-95.

Flanagan, Timothy, Edmund McGarrell, and Edward Brown. 1985. "Public Perceptions of the Criminal Courts: The Role of Demographic and Related Attitudinal Variables." *Journal of Research in Crime and Delinquency* 22, no. 1: 66-82.

Fletcher, Joseph F., and Paul Howe. 2000. "Canadian Attitudes toward the Charter and the Courts in Comparative Perspective." *Choices* 6 (May): 4-29.

Franklin, Charles H., and Liane C. Kosaki. 1989. "Republican Schoolmaster: The U.S. Supreme Court, Public Opinion, and Abortion." *American Political Science Review* 83 (September): 751-71.

Franz, Michael M., Paul B. Freedman, Kenneth M. Goldstein, and Travis N. Ridout. 2008. *Campaign Advertising and American Democracy*. Philadelphia: Temple University Press.

Freedman, Paul B., Michael Franz, and Kenneth M. Goldstein. 2004. "Campaign Advertising and Democratic Citizenship." *American Journal of Political Science* 48, no. 4 (October): 723-41.

Friedland, Michelle T. 2004. "Disqualification or Suppression: Due Process and the Response to Judicial Campaign Speech." *Columbia Law Review* 104 (April): 563-632.

Friedman, Barry. 2005. "The Politics of Judicial Review." *Texas Law Review* 84, no. 2 (December): 257-337.

Friedman, Lawrence M. 1998. *American Law: An Introduction*. Rev. ed. New York: W. W. Norton.

Geer, John G. 2006. *In Defense of Negativity: Attack Ads in Presidential Campaigns*. Chicago: University of Chicago Press.

Geyh, Charles Gardner. 2003. "Perspectives on Judicial Independence: Why Judicial Elections Stink." *Ohio State Law Journal* 64: 43-79.

———. 2006. *When Courts & Congress Collide: The Struggle for Control of America's Judicial System*. Ann Arbor, MI: University of Michigan Press.

Gibson, James L. 1991. "Institutional Legitimacy, Procedural Justice, and Compliance with Supreme Court Decisions: A Question of Causality." *Law and Society Review* 25: 631-35.

———. 1995. "The Resilience of Mass Support for Democratic Institutions and Processes in the Nascent Russian and Ukrainian Democracies." In *Political Culture and Civil Society in Russia and the New States of Eurasia*, edited by Vladimir Tismaneanu, 53-111. Armonk, NY: M. E. Sharp.

———. 1997. "Expectancy Theory and Institutional Decision Making: Thinking about How Norms Constrain Choices." Paper presented at the Second Annual Conference on the Scientific Study of Judicial Politics, Emory University, Atlanta, November 14-16.

———. 2002. "Truth, Justice, and Reconciliation: Judging the Fairness of Amnesty in South Africa." *American Journal of Political Science* 46, no. 3 (July): 540-56.

———. 2004. *Overcoming Apartheid: Can Truth Reconcile a Divided Nation?* New York: Russell Sage Foundation.

———. 2007. "The Legitimacy of the U.S. Supreme Court in a Polarized Polity." *Journal of Empirical Legal Studies* 4, no. 3 (November): 507–38.

———. 2008a. "Judicial Institutions." In *The Oxford Handbook of Political Institutions*, edited by R. A. W. Rhodes, Sarah A. Binder, and Bert A. Rockman, 514–34. New York: Oxford University Press.

———. 2008b. "The Evolving Legitimacy of the South African Constitutional Court." In *Justice and Reconciliation in Post-Apartheid South Africa*, edited by François du Bois and Antje du Bois-Pedain, 229–66. New York: Cambridge University Press.

———. 2010. "Public Images and Understandings of Courts." In *The Oxford Handbook of Empirical Legal Research*, edited by Peter Cane and Herbert M. Kritzer, 828–53. Oxford: Oxford University Press.

———. 2011. "A Note of Caution about the Meaning of 'The Supreme Court can usually be trusted . . . .'" *Law & Courts: Newsletter of the Law & Courts Section of the American Political Science Association* 21 no. (Fall): 10–16.

Gibson, James L., and Gregory A. Caldeira. 1992. "Blacks and the United States Supreme Court: Models of Diffuse Support." *Journal of Politics* 54, no. 4 (November): 1120–45.

———. 1995. "The Legitimacy of Transnational Legal Institutions: Compliance, Support, and the European Court of Justice." *American Journal of Political Science* 39, no. 2 (May): 459–89.

———. 1998. "Changes in the Legitimacy of the European Court of Justice: A Post-Maastricht Analysis." *British Journal of Political Science* 28, no. 1 (January): 63–91.

———. 2003. "Defenders of Democracy? Legitimacy, Popular Acceptance, and the South African Constitutional Court." *Journal of Politics* 65, no. 1 (February): 1–30.

———. 2009a. *Citizens, Courts, and Confirmations: Positivity Theory and the Judgments of the American People.* Princeton, NJ: Princeton University Press.

———. 2009b. "Knowing the Supreme Court? A Reconsideration of Public Ignorance of the High Court." *Journal of Politics* 71, no. 2 (April): 429–41.

———. 2010. "Judicial Impartiality, Campaign Contributions, and Recusals: Results from a National Survey." Paper delivered at the Fifth Annual Conference on Empirical Legal Studies, Yale Law School, November.

———. 2011. "Has Legal Realism Damaged the Legitimacy of the U.S. Supreme Court?" *Law and Society Review* 45, no. 1: 195–219.

———. 2012. "Campaign Support, Conflicts of Interest, and Judicial Impartiality: Can the Legitimacy of Courts Be Rescued by Recusals?" *Journal of Politics* 74, no1. (January): 1–17.

Gibson, James L., Gregory A. Caldeira, and Vanessa Baird. 1998. "On the Legitimacy of National High Courts." *American Political Science Review* 92, no. 2 (June): 343–58.

Gibson, James L., Gregory A. Caldeira, and Lester Kenyatta Spence. 2002. "The Role of Theory in Experimental Design: Experiments without Randomization." In "Experimental Methods in Political Science," special issue, *Political Analysis* 10, no. 4 (Autumn): 362–75.

———. 2003a. "The Supreme Court and the U.S. Presidential Election of 2000: Wounds, Self-Inflicted or Otherwise?" *British Journal of Political Science* 33, no. 4 (October): 535–56.

———. 2003b. "Measuring Attitudes toward the United States Supreme Court." *American Journal of Political Science* 47, no. 3 (April): 354–67.

———. 2005. "Why Do People Accept Public Policies They Oppose? Testing Legitimacy Theory with a Survey-Based Experiment." *Political Research Quarterly* 58 (June): 187–201.

Gibson, James L., Jeffrey A. Gottfried, Michael X. Delli Carpini, and Kathleen Hall Jamieson. 2011. "The Effects of Judicial Campaign Activity on the Legitimacy of Courts: A Survey-Based Experiment." *Political Research Quarterly* 64, (September): 545–58.

Gibson, James L., and Amanda Gouws. 1999. "Truth and Reconciliation in South Africa: Attributions of Blame and the Struggle over Apartheid." *American Political Science Review* 93, no. 3 (September): 501–17.

———. 2001. "Making Tolerance Judgments: The Effects of Context, Local and National." *Journal of Politics* 63, no. 4 (November): 1067–90.

Goldberg, Deborah, Craig Holman, and Samantha Sanchez. 2002. *The New Politics of Judicial Elections: How 2000 Was a Watershed Year for Big Money, Special Interest Pressure, and TV Advertising in State Supreme Court Campaigns.* Washington, DC: Justice at Stake Campaign (Brennan Center for Justice at NYU School of Law). http://www.justiceatstake.org/files/JASMoneyReport.pdf (accessed May 1, 2001).

Goldberg, Deborah, Sarah Samis, Edwin Bender, and Rachel Weiss. 2005. *The New Politics of Judicial Elections 2004: How Special Interest Pressure on Our Courts Has Reached a "Tipping Point"—and How to Keep Our Courts Fair and Impartial.* Washington, DC: Justice at Stake Campaign (Brennan Center for Justice at New York University School of Law).

Grosskopf, Anke, and Jeffrey J. Mondak. 1998. "Do Attitudes toward Specific Supreme Court Decisions Matter? The Impact of Webster and *Texas v. Johnson* on Public Confidence in the Supreme Court." *Political Research Quarterly* 51, no. 3 (September): 633–54.

Hall, Melinda Gann. 1992. "Electoral Politics and Strategic Voting in State Supreme Courts." *Journal of Politics* 54, no. 2 (May): 427–46.

———. 2001. "State Supreme Courts in American Democracy: Probing the Myths of Judicial Reform." *American Political Science Review* 95, no. 2 (June): 315–30.

Hall, Melinda Gann, and Chris W. Bonneau. 2011. "Attack Advertising, the White Decision, and Voter Participation in State Supreme Court Elections." Unpublished paper.

Hamilton, V. Lee, and Joseph Sanders. 1992. *Everyday Justice: Responsibility and the Individual in Japan and the United States.* New Haven, CT: Yale University Press.

Hansen, Mark. 1991. "The High Cost of Judging." *ABA Journal* 77: 44–48.

Hasen, Richard L. 2007. "First Amendment Limits on Regulating Judicial Campaigns."

In *Running for Judge: The Rising Political, Financial, and Legal Stakes of Judicial Elections*, edited by Matthew J. Streb, 15–33. New York: New York University Press.

Heagarty, J. Christopher. 2003. "Public Opinion and an Elected Judiciary: New Avenues for Reform." *Willamette Law Review* 39, no. 4 (Fall): 1287–1311.

Hibbing, John R., and Elizabeth Theiss-Morse. 2001. "Process Preferences and American Politics: What the People Want Government to Be." *American Political Science Review* 95, no. 1 (March): 145–53.

———. 2002. *Stealth Democracy: Americans' Beliefs about How Government Should Work.* New York: Cambridge University Press.

Hirsch, Matthew. 2006. "Swing Voter's Lament: At Least One Case Still Bugs O'Connor." Law.com, November 8, 2006. http://www.law.com/jsp/law/LawArticleFriendly.jsp?id=1162893919695 (accessed May 1, 2011).

Hoekstra, Valerie J. 1995. "The Supreme Court and Opinion Change: An Experimental Study of the Court's Ability to Change Opinion." *American Politics Quarterly* 23, no. 1 (January): 109–29.

———. 2000. "The Supreme Court and Local Public Opinion." *American Political Science Review* 94, no. 1 (March): 89–100.

———. 2003. *Public Reaction to Supreme Court Decisions.* New York: Cambridge University Press.

Hojnacki, Marie, and Lawrence Baum. 1992. "'New-Style' Judicial Campaigns and Voters: Economic Issues and Union Members in Ohio." *Western Political Quarterly* 45, no. 4 (December): 921–48.

Holbrook, Allyson L., Jon A. Krosnick, and Alison M. Pfent. 2007. "Response Rates in Surveys by the News Media and Government Contractor Survey Research Firms." In *Advances in Telephone Survey Methodology*, edited by James Lepkowski, N. Clyde Tucker, J. Michael Brick, Edith D. de Leeuw, Lilli Japec, Paul J. Lavrakas, Michael W. Link, and Roberta L. Sangster. New York: Wiley.

Huber, Gregory A., and Sanford G. Gordon. 2004. "Accountability and Coercion: Is Justice Blind When It Runs for Office?" *American Journal of Political Science* 48, no. 2 (April): 247–63.

Iyengar, Shanto. 2002. "The Effects of Media-Based Campaigns on Candidate and Voter Behavior: Implications for Judicial Elections." *Indiana Law Review* 35: 691–99.

Jacob, Herbert. 1988. *Silent Revolution: The Transformation of Divorce Law in the United States.* Chicago: University of Chicago Press.

Jackson, Donald W., and James W. Riddlesperger Jr. 1991. "Money and Politics in Judicial Elections: The 1988 Election of the Chief Justice of the Texas Supreme Court." *Judicature* 74 (December–January): 184–89.

Jamieson, Kathleen Hall, and Bruce W. Hardy. 2008. "Will Ignorance and Partisan Election of Judges Undermine Public Trust in the Judiciary?" *Dædalus* 137, no. 4 (Fall): 11–15.

Jamieson, Kathleen Hall, and Michael Hennessy. 2007. "Public Understanding of and Support for the Courts: Survey Results." *Georgetown Law Journal* 95, no. 4 (April): 899–902.

Johnson, Rick A., 2003. "Judicial Campaign Speech in Kentucky after *Republican Party of Minnesota* v *White*." *Northern Kentucky Law Review* 30, no. 3: 347–414.

Justice at Stake Campaign. 2001. "Justice at Stake Frequency Questionnaire." http://www.justiceatstake.org/media/cms/JASNationalSurveyResults_6F537F99272D4.pdf (accessed January 3, 2012).

———. 2004. "2004 State Supreme Court Election Overview," press release, November 9.

Kam, Cindy D., and Robert J. Franzese Jr. 2007. *Modeling and Interpreting Interactive Hypotheses in Regression Analysis*. Ann Arbor: University of Michigan Press.

Kelleher, Christine A., and Jennifer Wolak. 2008. "Explaining Public Confidence in the Branches of State Government." *Political Research Quarterly* 60, no. 4 (December): 707–21.

Kimball, David C., and Samuel C. Patterson. 1997. "Living Up to Expectations: Public Attitudes toward Congress." *Journal of Politics* 59, no. 3 (August): 701–28.

Kinder, Donald R., and Thomas R. Palfrey, eds. 1993. *Experimental Foundations of Political Science*. Ann Arbor: University of Michigan Press.

Kramer, Larry D. 2004. *The People Themselves: Popular Constitutionalism and Judicial Review*. New York: Oxford University Press.

Kritzer, Herbert M. 2001. "The Impact of *Bush v. Gore* on Public Perceptions and Knowledge of the Supreme Court." *Judicature* 85, no. 1 (July–August): 32–38.

———. 2005. "The American Public's Assessment of the Rehnquist Court." *Judicature* 89, no. 3 (November–December): 168–76.

———. 2007. "Law Is the Mere Continuation of Politics by Different Means: American Judicial Selection in the Twenty-First Century." *DePaul Law Review* 56, no. 2 (Winter): 423–67.

Kritzer, Herbert M., and John Voelker. 1998. "Familiarity Breeds Respect: How Wisconsin Citizens View Their Courts." *Judicature* 82 (September–October): 58–64.

Lau, Richard R., and Gerald M. Pomper. 2004. *Negative Campaigning: An Analysis of U.S. Senate Elections*. Lanham, MD: Rowman & Littlefield Publishers, Inc.

Lau, Richard R., Lee Sigelman, Caroline Heldman, and Paul Babbitt. 1999. "The Effects of Negative Political Advertisements: A Meta-Analytic Assessment." *American Political Science Review* 93, no. 4 (December): 851–75.

Lau, Richard R., Lee Sigelman, and Ivy Brown Rovner. 2007. "The Effects of Negative Political Campaigns: A Meta-Analytic Reassessment." *Journal of Politics* 69, no. 4 (November): 1176–1209.

Lehne, R., and J. Reynolds. 1978. "The Impact of Judicial Activism on Public Opinion." *American Journal of Political Science* 22: 896–904.

Liptak, Adam. 2010. "Former Justice O'Connor Sees Ill in Election Finance Ruling." *New York Times*, January 27, A17.

Mark, David. 2006. *Going Dirty: The Art of Negative Campaigning*. Lanham, MD: Rowman & Littlefield Publishers, Inc.

Markovits, Inga. 1995. *Imperfect Justice: An East-West German Diary*. New York: Oxford University Press.

Marshall, Thomas. 1989. *Public Opinion and the Supreme Court*. New York: Longman.

Mate, Manoj, and Matthew Wright. 2006. "Bush v. Gore and the Micro-Foundations of Public Support for the Supreme Court." Paper presented at the Annual Meeting of the American Political Science Association, Philadelphia, September 2.

McDermott, Monika L. 1997. "Voting Cues in Low-Information Elections: Candidate Gender as a Social Information Variable in Contemporary United States Elections." *American Journal of Political Science* 41 (January): 270–83.

McGuire, Kevin T. 2004. "The Institutionalization of the U.S. Supreme Court." *Political Analysis* 12 (Spring): 128–42.

Mendelberg, Tali. 2001. *The Race Card: Campaign Strategy, Implicit Messages, and the Norm of Equality.* Princeton, NJ: Princeton University Press.

Mondak, Jeffery J. 1993. "Public Opinion and Heuristic Processing of Source Cues." *Political Behavior* 15, no. 2 (June): 167–92.

Mondak, Jeffery J., and Shannon Ishiyama Smithey. 1997. "The Dynamics of Public Support for the Supreme Court." *Journal of Politics* 59 (November): 1114–42.

Murphy, Walter F., and Joseph Tanenhaus. 1990. "Publicity, Public Opinion, and the Court." *Northwestern University Law Review* 84: 985–1023.

Mutz, Diana C., and Byron Reeves. 2005. "The New Videomalaise: Effects of Televised Incivility on Political Trust." *American Political Science Review* 99 (February): 1–15.

Nicholson, Stephen P., and Robert M. Howard. 2003. "Framing Support for the Supreme Court in the Aftermath of *Bush v. Gore.*" *Journal of Politics* 65, no. 3 (August): 676–95.

Note. 2011. "Constitutional Law—First Amendment—Seventh Circuit Upholds Endorsement and Personal Solicitation Clauses of Wisconsin Code of Judicial Conduct—*Siefert v. Alexander*, 608 F.3d 974 (7th Cir. 2010)." *Harvard Law Review* 124: 1090–97.

Olson, Susan, and David Huth. 1998. "Explaining Public Attitudes toward Local Courts." *Justice System Journal* 20, no. 1: 41–61.

Overby, L. Marvin, Robert Brown, John Bruce, Charles Smith, and John Winkle. 2004. "Justice in Black and White: Race, Perceptions of Fairness, and Diffuse Support for the Judicial System in a Southern State." *Justice System Journal* 25, no. 2: 159–81.

Patterson, Samuel C., Randall B. Ripley, and Stephen V. Quinlan. 1992. "Citizens' Orientations toward Legislatures: Congress and the State Legislature." *Western Political Quarterly* 45: 315–38.

Persily, Nathaniel, and Kelli Lammie. 2004. "Perceptions of Corruption and Campaign Finance: When Public Opinion Determines Constitutional Law." *University of Pennsylvania Law Review* 153 (June): 119–80.

Pozen, David E. 2008. "The Irony of Judicial Elections." *Columbia Law Review* 108, no. 2 (March): 265–330.

Price, Vincent, and Anca Romantan. 2004. "Confidence in Institutions, Before, During, and After 'Indecision 2000.'" *Journal of Politics* 66, no. 3 (August): 939–56.

Primo, David M. 2002. "Public Opinion and Campaign Finance: Reformers versus Reality." *Independent Review* 7, no. 2 (Fall): 207–19.

Prior, Markus, and Arthur Lupia. 2008. "Money, Time, and Political Knowledge:

Distinguishing Quick Recall and Political Learning Skills." *American Journal of Political Science* 52, no. 1: 169–83.

Rahn, Wendy M., John Brehm, and Neil Carlson. 1999. "National Elections as Institutions for Generating Social Capital." In *Civic Engagement in American Democracy*, edited by Theda Skocpol and Morris P. Fiorina, 111–60. Washington, DC: Brookings Institution Press.

Rizzo, Louis, J. Michael Brick, and Inho Park. 2004. "A Minimally Intrusive Method for Sampling Persons in Random Digit Dial Surveys." *Public Opinion Quarterly* 68, no. 2: 267–74.

Robinson, Paul H., and John M. Darley. 1998. "Objectivist versus Subjectivist Views of Criminality: A Study of the Role of Social Science in Criminal Law Theory." *Oxford Journal of Legal Studies* 18, no. 3 (Autumn): 409–47.

Rottman, David B. 2007. "Campaign Oversight Committees and the Challenge of Perpetuating Ethical Judicial Elections." *Justice System Journal* 28 (January): 358–70.

Sample, James, Lauren Jones, and Rachel Weiss. 2007. *The New Politics of Judicial Elections 2006: How 2006 Was the Most Threatening Year Yet to the Fairness and Impartiality of Our Courts—and How Americans are Fighting Back*. Washington, DC: Justice at Stake Campaign.

Schotland, Roy A. 1985. "Elective Judges' Campaign Financing: Are State Judges' Robes the Emperor's Clothes of American Democracy?" *Journal of Law and Politics* 2: 57–167.

———. 2001. "Financing Judicial Elections, 2000: Change and Challenge." *Law Review of Michigan State University Detroit College of Law* 2001, no. 3: 849–99.

———. 2002. "Should Judges Be More Like Politicians?" *Court Review* 39 (Spring): 8–11.

———. 2007. "New Challenges to States' Judicial Selection." *Georgetown Law Journal* 95, no. 4: 1077–1105.

Schultz, David. 2006. "*Minnesota Republican Party v. White* and the Future of State Judicial Elections." *Albany Law Review* 69: 985–1011.

Schwartz, Herman. 2000. *The Struggle for Constitutional Justice in Post-Communist Europe*. Chicago: University of Chicago Press.

Shapiro, Robert Y. 2003. "Rebuttal to Ayres." In *Inside the Campaign Finance Battle: Court Testimony on the New Reform*, edited by Anthony Corrado, Thomas E. Mann, and Trevor Potter, 278–84. Washington, DC: Brookings.

Stark, Andrew. 2000. *Conflict of Interest in American Public Life*. Cambridge, MA: Harvard University Press.

Streb, Matthew J., ed. 2007. *Running for Judge: The Rising Political, Financial, and Legal Stakes of Judicial Elections*. New York: New York University Press.

Sullivan, John L., James E. Piereson, and George E. Marcus. 1982. *Political Tolerance and American Democracy*. Chicago: University of Chicago Press.

Tate, C. Neal, and Torbjorn Vallinder, eds. 1995. *The Global Expansion of Judicial Power*. New York: New York University Press.

Texas Office of Court Administration. 1998. *Public Trust and Confidence in the Courts and Legal Profession in Texas: Summary Report*. Austin: Texas Office of Court

Administration. http://www.courts.state.tx.us/publicinfo/publictrust/sumrpt.pdf (accessed December 27, 2004).

Tsebelis, George. 2000. "Veto Players and Institutional Analysis." *Governance* 13, no. 4 (October): 441–74.

Tyler, Tom R. 1990. *Why People Follow the Law: Procedural Justice, Legitimacy, and Compliance.* New Haven, CT: Yale University Press.

———. 2001. "A Psychological Perspective on the Legitimacy of Institutions and Authorities." In *The Psychology of Legitimacy: Emerging Perspectives on Ideology, Justice, and Intergroup Relations*, edited by John T. Jost and Brenda Major, 416–36. New York: Cambridge University Press.

———. 2006. "Psychological Perspectives on Legitimacy and Legitimation." *Annual Review of Psychology* 57: 375–400.

Vavreck, Lynn. 2007. "The Exaggerated Effects of Advertising on Turnout: The Dangers of Self-Reports." *Quarterly Journal of Political Science* 2: 325–43.

Walker, D. 1977. "Citizen Contact and Legal System Support." *Social Science Quarterly* 58, no. 3: 3–14.

Ware, Stephen J. 1999. "Money, Politics and Judicial Decisions: A Case Study of Arbitration in Alabama." *Journal of Law and Politics* 25, no. 4: 645–86.

Wenzel, James P., Shaun Bowler, and David J. Lanoue. 2003. "The Sources of Public Confidence in State Courts: Experience and Institutions." *American Politics Research* 31, no. 2: 191–211.

Whittington, Keith E. 2003. "Legislative Sanctions and the Strategic Environment of Judicial Review." *International Journal of Constitutional Law* 1, no. 3: 446–74.

Wyatt, Kristen. 2009. "Justices Making New Push to Abolish Elected Judges." Associated Press, December 10. http://www.google.com/hostednews/ap/article/ALeqM5ibf82ajYbNxG8SarZzCYCGE1GewD9CGN0G00 (accessed January 4, 2010).

Yates, Jeffrey L., and Andrew B. Whitford. 2002. "The Presidency and the Supreme Court after *Bush v. Gore*: Implications for Legitimacy and Effectiveness." *Stanford Law and Policy Review* 13, no. 1: 101–18.

COURT CASES

Alaska Right to Life Political Action Comm. v. Feldman. 2005. 380 F. Supp. 2d 1080 (D. Ala.).

Brief and Appendix for Respondents. 2002. At 15–19, Republican Party of Minnesota v. White, 536 U.S. 765 (No. 01–521).

Daggett v. Commission on Governmental Ethics and Election Practices. 2000. 205 F.3d 445 (1st Cir.).

Day v. Holahan. 1994. 34 F.3d 1356, 1360 (8th Cir.).

Family Trust Foundation of Ky., Inc. v. Wolnitzek. 2004. 345 F. Supp. 2d 672 (E.D. Ky.).

Gable v. Patton. 1998. 142 F.3d 940 (6th Cir.).

In re Dunleavy. 2003. 838 A.2d 338 (Me.).

In re Kinsey. 2003. 842 So. 2d 77 (Fla.).

In re Raab. 2003. 100 N.Y.2d 305 (N.Y.).

In re Watson. 2003. 100 N.Y.2d 290, 302 (N.Y.).

Kansas Judicial Watch. 2008. 519 F.3d 1107 (10th Cir.).

Kansas Judicial Watch v. Stout. 2006. 440 F. Supp. 2d 1209 (D. Kan.).

North Dakota Family Alliance, Inc. v. Bader. 2005. 361 F. Supp. 2d 1021 (D.N.D.).

Republican Party of Minnesota v. White, 416 F.3d 738 (8th Cir. 2005).

Republican Party of Minnesota, et al. v. Suzanne White, Chairperson, Minnesota Board of Judicial Standards, et al. 536 U.S. 765 (2002).

Siefert v. Alexander. 608 F.3d 974 (7th Cir. 2010)

Simes v. Arkansas Judicial Discipline and Disability Commission. 2007. 247 S.W.3d 876 (Ark.).

Weaver v. Bonner. 2002. 309 F.3d 1312 (11th Cir.).

INDEX

abortion policy as an election issue, 59,
192–93nn1–4
ads. *See* attack ads and political ads
Alaska, 144
Alaska Right to Life Political Action Comm.
v. Feldman, 144
Alito, Samuel, 16, 26, 68, 108, 203n4
American Association for Justice, 2
American National Election Study, 29
Ansolabehere, Stephen, 27, 184n18
Arkansas, 144
Aronson, Elliot, 189n20
attack ads and political ads: campaign
activity's influence on citizens' opinions, 23–24, 27, 187nn6–8; evidence that
attack ads have few consequences, 49,
53–54, 135; in experimental vignettes,
34; impact on court and legislative
legitimacy, 41, 54; nature of, 27–28;
reaction to ads politicized by interest
groups, 63; respondents' assessments of
broadcasted ads, 62–63, 193nn6–7; text
of ads, 61–62
authority versus legitimacy, 10, 86, 88,
183n8

Baird, Vanessa, 7–8, 197n15, 199–200n7,
201n18
Baum, Lawrence, 183n4, 183n7
Benesh, Sara, 14, 81, 90, 184n19, 185n27,
191n36, 191n38, 199n4
Bi-Partisan Campaign Reform Act
(BCRA), 29
Bonneau, Chris, 128, 140, 187n9, 199n3,
199n5, 199n6, 203n6, 204n8
Bopp, James, 143, 144, 186n32
Bowler, Shaun, 184n19
Boyea, Brent, 188n16
Brace, Paul, 188n16

Brandenburg, Bert, 88
Brehm, John, 110
Brennan Center, NYU, 2, 107
Brooks, Deborah Jordan, 23–24
Bush v. Gore, 6, 9, 16, 26, 108
Bybee, Keith, 91, 199n12

Caldeira, Gregory, 5, 7–8, 9, 10, 11, 16,
35, 63, 68, 96, 108, 183n9, 185nn26–27,
186n30, 188n15, 196n12, 197n14, 198n5,
198n8, 199n1, 201n18, 203n4, 204n9
campaign activity crossing the line
study: activities represented, 59–60,
192–93nn1–4; attack ads' influence on
citizens, 27–28, 187nn6–8; campaign
content experiment, 64–69, 194nn8–11;
campaign contributions' influence on
citizens, 28–29, 187–88nn9–15; conventional wisdom about, 23–24; hypothesis about the impact of politicized
campaign activity, 27; hypothetical
vignettes use, 58; impact of a candidate making a specific policy promise,
60–61, 193n5; policy commitments and
prejudgments' influence on citizens, 29;
reaction to politicized ads by interest
groups, 63; respondents' assessments
of broadcasted ads, 62–63, 193nn6–7;
study design, 57–58; text of ads, 61–62;
threats to impartiality from campaign
activity, 58–61
campaign content appropriateness experiment: differences in judged appropriateness according to the importance of
the issue, 66–67, 194n10; relevance of a
particular institution on judgments of
appropriateness, 67–68, 194n11; study
design, 63–64, 194n8; study findings,
68; views of appropriateness of any

219

campaign content appropriateness
experiment (*continued*)
candidate making policy promises,
64–66; why citizens object to policy
promises, 64–66, 194n9
campaign contributions: appearance of
corruption and, 28–29, 187–88nn9–15;
belief in a connection to decisions,
28; evidence of negative consequences
from, 135–36; in experimental vignettes,
31; impact on court legitimacy, 53; legal
developments since the *White* decision,
143–45
Campaign Media Analysis Group
(CMAG), 112, 183n6, 200n8, 201n19
Campbell, Donald, 189n18, 193n5
Cann, Damon, 14, 199n4
Canon 5B(1)(c), Kentucky Code of Judi-
cial Conduct, 186n32
Carlson, Neil, 110
Caufield, Rachel Paine, 105, 144
Choi, Stephen, 139, 199n5
Citizens United, 107
CMAG (Campaign Media Analysis
Group), 112, 183n6, 200n8, 201n19
Coleman, John, 188n14
commitment to an institution. *See* diffuse
support for the Kentucky State Supreme
Court
Congress, US, 3, 6–7, 90
Congressional Accountability for Judicial
Activism Act (2004), 6
Constitution, US, 6, 23
Cook, Thomas, 189n18, 193n5
corruption and campaign contributions,
28–29, 187–88nn9–15

*Daggett v. Commission on Governmental
Ethics and Election Practices*, 145
Darley, John, 189n19
Day v. Holahan, 145
diffuse support for the Kentucky State
Supreme Court: administrators' interest
in constituents' views, 70, 194–95nn2–3;

citizens' awareness of and satisfaction
with state political institutions, 72–75,
195nn4–13; comparison between attitudes toward the courts and the legislature, 80–81; definition of diffuse support
for an institution, 5; determinants of
institutional support, 82–86, 197n19,
197n20; discussion and concluding comments, 85–86, 197n21; knowledge of the
court related to support for or awareness
of it, 74–75, 81–82, 195–96nn10–13; measuring institutional loyalty, 75–76, 77t,
78–81, 80t, 83t, 96–97, 169, 197nn14–15;
statistical analysis of survey responses,
79–80, 197nn16–18; study design, 71–72;
summary, 82

Easton, David, 5
elections and court support in Kentucky:
ad campaigns and politicization of
the election, 112–14, 200nn8–11; ad
exposure effects, 120, 121t, 201nn20–23;
ad partisanship and perceptions of
unfairness, 120–21, 201nn24–25; assessments of the advertisements, 118–19,
201n19; district races, 112; means of ad
exposure and, 121–24, 201–2nn26–29;
measurement of institutional loyalty,
115, 116–17t, 118, 200–201nn17–18; public
attentiveness to and knowledge of the
elections, 114–15, 175–79, 200nn12–16;
research design, 111; statistical confidence in self-reported variables, 124–25;
summary, 125, 202n30. *See also* judicial
elections
electoral accountability in judicial
elections: accountability as a source
of legitimacy, 88; appropriateness of
policy talk during elections, 132; basis
of judging state selection systems, 139,
203–4nn7–8; conclusion on purity
of elections, 140–41; evidence that
attack ads have few consequences, 135;
evidence that campaign contributions

General Social Survey, 9
Georgia, 143
German Federal Constitutional Court, 17, 90
Germany, 185n22
Geyh, Charles, 22, 140, 141
Gibson, James, 5, 7–8, 9, 10, 11, 16, 35, 41, 63, 68, 82, 83, 84, 85, 96, 105, 108, 109, 115, 118, 183n9, 185n27, 186n30, 187n5, 188n15, 196n12, 197n14, 197n17, 198n5, 198n8, 199n1, 199n4, 201n18, 202n27, 203n1, 203n4, 204n9
Goldstein, Kenneth, 187n8
goodwill requirement for legitimacy, 5, 183n10
Grosskopf, Anke, 54
Gulati, Mitu, 139, 199n5

Hall, Melinda Gann, 31, 128, 138, 140, 187n9, 199n3, 199n5, 199n6, 203n6, 204n8.
Hardy, Bruce, 98
Hasen, Richard, 56
Heagarty, J. Christopher, 90
Hibbing, John, 3
Hoekstra, Valerie, 187n4
Hojnacki, Marie, 183n7

impartiality. *See* judicial impartiality
In re Dunleavy, 144
In re Kinsey, 144
In re Raab, 144
In re Watson, 144
institutional legitimacy. *See* judicial legitimacy
institutional support: analysis approach, 82–83; knowledge of the courts related to, 97–98; legitimacy views related to democratic values and level of education, 84, 85f, 197n20; measurement of institutional loyalty, 75–76, 77t, 78–79, 173–74, 197nn14–15; variables not connected to court support, 84–85; variance in court attitudes, 83–84,

197n19. *See also* diffuse support for the Kentucky State Supreme Court
Iyengar, Shanto, 27, 184n18

Jacob, Herbert, 197n1
Jamieson, Kathleen Hall, 98
JaS (Justice at Stake), 15, 19, 91, 187–88nn10–11
judicial campaigns: conditional effects of judicial expectations, 125–27, 202n32; current style of campaigning, 105; discussion and concluding comments, 127–28; expectancy theory applied to, 106, 110–11, 199n7; finding that elections enhance legitimacy, 107; impact of state Supreme Court elections on court support (*see* elections and court support in Kentucky); inappropriate activity study (*see* campaign content appropriateness experiment); overview of past research on effects on legitimacy, 107–10, 199nn1–6; predictions of negative impacts from, 2–3, 105, 129; previous studies examining effects of campaign activities, 184nn17–18; research deficiencies concerning, 106; threat of politicized judicial campaigns, 26–27, 187n5
judicial elections: citizens' perceptions of judicial impartiality and, 3–4; electoral accountability and (*see* electoral accountability in judicial elections); finding that elections enhance legitimacy, 107; impact of state Supreme Court elections in 2006 (*see* elections and court support in Kentucky; Kentucky State Supreme Court); interest in influencing the outcomes of, 2; issue of permitting policy debates in elections, 3; judges' free-speech ruling by Supreme Court, 1, 2–3, 183n7
judicial impartiality: attack ads' influence on legitimacy, 27–28, 41, 54,

Kelleher, Christine, 185n27
Kentucky Judicial Campaign Conduct Committee (KJCCC), 113, 200n11
Kentucky State Legislature: affect toward, compared to other institutions, 73–74, 195nn4–9; comparison attitudes toward the courts, 80–81; evaluation of its performance, 72; generalizability of findings about, 16–17, 19–20, 137–38; levels of asserted awareness, 72
Kentucky State Supreme Court: elections and court support (*see* elections and court support in Kentucky); rationale for studying, 17–18, 143, 144, 186n31; support of by citizens (*see* diffuse support for the Kentucky State Supreme Court)
knowledge of the courts: connection between expectations and knowledge of the courts, 98–101, 198n10; national data, 196n13; public attentiveness to and knowledge of the elections, 114–15, 175–79, 200nn12–16; relation of knowledge of the court and support for it, 81–82, 97–98; relationship between knowledge of and awareness of, 74–75, 195–96nn10–13
Kritzer, Herbert, 184n14

Lammie, Kelli, 29, 188n13
Lanoue, David, 184n19
Lau, Richard, 27, 184n18, 199n3
legislatures. *See* state legislatures
loyalty to an institution: contribution to perceptions of politicization, 41–42; degree that it exists for the courts, 70, 71; measuring indicators of attitudes, 115, 116–17t, 118, 200–201nn17–18; measuring institutional loyalty, 75–76, 77t, 78–81, 80t, 83t, 96–97, 169, 197nn14–15; reservoir of goodwill likened to, 5, 8. *See also* diffuse support for the Kentucky State Supreme Court

Maag, Gordon, 27
Maine, 144
Manna, Paul, 188n14
mechanical jurisprudence theory, 9
Mendelberg, Tali, 27
Minnesota, 145
minority rights, 5
Mondak, Jeffery, 54

national data: generalizability of state findings to, 136–38, 203nn5–6; impact of campaign contributions on legitimacy, 48, 191n35; impact of policy commitments on legitimacy, 48
national level data derived from Kentucky results: analysis of the national data, 47–49, 191nn33–35; applicability of the data, 43–44; dependent variable, 44–45, 191n30; manipulation checks, 45–47, 168–70, 171, 191nn31–32; subnational differences when judges are not elected, 49–52, 191–92nn36–40
National Replication Survey, 19–20
Neeley, Josiah, 143, 144
negative advertising. *See* attack ads and political ads
New York, 144–45
North Dakota, 144
North Dakota Family Alliance, Inc. v. Bader, 144

O'Connor, Sandra Day, 23, 107, 183n2, 187n1
Ohio, 138, 183n7

partisanship: ads' influence on perceptions of, 120–22; American's view of, 93, 125–27; possibility that it does not create perceptions of unfairness, 119; view that judges should represent majority opinion, 101
Pennsylvania Supreme Court, 109, 203n1
Persily, Nathaniel, 29, 188n13

CHICAGO STUDIES IN AMERICAN POLITICS

A SERIES EDITED BY BENJAMIN I. PAGE, SUSAN HERBST,

LAWRENCE R. JACOBS, AND JAMES DRUCKMAN

Series titles, continued from frontmatter: